GREEK DRAMA AND DRAMATISTS

The history of European drama began at the festivals of Dionysus in ancient Athens, where tragedy, satyr-drama and comedy were performed. Understanding this background is vital for students of classical, literary and theatrical subjects, and Alan H. Sommerstein's accessible study is the ideal introduction.

The book begins by looking at the social and theatrical contexts and different characteristics of the three genres of ancient Greek drama. It then examines the five main dramatists whose works survive – Aeschylus, Sophocles, Euripides, Aristophanes and Menander – discussing their styles, techniques and ideas, and giving short synopses of all their extant plays.

Additional helpful features include succinct coverage of almost sixty other authors, a chronology of significant people and events, and an anthology of translated texts, all of which have been previously inaccessible to students. An up-to-date study bibliography of further reading concludes the volume.

Clear, concise and comprehensive, and written by an acknowledged expert in the field, *Greek Drama and Dramatists* will be a valuable orientation text at both sixth form and undergraduate level.

Alan H. Sommerstein is Professor of Greek at the University of Nottingham, where he is also Director of the Centre for Ancient Drama and its Reception. He is the author of *Aeschylean Tragedy* (1996) and has produced editions of Aeschylus' *Eumenides*, and of all eleven comedies of Aristophanes.

GREEK DRAMA AND DRAMATISTS

Alan H. Sommerstein

London and New York

First published 2000 in Italian translation
as *Θέατρον: Teatro greco*
(tr. F. De Martino) by Levante, Bari

First published in English 2002
by Routledge
11 New Fetter Lane, London EC4P 4EE

Simultaneously published in the USA and Canada
by Routledge
29 West 35th Street, New York, NY 10001

Routledge is an imprint of the Taylor & Francis Group

© 2002 Alan H. Sommerstein

Typeset in Garamond 3 by
Keystroke, Jacaranda Lodge, Wolverhampton
Printed and bound in Great Britain by
TJ International, Padstow, Cornwall

British Library Cataloguing in Publication Data
A catalogue record for this book is available from the British Library

Library of Congress Cataloging in Publication Data
Sommerstein, Alan H.
[Theatron. English]
Greek drama and dramatists / Alan H. Sommerstein
p. cm.
1. Greek drama—History and criticism. 2. Theater—Greece
—History—To 500. I. Title.
PA3131 .S8813 2002
882'.0109—dc21   2001045713

ISBN 0–415–26027–2 (hbk)
ISBN 0–415–26028–0 (pbk)

CONTENTS

CONTENTS

CONTENTS

ACKNOWLEDGEMENTS

This book is a revised English version of *Θέατρον: Teatro greco*, which was published (in an Italian translation by Professor Francesco De Martino) by Levante Editori, Bari, in 2000. I am most grateful to Professor De Martino and Levante Editori for kindly giving permission for the work to be published in English, to Routledge editor Richard Stoneman and his assistant Catherine Bousfield, and to their anonymous reader for the many improvements (s)he suggested.

Alan H. Sommerstein
Nottingham, June 2001

1

HISTORY OF THE DRAMATIC GENRES

INTRODUCTION

Ancient Greek drama comprises three principal genres: tragedy, satyr-drama and comedy.[1] These resemble each other in many ways, and were performed at the same festivals, but each had its own distinguishing features, which are so clear-cut that when a new papyrus fragment of a hitherto unknown dramatic text is discovered it is nearly always possible to assign it to its correct genre on the basis of language, metre and content. In what follows, therefore, it will be necessary to discuss both those features which the three genres shared (including the physical and institutional environments in which they were performed) and those which distinguished them from each other.

We can be sure that role-playing activities, perhaps of a ritual or semi-ritual nature, were part of Greek life, as they are part of the life of almost all peoples, from the earliest times; we know that choral dancing was familiar in Homer's world; and archaic art portrays many groups of costumed dancers, often fantastically garbed (e.g. as birds, satyrs, or horsemen complete with hobby-horses), often grotesquely padded. But we do not know how or where these performances metamorphosed into something that can truly be called *drama* – an enactment of a story (whether adapted from a familiar myth, or freely invented) in which each performer, or group of performers, represents (at any given time) a person or persons in the framework of the story, speaking or singing the words of a more or less fixed text. The origins of drama were already disputed in Aristotle's day. Our evidence suggests, however, that the crucial time

---

1 We know of at least two other forms of dramatic performance that existed in the classical period – mime and *phlyax* drama – but no complete examples of these have survived.

was the sixth century BC, and the crucial area a strip of territory extending roughly east and west from Attica, through Megara and the Isthmus, to Sicyon and Phlius in the north-eastern Peloponnese. According to Herodotus (5.67.2), 'tragic choruses' had once sung of the misfortunes of Adrastus at Sicyon, until the tyrant Cleisthenes (*fl.* 600–570) transferred them to the cult of Dionysus; Phlius, further inland, was the birthplace of Pratinas, the first great satyr-dramatist (who, to judge by changes in the iconography of satyric scenes in Attic art, may have moved to Athens around 520); Megara claimed to have originated both Athenian comedy (through the alleged founder of the genre, Susarion, traditionally dated *c.*570) and Sicilian comedy (through its colony of Megara Hyblaea, where Epicharmus was supposed to have been born *c.*550); while the founder of Athenian tragedy, Thespis, came from Icaria in eastern Attica, and is reported to have won the first official tragic competition at Athens *c.*533. Some of these traditions are based on shaky evidence, but their geographical coherence strongly suggests that this area did have a vital role in the origins of Greek drama, though very likely Corinth, long the cultural centre of the region (and the mother-city of Syracuse, where Epicharmus lived and worked as an adult), was more important in the process than the traditions indicate.[2] In Attica these early dramatic performances appear to have been particularly associated with the Dionysiac cult-centre of Icaria, and it may be significant that the east of Attica was the home territory and main power base of the tyrant Peisistratus under whose rule our sources place Thespis' activity.

It is only from the end of the sixth century that the history, as opposed to the prehistory, of Greek drama can be said to begin. When the records of the dramatic and dithyrambic contests at the Athenian City Dionysia were eventually published on stone, they seem to have been taken back to 501, perhaps because the festival was reorganized at that time to conform with the recent redivision of the citizen body into ten artificial 'tribes'; Aeschylus made his debut two or three years later, and the earliest tragedy whose date is known, Phrynichus' *Fall of Miletus*, was produced in 493. From then until the mid-third century Athens was the premier home of Greek drama. In the first generation, to be sure, Syracuse outshone Athens in comedy, but by 470 even Syracuse was importing Athenian dramatic talent, and as drama gradually became a leading form of art and entertainment throughout the Greek world it also became one of the prime

---

2 Indeed a few Corinthian vase-paintings of the early sixth century do seem to show costumed and/or padded performers enacting, in comic rather than serious fashion, roles in either mythical or fictitious stories.

promoters of Athenian cultural prestige. At first this applied mainly to tragedy, because of the topical and parochial nature of most of the best fifth-century Athenian comedy; but as the nature of comedy changed in the fourth century its international popularity rose, and in the early Hellenistic period the by now ubiquitous touring companies of actors were as likely to be performing Menander as Euripides. By this time a theatre was almost an essential part of the civic infrastructure of a Greek *polis*, wherever it might be, and the dramatic arts were beginning to catch on among some of the 'barbarians' as well (at Rome the first tragedies and comedies on the Greek model were produced in 240). But by this time, also, the creative phase of drama in the Greek world was coming to an end. The last dramatist generally ranked in the highest class, Philemon, died at the age of ninety-nine *c*.263; competitions for new tragedies and comedies, at Athens and elsewhere, continued long after, but few if any of the plays that won them were performed or read by later generations. From the time of Augustus evidence for the production of new plays in the traditional genres becomes thin; there is a limited revival *c*.AD 125–175 – doubtless associated with the general renaissance of Greek culture in and after the reign of Hadrian – but after AD 200 the record goes dead until the reign of Julian (361–363), when (no doubt with official encouragement) comedies were put on stage in which Christians and Christianity were satirized, and, by way of response (to the emperor's great annoyance), one Apollinaris made the first of several abortive attempts to create a Christian tradition of tragedy and comedy on biblical themes.

By and large, from the mid-third century BC onwards, drama became for educated Greeks a treasured cultural possession from the glorious past to which they looked back with increasing nostalgia; it was still performed, but even more it was read, and made the subject of large-scale commentaries and intensive scholarly research. From the first, and increasingly, this activity was concentrated on three tragic dramatists – Aeschylus, Sophocles, Euripides – who had been singled out as classics at Athens as early as the fourth century BC, when official standard texts of their plays had been designated for archival preservation and public performance, and five comic dramatists – Epicharmus, Cratinus, Eupolis, Aristophanes, Menander. About AD 300 Epicharmus, Cratinus and Eupolis virtually disappear from the canon (though there is one papyrus of Eupolis from *c*.400), and knowledge of the other major fifth-century dramatists becomes more and more confined to a selection of plays (seven each for Aeschylus and Sophocles, ten for Euripides, eleven for Aristophanes) which may have been favoured for school use. Menander does not seem to have been studied in schools, but remained popular with the adult reading public, at least in Egypt; the impressive Cairo codex, containing at least five plays, dates from the fifth century AD.

The eighth century saw an almost complete break in the study and copying of pagan Greek poetry in the Byzantine Empire. When interest revived in the middle of the ninth century, texts of Menander were no longer to be found; those of Aeschylus, Sophocles, Euripides and Aristophanes now began to be recopied, and all the plays included in the selections mentioned above, together with nine additional plays of Euripides preserved by a lucky chance from what had once been a complete edition in alphabetical order, survived the next six centuries to be included in the first printed editions, which appeared between 1494 and 1546.

As the revival of Greek learning in the West began to bring Greek drama back into educational curricula, attempts also began to be made to produce it; Aristophanes' *Wealth* was performed in German schools as early as 1521. In the sixteenth and seventeenth centuries more than one attempt was made to recreate an equivalent of Greek tragedy as a living, vernacular art-form. In Italy the so-called *Camerata Fiorentina* of the late sixteenth century, and following them Claudio Monteverdi, mistakenly supposing that the text of Greek tragedy was all sung, by one of the sublimest errors in the history of human culture created opera; in France, Corneille and especially Racine were as imaginatively flexible in their adaptation of Euripidean story material as they were rigid in maintaining the supposed Greek conventions of unity of time and place; in England the scholar-poet John Milton, thinking of drama primarily as a species of poetry, created in *Samson Agonistes* a form of tragedy-for-the-reader, complete with chorus, which found many imitators but produced no other great work. The direct impact of Greek drama on modern Western culture only became clearly perceptible about 1800, initially in Germany where a whole series of classic translations were published in the following few decades; then from about 1880 Greek tragedy, and subsequently comedy too, invaded the professional and amateur stage, which has been fascinated with it ever since, so that today Euripides, for example, is probably seen in any given year by more people than saw all the productions of his plays in Athens during his own lifetime.

FESTIVAL, THEATRE, PERFORMANCE

In classical Athens, every dramatic performance formed part of a religious festival held either by the state or by a local community; and our evidence strongly suggests that this was always and everywhere the normal pattern. This in no way proves that dramatic performances were thought of as 'ritual' events, any more than were (say) athletic contests, which likewise were always part of a religious festival. What it does prove is that dramatic performances were *public* and *civic* events.

Modern dramatic performances (taking the term in a broad sense) are of two kinds. In one variety (film, video, television) the spectators are separated in space and time from the performers, and often also from each other; they are essentially passive consumers of a prepackaged product. Even in the other (live theatre in its various forms), where performers and spectators are in one place, the spectators are normally just a chance assemblage of ticket-buying individuals. Sometimes, to be sure, a production is closely associated with a particular subcommunity (e.g. a school, a church, a village) and involves all or most of its members either as performers, ancillaries or spectators; but theatrical events of that type are not normally considered to be of central importance either to the art of theatre or to society in general.

In classical Athens, on the other hand, dramatic performances were essentially and in principle events for the whole community. This indeed was one reason, even had there been no others, why they formed part of religious festivals. In the absence of adequate artificial lighting, performances had to be held by day, and religious festivals were the only days when non-leisured citizens could attend them. Not all Athenian citizens can have watched the performances, and probably not all cared to, particularly since (probably from the 440s on) they had to pay an entrance fee of 2 obols per person per day (at a time when 6 obols was a good daily wage for a family man). Nevertheless, even allowing for the presence of a large number of resident and visiting foreigners, and of boys under eighteen (but few slaves, and probably few women[3]), the theatre audience (of about 15,000) must always have included a substantial proportion of the Athenian citizen body – probably never less than 20 per cent, and often as much as 40 to 50; it is likely that in general more citizens would be present in the theatre than were present at the political

---

3 That some women attended the theatre is shown by passages in Plato's *Gorgias* (502b–d) and *Laws* (658a–d, 817b–c), and by one passage in Aristophanes' *Lysistrata* (lines 1050–1) where the chorus, pretending to offer the audience gifts of money, ask 'every man and woman' to let them know if they want some. On the other hand, none of the many other passages in comedy addressed to, or referring to, the audience makes any mention of the presence of women, and more than once in Aristophanes it is taken for granted that when a citizen goes to the theatre his wife stays at home. These apparently conflicting data can be reconciled on the assumption that while women were not officially barred from attending the performances, relatively few actually did so, and even fewer among those of citizen status.

assemblies on the Pnyx a few days before or after. No wonder that in Old Comedy characters and chorus regularly address the audience as if it were identical with the Athenian people.

Many spectators, too, will have had experience of performing in the same theatre: the dramatic and dithyrambic choruses at the City Dionysia alone, in a peacetime year in the third quarter of the fifth century, comprised 665 men and 500 boys, all of citizen status, and on plausible assumptions about demography and behaviour it is not at all unlikely that a *majority* of the adult citizens who watched the performances in the Theatre of Dionysus had at some time taken part in them – quite apart from those whose fathers, brothers or sons had done so. Actors playing individual roles (and also musical accompanists) were professionals (and were not always Athenians), but these specialists numbered, for all the performances at the City Dionysia, no more than fifty-seven.

One must not suppose, however, that the theatre audience was a sober assemblage of the earnest and intelligent. Their average level of education may have been higher than that of the whole citizen body, but even the educated were on holiday – and a Dionysiac holiday at that – and they had numerous children and teenagers among them, which the assembly on the Pnyx did not. Indeed, in their numbers, their average age, their gender imbalance, their liking for alcoholic refreshment, their tendency to make unruly noises and sometimes to throw missiles at performers who displeased them, and the authorities' need to subject them to vigorous policing, the spectators at the Theatre of Dionysus are perhaps better compared with those at a present-day football stadium than with those at a present-day theatre or opera house.

The state festivals at which drama was produced were the City Dionysia and the Lenaea. The Lenaea, an ancient festival common to many Greek communities, was held in the month of Gamelion (January–February); the City (or Great) Dionysia, a more recent creation (very possibly instituted, or at least utterly transformed, by Peisistratus), began on the tenth of Elaphebolion (March–April) and lasted four or five days. The Dionysia fell at the beginning of the good sailing season, and attracted many visitors from abroad; in the days of the Athenian Empire, its subject states sent delegations to the festival bringing their annual tribute payment, military contingents to serve in the year's campaigns if any, and a phallus to be carried in the festival procession. The Lenaea, by contrast, was attended almost exclusively by the resident population of Attica, citizen and non-citizen.

Both festivals were in honour of the god Dionysus, who always remained the god of drama *par excellence* throughout the Greek world (so that the international actors' guild of Hellenistic days was called the 'Artists of

Dionysus'). His association with drama probably derived from older associations with masking and costume (as in satyric dances, and in the Attic myth of Erigone), and with competitions in song and dance (notably the dithyramb, a major musical/poetic form from at least the seventh century). Since masking, costume, song, dance and competition were essential features of all the dramatic genres, their Dionysiac character was guaranteed regardless of their subject-matter. Satyr-drama was Dionysiac in theme by its very nature, for satyrs were the servants or companions of Dionysus. Comedy's Dionysiac features were implicit in its name ('song of a band of drunken revellers'), and throughout its history it set great store by the joys of wine, the spirit of communal merrymaking, and the Dionysiac emblem of the phallus and all it represented; it was a very apt coinage when an unknown comic poet rechristened comedy *trugōidiā*, 'song of new wine', to emphasize both the kinship and the contrast between it and tragedy (*tragōidiā*). It was less obvious why the often bloody and sombre tales of tragedy should be enacted under Dionysus' auspices, and it became a catchphrase that tragedy was 'nothing to do with Dionysus'; attempts to explain the paradox continue.

At first official dramatic performances took place only at the City Dionysia, tragedy from c.533, satyr-drama from c.520, comedy from 486. In the time of Pericles, competitions were instituted at the Lenaea also, first in comedy (from about 442), then, about ten years later, in tragedy also. The tragic competition at the Lenaea never attained great importance, though Sophocles appears to have won it several times; the comic competition, on the other hand, was from the first almost equal in prestige to that at the City Dionysia – though there is some (disputed) evidence that comic dramatists who finished low in the Dionysia rankings in one year were, so to speak, 'relegated to the second division' and allowed to produce only at the Lenaea (if at all) in the following year.

For all, or virtually all, the performances were *competitive* – like most exhibitions of artistry and prowess held on festival occasions in the Greek world. At the City Dionysia, from 486, there were two competitions, one in tragedy plus satyr-drama, the other in comedy. For each competition it was the responsibility of the magistrate in charge of the festival (the so-called eponymous archon) to choose the persons who would be allowed to compete, three for the tragic contest and five (perhaps sometimes reduced to three in wartime) for the comic; applicants were said to have 'asked for a chorus', and the successful ones were 'given a chorus'. Officially their role was that of *didaskalos*, 'trainer' of the chorus; in reality it was far wider. The *didaskalos*, as a rule, did far more than rehearse the chorus (and the actors) in their words, melodies and dances (and the piper in his accompaniment); he was also the poet and dramatist and composer and

7

choreographer who had created them, the director who chose costumes, masks, properties and scenic effects, and blended everything together into a complete dramatic experience, and, in early days, the principal actor as well. From the 460s on, some specialization began to creep in. Sophocles early ceased to act in his own plays, others followed suit, and by about 450 acting had become a separate profession and there was a separate prize for the best tragic actor at the City Dionysia; later the routine work of choral rehearsal was often hived off to a *chorodidaskalos*, and in comedy, where the director's job was extremely demanding and required great precision in the planning and timing of movements and actions, it was common practice, especially in the late fifth century, for productions to be mounted by a two-man team, one partner writing the words, the other (the official *didaskalos*) taking most of the directorial responsibility. Aristophanes was particularly fond of this arrangement, and ten of his forty plays (including at least four of the eleven that survive) are known to have been directed by others. The *Fasti* record the name of the winning *didaskalos* whether or not he was the scriptwriter, but when reading-texts of plays went into circulation they normally bore the scriptwriter's name.

The financing of dramatic productions – like that of other important state activities such as the maintenance of warships – was effected mainly through a remarkable combination of sponsorship and taxation, the Athenian system of 'liturgies' (*leitourgiai*, 'public works'). The state provided the fixed equipment of the theatre, and paid fees to the *didaskaloi* and also to some or all of the actors taking individual parts; everything else was the responsibility of the rich man who had been designated by the archon, or had volunteered to serve, as *chorēgos* (literally 'chorus leader'). His remit was to make sure that 'his' chorus was ready to compete on the day, and that all the equipment and training needed to make the production effective and impressive were duly provided. The role of *chorēgos* was an expensive one. A tragic *chorēgiā* in 410 cost 3,000 drachmae, and eight years later the same man spent 1,600 drachmae on a comic chorus: even the lesser sum was five times as much as a building worker could expect to earn in a year. Although conscription was sometimes necessary, there were many for whom the expense was well worth it, whether because of the chance of gaining the glory of victory, or because it was good for one's reputation to be seen to be giving munificently of one's resources for public benefit. The *chorēgiā* was abolished during the rule of Demetrius of Phalerum (317–307), and thereafter the funding of dramatic productions was the responsibility of a state official.

When the festival came, each comic chorus performed one comedy, while each tragic chorus performed (in the fifth century) three tragedies and one satyr-play (or, at the Lenaea, two tragedies). The contests were judged by a panel of ten, whose votes were very likely to be influenced (as many remarks in comedy indicate) by the perceived preferences of the audience as a whole.

The theatre itself was near the heart of the city, close up against the south face of the Acropolis in an area associated with some of Athens' oldest cults; when the audience of Aeschylus' *Persians* in 472 heard the ghost of Darius denounce his son for having destroyed Greek temples, the sacked Acropolis was just behind and above them.

In the fifth century the performing space was centred on the dance-floor (*orchēstrā*) which was normally occupied by the chorus. The shape of the fifth-century *orchēstrā* is disputed; in fourth-century theatres it was normally circular, but the evidence of early theatres in outlying parts of Attica and elsewhere, and some rather ambiguous traces in the Theatre of Dionysus itself, have led many scholars, since 1974, to believe that in the fifth century it was an elongated, shallow quadrilateral – though it is not clear how dithyrambic choruses of fifty, dancing in circular formation, could have performed in such a space. In the centre of the *orchēstrā* was an altar, later called the *thymelē*; sometimes in tragedy, less often in comedy, this is pressed into dramatic service as a focus of ritual activity or a place of refuge for suppliants, especially in the earlier plays of Aeschylus where it appears to be set on a mound definitely, though not very greatly, higher than the *orchēstrā* floor. Passages to right and left (called *eisodoi* in the fifth century, sometimes called *parodoi* by modern writers) served for the entry and exit of chorus and characters; in Hellenistic times, and probably in Menander, the two directions had acquired conventional significances (audience's right = towards the city centre, audience's left = towards harbour or countryside), but even Menander never *relies* on such a convention to give his audience information not provided otherwise, and in the fifth century all we can reasonably assume is that where the contrast between two or more offstage locations was important to a play, the director would make sure that each *eisodos* was consistently associated with one of these locations.

In Aeschylus' earlier plays, down to *c*.463, there is no sign of any further scenic structures or equipment (except perhaps an underground passage beneath the *orchēstrā* to enable actors playing ghosts and similar apparitions to reach the altar-mound). By 458, however, in the *Oresteia*, we find that behind the *orchēstrā* there is a building. There may always have been some kind of booth (Greek *skēnē*) to serve as a rest-room for the actor(s) and a store for properties; now this booth, while retaining its original functions and also (as later evidence shows) its name, is enlarged, equipped with access to its roof (as at the beginning of Aeschylus' *Agamemnon*), doors and (perhaps later) a window, and brought into dramatic use, normally representing the dwelling of one or more of the leading characters – palace, private house, army hut, temple, cave, according to what the play might require. Painted scenic decor (*skēnographia*) is said to have been introduced about this time, probably in the form of panels hung on the front of the *skēnē* to help make clear the nature and location (urban, rural, seashore) of the dwelling it represented. The early *skēnē* may or may not have been on a platform raised above the level of the *orchēstrā* and approached by steps; if there was such a platform, the evidence of play-texts suggests that it was made appreciably higher *c*.418. In plays like Aristophanes' *Frogs* and Sophocles' *Oedipus at Colonus*, both written in 406/5, access from *skēnē* to *orchēstrā* and vice versa nevertheless remained easy; but as the dramatic importance of both tragic and comic choruses dwindled in the fourth century, the segregation of actors' and choral space became virtually complete, and in many theatres the actors' platform, and the entrance to the *skēnē*, came to be as much as 3 or 4 metres above ground level (though some passages of New Comedy suggest that in Athens at least, interaction between characters and chorus was still thought of as possible in the early third century).

Associated with the *skēnē* were two special-effects devices. One, usually referred to as the *ekkyklēma* ('rolling-out'), was used primarily to display indoor scenes to the audience, though in satyr-drama and comedy it could also serve a variety of other purposes; it probably consisted simply of a wheeled trolley which could be pushed (or sometimes pulled) out through the central door of the *skēnē*. It is used, for example, in Aeschylus' *Agamemnon* to display the tableau of Clytaemestra standing sword in hand over the corpses of Agamemnon (sprawled in a bathtub) and Cassandra; in Menander's *The Curmudgeon* (*Dyskolos*) to enable the audience, and the young lover Sostratus, to hear a conversation between Cnemon, ill in bed, and his stepson Gorgias; in Aristophanes' *Peace* to stage the rescue of the goddess Peace, hauled out of the 'deep cave' in which War has imprisoned her; and in his *Knights* merely as a convenient way to get an unwanted character offstage: 'Roll me within, ill-starred one that I am!' cries the discomfited Paphlagon in mock-tragic tones, the trolley is pushed out, and a moment later he collapses on it and it disappears into the *skēnē*.

The second special-effects device was the flying-machine (*mēchanē*), a crane (as used in building) whereby characters making airborne entries could be swung onstage – characters like Bellerophon on his winged horse, Perseus with his winged sandals, or the divinities (*dei ex machina*) who often intervene at the end of a tragedy to impose a solution and tell the characters their future fate. The earliest tragedy in which it is universally accepted that the *mēchanē* was used is Euripides' *Medea* (431), but there is good reason to believe that Euripides is playing on an existing *deus ex machina* convention, and there is evidence that Aeschylus used the *mēchanē* at least twice in his last years.

All forms of drama were performed by a troupe of the same basic structure:

1   *The chorus*, the essential and original nucleus of the performance. Although the signal for the commencement of a play was the herald's call to the *didaskalos*, 'Bring on your chorus', the chorus normally entered only after the play had been in progress for some time; in Hellenistic drama their entry marked the end of the first of the five acts (*merē*, 'parts') into which all plays were by then divided. Once the chorus had arrived they usually remained throughout, their exit marking the end of the play, though occasionally they departed and later returned. In classical tragedy they usually represented a group of persons who had little power over events (such as women, old men, sailors) but who stood to be deeply affected, for good or ill, by the actions of the principal characters. In satyr-drama the chorus invariably consists of satyrs. In Old Comedy they often had bizarre identities (e.g. clouds, birds, cities) and showed strong partisanship for or against leading characters, as well as addressing the audience on behalf, or in the name, of the author. By Aristotle's time the tragic chorus was tending to degenerate into an 'ineffective lamenter [which] does no more than express sympathy' (*Problems* 922b26–27), and in Menander's comedies the choruses represent mere crowds of drunken revellers, who dance and probably sing between acts, but of whom the characters take no notice except at their first entry; their lyrics, if any, were not included in the published scripts, which merely have the note *chorou* '[performance] of the chorus' at the appropriate points. The chorus of tragedy were at first twelve in number, later fifteen; the chorus of comedy numbered twenty-four; in the Hellenistic period both were drastically cut down. The chorus were led on, and accompanied throughout the performance, by a musician playing on the double reed-pipe (*aulos*, often misleadingly rendered 'flute'). They normally danced in rectangular formation (though some passages clearly require circular or irregular dances), and sang in unison; the tight and sometimes obscure syntax of some choral songs, especially by Sophocles, is evidence that their words must almost always have been distinctly heard, since otherwise they would have been unintelligible to many. A few papyrus fragments of Euripidean choral songs have survived with musical notation. The leader of the chorus (*hēgemōn* or *koryphaios*) had considerable responsibility, in the absence of a conductor, for the moment-to-moment management of

the chorus in actual performance; he also regularly had a small speaking part (additional to those of the actors proper), though he would hardly ever be assigned a long set speech. Some plays had a second chorus with a different identity, usually appearing only in a single scene; in others the chorus for a longer or shorter period divide into two antagonistic halves (all known examples are in comedy), but apparently always reunite before the end of the play.

2   The actors (Greek *hypokritai*, perhaps originally meaning 'respondents', which may refer to their role in the 'epirrhematic' form of dialogue between actor and chorus, common in Aeschylus, in which the chorus sing a series of short stanzas, to each of which the actor responds with a few spoken lines). In early times there was only a single actor; in tragedy Aeschylus is said to have added a second, Sophocles a third (used by Aeschylus in his last years). There seems always to have been a limitation on the number of speaking actors, doubtless a rule of the competition to ensure a measure of equality between the contestants, but the limit varied from genre to genre and must sometimes have been increased or reduced; there was never any limit on the number of speaking *parts*, which ranges, in surviving plays, from two to twenty-two. All surviving tragedies of Sophocles and Euripides can be performed by three speaking actors; normally the parts are so arranged that each can be played by the same actor throughout, but Sophocles' *Oedipus at Colonus* is an exception. Satyr-plays also regularly require three actors, but one of them always takes the role of Silenus, 'father' of the satyrs; from what survives of Aeschylean satyr-plays it seems likely that in the days of two-actor drama the Silenus part did not count towards the quota of two. In comedy, almost all Aristophanes' surviving plays require four actors (none more); a century later, on the other hand, we find that every play of Menander can be performed by three actors (provided we assume that any role may be split between two or even all three of them), and comic, as well as tragic, companies performing at Delphi in the third century had only three members. From the time when acting became a separate profession, one actor in each play was always regarded as the most important (he was later called the *prōtagōnistēs*, 'first contestant'); in ancient scholarly synopses he is spoken of as having 'acted the play' as if he did it all himself, and he alone was a contender for the acting prize. By the mid-fourth century the actors in a company formed a strict hierarchy, and we find the third (out of three) being called the *tritagōnistēs*. Small singing parts for children were always exempt from any limitation on the number of actors, no doubt because otherwise a dramatist who wanted to use one would

have been unfairly handicapped, child performers being unable to take adult parts.

3 *Mutes*. Restrictions on the number of actors applied only to those with speaking parts, and author and director were free to populate the acting area with as many non-speaking performers as their artistic discretion, and the purse of the *chorēgos*, would tolerate. In tragedy, persons of high status would normally be accompanied by attendants; in Old Comedy occasions for the employment of mutes are numerous and varied – Aristophanes' *Wasps*, for instance, has non-speaking parts for half a dozen citizens, about the same number of domestic slaves, one nude woman (see below), perhaps six or twelve young boys, one donkey, one dog and its puppies, three dancing crabs and one non-dancing one, and a collection of kitchen utensils.

All the performers were male. Originally, we are told, the parts they played were all male as well, until the tragedian Phrynichus first introduced female characters and choruses. They wore tight bodysuits over which they put on costumes appropriate to genre and character; actors playing female roles would have their bodysuits suitably padded, as indeed (so vase-paintings and statuettes show us) would many of those playing male roles in comedies and satyr-plays where fatness was considered funny. It has often been doubted whether the naked young females (prostitutes, goddesses or allegorical figures like Treaty and Reconciliation) who appear towards the end of several of Aristophanes' comedies, often being presented as a sort of prize to the chief male character, could really have been nothing more titillating than men dressed up as naked young females; but quite apart from the practical consideration that the weather might be very cold (especially at the Lenaea), artificial has the advantage over natural nudity, in a very large theatre, in that it can be made more easily visible by exaggeration of primary and secondary sexual characteristics. Similarly, even though natural male nudity was an everyday feature of life, only artificial male nudity, in the exaggerated form of the comic or satyric phallus (see pp. 22, 30), was to be found in the theatre.

All actors, chorus members and mutes wore masks – or rather headpieces, since they covered most of the head and included hair. The mask could tell the audience a good deal about a character's gender, age, social status, sometimes his ethnic origin (an Egyptian would have a dark complexion, a Thracian might have red hair), and possibly his personality (by the Hellenistic period, if not earlier, certain mask-types had acquired strong associations with particular character-types, as happened two millennia later in the Italian *commedia dell'arte*); but its prime function (except in the case of choruses) was simply *to be different* from every other mask in the play. Masking made it easy for the same actor to play several different parts, sometimes in interlaced order, without risk of confusion; for a corpse, like that of Ajax, to remain onstage for a long period without immobilizing a live actor (a dummy would be accoutred in the appropriate mask and costume – a severely practical reason for the convention that violent deaths never took place onstage); and, when necessary, for the same part to be taken by different actors in the course of a play. A larger-than-life, boldly coloured mask would also be much easier to see, far back in a large theatre, than a face would be, and would make its wearer easier to distinguish from other characters appearing in the same or in a previous scene. In Old Comedy, when a living person, such as Socrates or Euripides, was presented as a character on stage, his mask would at least sometimes be a caricature portrayal of the individual concerned; but the dramatists never seem to have *relied* on such portrait-masks alone to identify the characters for their audiences. The only characters who could sometimes be identified by their appearance alone, without any verbal clues, were the better-known gods and a few heroes, like Heracles, who were traditionally portrayed with very distinctive attributes.

All drama was composed in verse (with a few trivial exceptions in comedy when mock prayers, laws, treaties, etc. were recited in prose), but drama was unique among Greek poetic genres in the enormous variety of verse-forms that it could employ within a single composition.

Common to all forms of drama was the iambic trimeter (a line of three metrical units or *metra* each of the form ×– ◡ –) which was the standard verse-form for spoken dialogue (though the detailed rules for its use differed between the genres, and changed somewhat over time).

The *lyric* metres of choral songs were of almost all the major types existing in any form of Greek poetry at the time (and one or two, like the *dochmiac* ×– –×–, typical of highly emotional moments, which hardly existed outside drama). Most choral songs were *strophic*; that is, they consisted of stanzas grouped in pairs, each pair consisting of a *strophe* and an *antistrophe* which were identical (or virtually so) in metre and presumably also in music and choreography. Some strophic songs included occasional unpaired stanzas, usually at the end (and then called *epodes*); some choral (and more solo) songs, especially in the late fifth century, had no strophic structure and are termed *astrophic*.

Intermediate between the spoken iambics and the sung lyrics was a form of delivery called *parakatalogē* ('accompanied recitation') by some ancient writers and 'recitative' by some modern ones; it is not clear whether this would today be classified as a variety of speaking or as a variety of singing, but it was certainly accompanied by the piper and delivered in much stricter rhythm and tempo than were the spoken iambics. This form of delivery will here be called 'chant'; it is particularly associated with two metrical patterns, the *anapaestic* (based on *metra* of the form ∪∪ −∪∪− and variants, all giving a 4/4 rhythm) and the *trochaic* (based on *metra* of the form ∪−∪ x). Chanted trochaics are almost always *tetrameters* (lines of four, or rather 3¾, *metra*), a metre typical (according to Aristotle, *Poetics* 1449a21−23) of the earliest tragedy and satyr-drama, but frequent in comedy also. Chanted anapaestic tetrameters are found mainly in comedy, but common in all genres are long continuous runs of anapaestic *metra*, often associated with entries and exits especially of the chorus (and often called 'marching anapaests' by modern scholars). The division between chanted and spoken delivery is usually well marked, though occasionally doubt arises when isolated iambic trimeters appear in a lyric context; the boundary between chant and song is fuzzier, since the chanted line-patterns are combinations of shorter units frequent in song, and (especially in comedy) one type of delivery may pass gradually into the other without any clear break.

TRAGEDY

Tragedy (*tragōidiā*) is a performance by *tragōidoi*, etymologically 'he-goat singers'. It is not known how the performance and the performers came to be so called, and there is no sign that either dramatists or spectators in the fifth and fourth centuries were conscious of the etymology or thought it in any way relevant to their understanding of the genre.

The earliest ideas we can trace about the nature of tragedy seem to conceive it as centred essentially on *suffering*. It is significant that the earliest 'tragic' choruses we know of − the pre-dramatic ones at Sicyon, before their reform by Cleisthenes in the early sixth century − are reported to have 'honoured Adrastus [by singing] about his sufferings'. And the sufferings of great figures of the heroic age remained the staple of tragedy throughout its history.

This simple formula provided tragic dramatists with enormous scope for variety and innovation. There was no significant character in heroic saga who had not undergone suffering and sorrow at some time in his or her life; and there was no obligation on the dramatists to avoid stories already treated by others. On the contrary, they often went back to these − more and more often as judgements came to be formed about which myths were most suitable for tragic treatment and as public familiarity with the vast inherited corpus of story possibly diminished in the fourth century; and when they did so they nearly always altered the story, sometimes in quite fundamental ways, as we can see whenever we are able to compare one tragic version of a story with another, or with earlier poetic or artistic representations of the same story. Many myths, whose tragic versions have become so familiar to us that we think of them not just as one variant of the story but as *the* story, probably never existed in those forms before the tragedians got to work on them. Nobody before Euripides, for example, had thought of Medea as avenging herself on Jason by deliberately killing their children; contrariwise, everybody before Sophocles had thought of Deianeira's killing of her husband Heracles as a wilful murder motivated by jealousy – Sophocles makes it the accidental result of a well-meaning attempt to win back his love by magic, and if anyone murders Heracles in his version it is the long-dead centaur Nessus who lied to Deianeira about the magic ointment.

From this basic fact about dramatists' attitude to myth, there follow three important critical principles. In the first place, it is hardly ever safe to explain any event in a tragedy by saying that it was 'an unalterable part of the saga and [the dramatist] was bound to include it';[4] the words I have quoted were written, by Philip Vellacott,[5] about one of the most famous events in all of Greek legend, 'the self-blinding as the result of the discovery' (by Oedipus that he is guilty of parricide and incest) in Sophocles' *Oedipus the King* – forgetting that we happen to know that in the *Oedipus* of Euripides, Oedipus was blinded *forcibly* by the servants of Laius, at a time when he was not yet known to be Laius' son. Secondly, when attempting to reconstruct a lost play, we cannot assume that it contained incidents parallel to those in a surviving play based on the same story; we can, in fact, be virtually certain that there were fundamental differences, though we may not be able to tell what these were. Thirdly, by the same token, we cannot assume that the audience of a tragedy, because they knew 'the myth', knew from the start of the play how it would end. There was no such thing as 'the myth' in the sense of a fixed canonical story; there were only variant versions of it, and all the audience knew for certain was that the variant they were going to see would in at least some ways be entirely new. Even where an event really was unalterable

---

4 Aristotle, to be sure, wrote that 'it is not possible to abolish the stories that have been handed down, such as that of Clytaemestra being killed by Orestes or Eriphyle by Alcmeon' (*Poetics* 1453b22–25); but while some mythical data were certainly much less alterable than others, we can never take it for granted that *any* piece of mythical data was absolutely unalterable. In Homer's *Odyssey*, where the revenge of Orestes is a prominent theme, it is never mentioned that he killed Clytaemestra, and the great scholar Aristarchus seriously entertained the possibility that the reader was meant to assume he did not.

5 *Sophocles and Oedipus* (London, 1971), p. 234.

(or at least was never to our knowledge actually altered), the dramatist might still play with the *possibility* of altering it. This may well happen in Sophocles' *Electra*, where during the first third of the play there is no specific indication that anyone is thinking of killing Clytaemestra, and many spectators may be wondering whether Sophocles is going to create a new version of the myth in which she is not slain by her son but commits suicide; in the middle third it seems increasingly likely that a matricide will indeed be committed – but committed by Electra, a possibility which is forestalled only by the arrival of Orestes on the scene before she is able to take any action.

The horrendous acts of Orestes or of Oedipus are typical instances of a pattern endemic to tragedy. It was already observed by Aristotle (*Poetics* 1453b19–1454a9) that tragedy – in marked contrast to Homeric epic – was particularly fond of situations in which someone either kills, or narrowly avoids killing, a close member of his or her family. This generalization can be extended to two other kinds of death which could in different ways be seen as monstrously unnatural: suicide (which, like the killing of a kinsman, involves shedding one's own blood) and human sacrifice (known in heroic saga, unknown in fifth-century reality). Of twenty-eight surviving fifth-century tragedic dramas, there are twenty-five in which one of these three kinds of death occurs or is narrowly averted. Aristotle's explanation is that incidents of this kind are particularly apt to arouse the tragic emotions of pity and fear; at any rate they become, at the latest with Aeschylus, an all but essential feature of the genre.

The dichotomy just referred to between the *occurrence* and the *narrow avoidance* of a horrific act implies that there could be two basic types of tragedy – or, better, four:

1   A horrific act is performed and leads to, or itself constitutes, a lamentable catastrophe. Many of the most famous tragedies fall into this category, including Aeschylus' *Seven against Thebes* (the mutual killing of Eteocles and Polyneices), Sophocles' *Oedipus the King* (the suicide of Iocaste plus the self-blinding of Oedipus) and *Antigone* (the suicide of Antigone, Haemon and Eurydice, and Haemon's attempt to kill his father), Euripides' *Medea* (Medea's murder of her children), *Hippolytus* (Phaedra's suicide and Theseus' fatal curse on his son) and *Bacchae* (Pentheus torn in pieces by the bacchants led by his mother); it may fairly be called the typical form of tragedy, and as early as 425 BC 'tragic anguish' can mean 'excruciating anguish' (Aristophanes, *Acharnians* 9).

2   A horrific act is performed, but the survivors eventually reach an equilibrium that gives hope for the future. This pattern is particularly

suited to the broad canvas of the Aeschylean trilogy (see 'Aeschylus', p. 39), and the classic instance of it is the Oresteia, where after the murder of Thyestes' children by their uncle, of Agamemnon by his wife, of Clytaemestra by her son, as well as the sacrifice of Iphigeneia, the trilogy culminates in the inauguration at Athens of a new system of justice which acquits Orestes and gives Athens the prospect of future prosperity and glory. Similarly, in the lost ending of Aeschylus' Danaid trilogy the murder by the Danaids of all but one of their bridegrooms almost certainly led eventually, through the intervention of Aphrodite, not to further disaster but to their remarriage and the establishment of a new royal house in Argos from which the great heroes Perseus and Heracles would spring. Later plays belonging to this general type include Sophocles' Ajax, which begins with the disgrace and suicide of Ajax but ends with the intervention of Odysseus, once his greatest enemy, to secure his honourable burial, and Euripides' Madness of Heracles, where Heracles, having killed his wife and children in a divinely imposed fit of madness, on recovering his sanity rejects suicide and goes with his friend Theseus to rebuild his life.

3   A horrific act is narrowly avoided, and the action ends satisfactorily for everyone (except possibly some clearly villainous character). According to Aristotle (Poetics 1453a30–35) this was the most popular form of tragedy in the mid- to late fourth century (and regarded by some of his contemporaries as the best) – and certainly a spectacular example of it, Euripides' Orestes, has more known fourth-century revivals than any other fifth-century tragedy. In this play Orestes, Electra and Pylades, who have been sentenced to death for the killing of Clytaemestra, at first are ready to end their own lives as demanded but then murder Orestes' aunt Helen (or so they think), take her daughter Hermione hostage, and threaten to destroy Hermione, themselves and the royal palace by fire – until a deus ex machina appears, reveals that Helen is not dead after all, and imposes a solution one of whose terms is that Orestes shall marry Hermione! Such plots would today probably be called melodramatic (or even tragicomic) rather than tragic; Aristotle thought their proliferation was encouraged by 'the feebleness of audiences' who found unbearable the deeply disturbing implications of tragedy of type (1). The earliest surviving examples are Euripides' Ion and Iphigeneia in Tauris, both dating from shortly after 415, but some reconstructible Euripidean plays of earlier date seem to belong to the same type, including Stheneboea (early 420s?) and Cresphontes (middle 420s?). Sophocles' Philoctetes (409), though very different in many ways, may also be assigned to this

group. One play of the same period, Euripides' *Helen*, hardly even comes near to containing any horrific deaths; all we get is what can be called a token bow to convention when, after Helen and Menelaus have escaped from Egypt, the wicked king Theoclymenus resolves to kill his sister who had helped them, but is baulked first by a heroic slave who is ready to lay down his own life, and then by the intervention of two *dei ex machina*.

4   A horrific act is narrowly avoided, but a lamentable catastrophe ensues nevertheless. In this case the audience is in a sense being double-bluffed: first they expect the horror to occur, then when it fails to occur they expect a non-disturbing ending which in turn does not materialize. The only surviving example of this pattern is Euripides' *Andromache*. A quarrel between Hermione and Andromache (respectively wife and concubine of Neoptolemus) almost leads, in Neoptolemus' absence, to the execution of Andromache and her child by order of Hermione's father Menelaus; the victims are rescued by Neoptolemus' grandfather Peleus, and the shamed Hermione is on the point of suicide – when her ex-fiancé Orestes arrives, she runs off with him, and he arranges for Neoptolemus to be murdered at Delphi.

The plots of tragedies were almost invariably conceived within the framework of heroic saga, the major characters being established figures from the saga cycles, the dramatic action either constituting, or being clearly placed in temporal and causal relation to, well-known incidents in their careers. Two attempts – possibly three – were made to break away from this convention. In 493 Phrynichus dramatized the capture of Miletus by the Persians, which had happened only a few months previously (and which many Athenians believed they could have prevented had they sent help to the Milesians when asked); afterwards he was fined ('because he had reminded the Athenians of their own troubles', according to Herodotus 6.21.2) and future productions of the play were banned. Seven years later the introduction of comedy to the City Dionysia provided a more suitable vehicle for a drama that commented directly on current affairs.

A more successful, but in its nature temporary, flowering of tragedy on contemporary themes came in the aftermath of the Persian Wars. The day of Marathon, the months from Thermopylae to Plataea, were among the rare occasions when history, as it were, rises to the stature of legend, when men feel that they are performing and witnessing deeds that deserve to rank with those of the age of heroes. Since, however, tragedy was a genre that told of suffering rather than of triumph, both the tragic productions that we know of on the Persian Wars – that by Phrynichus, probably in

19

476, and the surviving *Persians* of Aeschylus in 472 – presented the war not as an Athenian or Greek victory, but as a Persian or Asian disaster. There was never another such moment in ancient Greek history, and contemporary tragedy was never tried again, though in the early Hellenistic period some tragedies were written around figures of the historical past such as Themistocles or Gyges of Lydia.

The third breakaway was, or may have been, attempted by Euripides' younger contemporary Agathon when he wrote a play, probably called *Antheus*, whose plot and characters were entirely invented. At least such is the assertion of Aristotle (*Poetics* 1451b21–23), who implies that this was not the only play of its kind; but there is some evidence that the stories of these plays were not fictions, but obscure, perhaps local myths known to very few people. At any rate, if there were indeed tragedies of this kind they remained very rare, and we can identify no other example.

The basic structural rhythm of all forms of Greek drama was an alternation between scenes of spoken dialogue by actors (or by an actor and the chorus leader) and songs by the chorus, often but not always when no one else is on the scene. Traditionally this alternation is described in terms to be found in Aristotle's *Poetics* (1452b15–25). The first choral song is called the *parodos* ('arrival'), and subsequent ones *stasima* ('standing songs', i.e. songs sung after the chorus had stationed itself in the *orchēstrā*); the spoken scene which in most plays precedes the entry of the chorus is the *prologos* (prologue), and spoken scenes between choral songs are *epeisodia* ('additional entrances', i.e. scenes marked off by the entrance of actors in addition to the chorus); the term *exodos* ('exit') denotes all that part of the play that follows the last full choral song. Another term in this tradition is *kommos* (literally 'lament'), defined in the *Poetics* as a 'lament uttered jointly by the chorus and from the *skēnē*', but used more broadly by more recent critics to denote any lyric or mainly lyric passage in which both chorus and actor(s) participate (a modern alternative is *amoibaion*, 'exchange'). This terminology is unsatisfactory but is still widely used, especially to refer to choral songs; it does not provide an entirely adequate account of the structure of every play, but neither do any of the alternative patterns of analysis which have been developed in modern times. An important omission is the solo song by an actor, or *monody*, typical especially of late fifth-century tragedy, which may effectively take the place of a choral song; in this period it also becomes common for the *parodos* to take the form of a lyric dialogue between the chorus and one or more principals. Other important recurring structural elements include the *epirrhematic exchange* (see p. 12), which after Aeschylus tends to be replaced by less rigidly constructed *amoibaia*; the *rhesis*, or long set speech by a single character, a subtype of which is the *messenger-speech* narrating to

20

characters and audience events that have taken place 'offstage'; the *agon* or debate between two characters, including normally a *rhesis* by each (an occasional option in Aeschylus and Sophocles; Euripides has one in almost every play); *stichomythia* ('line-talk'), a highly stylized form of dialogue in which each speech consists of exactly one single line (with a variant, *distichomythia*, in which speeches are of two lines); and *antilabe* ('take-over'), in which, contrary to normal tragic practice, one speaker interrupts or answers another in the middle of a line (usually at moments of heightened tension).

Tragedy rigidly upheld the convention (sometimes, rather misleadingly, called the 'dramatic illusion') that the words and actions of the *dramatis personae* must be appropriate to their fictive situation and must show no awareness of the occasion of performance or of the presence of spectators. This convention can occasionally be stretched, as towards the end of the *Oresteia* when much that is said, though formally of timeless significance, very obviously addresses Athenian concerns of 458 BC, and Athena explicitly addresses one speech (*Eumenides*, lines 681–708) to 'my citizens for the future'; but it is never actually broken. Consequently, once the brief post-Persian Wars period ended, it was impossible for tragedy to deal directly with specific political issues in the narrow sense; reference to current affairs has to be made, if at all, by way of generalization, prophecy or oblique allusion. Fifth-century tragedy is, however, constantly concerned with issues that are political in the broader sense that they are vital to the lives of humans in a *polis* society (often in any society) – among many others, the relations of men and women and the nature and responsibilities of marriage; the problems an exceptional leader and an egalitarian community may have with one another; the extent to which the *polis* is entitled to override traditional family and other loyalties; the justification, ethical or pragmatic, of a ruthless *Realpolitik*, or of the traditional rule 'help your friends and harm your enemies'; the treatment of defeated enemies; the social repercussions of the ethical teaching of the sophists, or of the rise of new, often exotic religious cults. And beyond this, tragedy just as constantly explored the contradictions inherent in the human condition itself; portraying as it often did events of almost inconceivable horror, it posed questions about the nature of a world in which such things can happen, and of the gods who control that world. Each of the great dramatists gives a different response to these questions ('response' rather than 'answer', because 'answer' might suggest that the problems have been solved). By and large, Aeschylus' response is that the worst evils in the world are caused by wilful human action, which often has effects spreading far beyond the harm originally intended by the perpetrator. Sophocles encourages us to perceive an overall pattern and logic in the universe that has, one might say, a kind of terrible beauty about it even if it cannot satisfy the demands of our moral sense, while at the same time he also makes us feel that sometimes a human *refusal* to conform meekly to this logic, ultimately futile as it may be, is nevertheless a mark of greatness. Euripides, in his tragic (as distinct from his melodramatic) plays, is the bleakest of the three, seeing in the evils of our existence no logic but only caprice; but frequently crushing and undeserved disaster is made a little more bearable by human love, whether among family (e.g. the final reconciliation between Theseus and Hippolytus) or between friends (e.g. Heracles, Theseus and Heracles' foster-father Amphitryon at the end of *The Madness of Heracles*).

SATYR-DRAMA

Satyrs (*satyroi*), also called silens (*silēnoi*), were a class of male beings of popular belief who notably failed to fit into the usual tripartite classification of the animate world into gods, humans and beasts. They were followers and servants of Dionysus, they engaged at every opportunity in the amorous pursuit of the minor goddesses known as nymphs, and they do not appear to have been thought of as mortal – but they were not gods, and were not worshipped. Their appearance was imagined as in most respects human – but they were less than fully human, for they lacked all moral sense and all higher spiritual qualities, knew nothing of society, property, family or work, and lived in the wilds. They were beastlike in certain aspects, notably (in the archaic and classical periods) in possessing a horse's tail and in their uncontrolled lust (symbolized by their outsize, permanently erect phallus) – but they could at least sometimes be imagined as possessing a human and even superhuman cleverness.

Satyrs seem to have been early associated with ritual and festal dressing-up and masquerade, especially on Dionysiac occasions; it is thus not surprising that once a masked and costumed Dionysiac drama became established, there soon arose a variety of it in which satyrs played a central role. Its creator is said to have been Pratinas of Phlius (see pp. 2, 60), and artistic evidence suggests that the genre reached Athens around, or shortly before, 520. We do not know what official place satyr-drama had in the City Dionysia, in these early days; but at least from the start of Aeschylus' career *c*.499, it had been wholly incorporated into the tragic competition. Each contestant was required to produce three tragedies and one satyr-play; we can safely assume that the same chorus, actors and piper performed all four plays. In general this pattern continued throughout the fifth century, though at least once a dramatist was allowed to present a light tragedy (Euripides' *Alcestis*, 438) in lieu of a satyr-play. When the three tragedies had formed a connected 'trilogy' presenting episodes of a single story, the satyr-play often dramatized another episode of the same story, though not necessarily continuing sequentially on from the three tragedies: Aeschylus' *Oresteia* (murder of Agamemnon, revenge taken by his son Orestes, Orestes' flight and eventual acquittal at Athens) was followed by the satyr-play *Proteus* (adventures of Agamemnon's brother Menelaus in Egypt), while his Theban trilogy (*Laius, Oedipus, Seven against Thebes*) was followed by *The Sphinx* whose story fell, in the sequence of the legend, between those of *Laius* and of *Oedipus*.

This is the only known ancient Greek poetic/musical competition in which entrants were required to make presentations in two different genres. It is possible that the linking of the two was due to a feeling that tragedy, whatever its origins, was now usually 'nothing to do with Dionysus', and that a performance in honour of this god ought to contain at least one component that was more clearly associated with him; but this cannot be the whole story for, as *Alcestis* shows, the inclusion of a satyr-play was not in any sense a religious obligation, and the practice could not have lasted as long as it did had not the leading dramatists found it suited them artistically and/or appealed strongly to their audiences.

There were more senses than one in which tragedy had come to be 'nothing to do with Dionysus'. Not only did it usually enact stories in which Dionysus was not involved, but more importantly these stories, especially as they were treated in tragedy, were prima facie highly unsuitable for a festival in honour of a god associated more than any other with joyful celebration. The satyrs were beings whose sole aim in life was pleasure, and a play about their doings formed an appropriate transition from the grim spectacles of tragedy back to the festive mood. It is probably significant that a very common pattern in satyr-drama is the *return* of the satyrs from an abnormal activity to their normal role as revellers attendant on Dionysus.

The recipe for making a satyr-play, in the fifth century, was this. Take a suitable episode from myth. Ensure that it has, or can be made to have, a happy ending (for those characters who have engaged the audience's sympathy; not necessarily for the satyrs). Ensure that it contains some of the following ingredients, and if not, mix some in: sex, babies, resurrection, athletics, new inventions or discoveries, and an ultimately abortive attempt by the satyrs to follow a new and unaccustomed occupation, or by someone else to make them do so. Stir in a chorus of satyrs, together with their 'father', Silenus, who is an obligatory character in every satyr-play. He may originally have been the leader of the chorus, but by Sophocles' time he was a distinct character played by one of the actors.

23

Stew the whole mixture together, allowing the satyrs to impart a farcical, selfish, amoral flavour to the dish, and serve as dessert to the tragic banquet.

Until the twentieth century only one satyr-play, Euripides' *Cyclops*, was known by anything more than references and short quotations in other ancient writings; it had survived by the accident of the alphabetical position of its title (see p. 4). Papyrus discoveries have enabled us to get some idea of what satyr-drama may have been like in the hands of Aeschylus and Sophocles, though none of the rediscovered texts is anything like complete.

One of these rediscovered plays, Sophocles' *The Trackers* (*Ichneutai*), contains within its preserved portions almost all the typical ingredients of satyr-drama. It is written around the birth-legend of the god Hermes, who on the first day of his life invented the lyre, stole Apollo's cattle, and avoided Apollo's vengeance by making a gift of the lyre to him. The scene is Hermes' birthplace, Mount Cyllene in Arcadia. Our text begins with Apollo proclaiming a reward to whoever helps him find his lost cattle. Silenus, on behalf of the satyrs, offers to do so, and Apollo promises them gold and freedom. The satyrs search like hounds (or, as Silenus puts it, they crawl around on their stomachs like hedgehogs), and quickly find tell-tale hoofprints – but soon they are terrified out of their wits by a mysterious noise. Their own loud cries and foot-stamping dances presently bring the local nymph, Cyllene, out of her cave. She asks them why they have 'changed from the toil with which you used to gratify your master' (Dionysus), and is clearly afraid that they have come to rape her; they assure her that all they want is an explanation of the noise, and she tells them about the birth of Hermes and how he made a lyre out of a tortoise-shell (this takes some explaining as the satyrs do not know what a tortoise is); that is what is making the noise. The satyrs are now certain that Hermes is the cattle-thief (because Cyllene has told them that cows' leather was used in the making of the lyre), but Cyllene refuses to believe them (not least because she herself is currently nursing Hermes on behalf of his mother Maia). This is as far as the papyrus intelligibly takes us, though some later scraps indicate (as we might anyway have expected) that Apollo appeared again; very likely the climax of the play was the appearance of Hermes (full-grown at the age of six days) and his presentation of the lyre to Apollo, who may have made beautiful music with it immediately; the satyrs may have claimed their reward, but they certainly will not have got the gold, and probably not their freedom either.

The costume of dramatic satyrs is well known from art. It had three constant elements: short breeches (sometimes hairy, sometimes smooth) worn over the usual theatrical bodysuit; a horse's tail; and a large, erect phallus pointing upwards at 45 degrees or so. The masks tend to have black beards, bald and rather domed foreheads, pointy ears, and diminutive snub noses – the last three all regarded as ugly features. Silenus, being the satyrs' father, has a similar but much older-looking mask with a white beard. The dramatic and poetic structure of satyr-drama was broadly similar to that of tragedy, but the lyrics were usually much shorter and rhythmically simpler, and an entire play would often be little more than half the length of an average tragedy.

The language of satyr-drama see-saws between a level close to that of tragedy and one permitting reference to undignified animals and objects and (usually in euphemistic or metaphorical terms) to sexual and excretory activities, and the use of word-types (especially diminutives) not found in tragedy; there is some tendency for these low-register linguistic features to be put in the mouths of the satyrs rather than of 'heroic' characters like Odysseus.

Satyr-drama continued to be written and performed as long as tragedy and comedy did, and Horace in the *Ars Poetica* has much to say about it (lines 220–250); but from the fourth century onwards it seems to have lost its close association with tragedy. Fragments of satyr-plays from the 330s and 320s suggest that it had acquired features of Old Comedy such as personal satire and explicit recognition of its own status as a performance; by that time, too, satyr-plays were no longer part of entries for the tragic competition. For a time at the City Dionysia only one satyr-play was performed, as an *hors d'oeuvre* to the major dramatic competitions; but from the mid-third century, both at Athens and elsewhere, the normal practice was to have separate competitions in tragedy, satyr-drama and comedy, sometimes with the same dramatists presenting all three.

OLD COMEDY

Comedy (*kōmōidiā*) is etymologically the song of a *kōmos*, a rowdy, drunken band of revellers moving unsteadily and noisily through the streets, singing as they go, in search of a symposium into which they can burst uninvited. It is easy to believe that from early times the songs of some *kōmoi* tended towards insult, abuse and satire, and it may have been this tradition that took formal poetic shape in the iambic insult-poetry of Archilochus and Hipponax in the northern and eastern Aegean; in recent years there has been increasing recognition of the influence of this genre on Old Comedy. At Athens informal insult-songs had a recognized place in the celebration of the Eleusinian Mysteries; it is possible that in the late sixth and early fifth centuries this 'iambic' tradition was blending with the Dionysiac tradition of the mimetic chorus and producing, on the fringes of the City Dionysia, unofficial quasi-dramatic performances which were becoming a regular feature of the occasion. At any rate, in 487/6 a competition in *kōmōidiā* became part of the official programme of the festival. This was the only wholly new poetic contest that we know to have been introduced at the City Dionysia in the two centuries between its reorganization near the end of the sixth century (see p. 2) and the end of the great age of Athenian drama *c*.263. Its introduction may have been a political move, designed – like the start of a series of annual ostracism votes, and the substitution of lottery for election in the choice of the principal magistrates, both in 487 – to limit the power of the interrelated elite family groups who had always dominated Athenian public life, and if so it is likely to have been Themistocles who proposed or at least inspired it: comic drama was given official status as a weapon of left-wing[6] political agitation.

It may, however, have lost this role before long: Magnes, the leading comic dramatist of the 470s and 460s, seems to have been remembered mainly for his music and his farmyard imitations (see Aristophanes, *Knights*, lines 520–525). One suspects that comedy was in the doldrums. Its original *raison d'être* had disappeared with the Persian Wars, the end of the factional struggles of the 480s, new political alignments, and finally the ostracism of Themistocles in the late 470s, and it seems not to have found a new one; Magnes reigned unchallenged because no poet of high quality was interested in comedy, and the genre seemed likely to degenerate into a downmarket form of entertainment mainly of interest to children.

In the 450s something changes. Within a few years several new names appear, most notably that of Cratinus, and so do new themes: we can detect a blending of the Athenian comic tradition established by Magnes with the rediscovered tradition of satire and invective in iambic verse, and, most significantly, with the tradition of comic drama that had grown up, more or less independently, in Sicily.

The outstanding figure in this Sicilian tradition had been Epicharmus. Despite significant papyrus discoveries, we know little about the structure of his plays (we do not even know for sure whether they had a chorus); but we know on the one hand that they sometimes made explicit reference to contemporary persons or events, on the other that a large proportion

---

6 By a 'left-winger', in relation to ancient Athens, I mean one who favoured the active use of the power of the state to reduce or eliminate privilege and inequality among its adult male citizens, and by a 'right-winger' one who favoured the active use of the power of the state to maintain or extend such privilege and inequality.

of them were burlesques of episodes from myth. Turns of phrase and types of plot (such as conflicts between a hero and a monster, e.g. Heracles and Pholus, Odysseus and the Cyclops) pass from Epicharmus to Cratinus and, later, Aristophanes. It is likely that Old Comedy owes to Sicilian comedy the strong vein of fantasy that runs through it, enabling its characters to achieve the impossible with ease and often without even requiring divine assistance.

The iambic tradition encouraged Athenian dramatists to revive the practice of direct, often vicious personal attacks on prominent contemporary individuals. And, at the latest in the 440s when our textual material becomes slightly less scanty and we are able to assign approximate dates to plays, we can see a strong selectivity in the individuals chosen for attack. The political stance of comedy has been reversed. From now till 404, at least, comedy belongs politically to the Right – attacking Pericles and those of his successors who relied mainly on the support of the poor, but being comparatively soft on their opponents who are occasionally sympathized with or even praised; ridiculing such democratic practices as the payment of jurors; urging their audiences (when at all possible) to understand the Spartan point of view. Either comedy was now attracting highly educated (and therefore wealthy) poets who thought right-wing thoughts because that was natural in their social milieu, or the dramatists were accommodating to an audience that was more right-wing than formerly because the entrance fee had been increased, or (likely enough) both factors were at work. In 440/39 an attempt was made to draw comedy's political teeth, when an Assembly decree prohibited the slander in comedy of named individuals; the next couple of years may have been a fruitful period in the development of new styles in comic drama that were to have a long life and eventually, in modified forms, to take over entirely, but the decree was repealed in 437/6, at a time when Pericles was under strong political pressure. Later some politicians, notably Cleon between 426 and 423, tried to intimidate comic dramatists by prosecuting them under the general law, but with no success. In practice the Athenian comic dramatist, like the Athenian politician himself, had total freedom of speech.

At any rate, by the 440s Old Comedy has taken shape, a shape which remains recognizable for about half a century before gradually disintegrating. It has three fundamental characteristics that remain typical of Athenian comedy in all its subsequent developments. One is that in comedy, as in satyr-drama, there may be no profound disasters (though deplorable characters like *sykophantai* [informers] may be punished by a symbolic or even, very occasionally, an actual death). A second, which also links comedy with satyr-drama, is that the ethos of comedy is strongly

Dionysiac; but whereas the satyrs seek Dionysiac fulfilment purely for themselves, even father and children being ready to betray each other, the ideal world of comedy is a world in which people seek pleasure for themselves *and others*, as inclusively as possible. Those who deny pleasure to others,[7] or try to monopolize it at others' expense, are enemies of the comic spirit, and must be either converted or suppressed.

The third key characteristic of comedy, which separates it from both the other dramatic genres, is that comedy *exists in present time*. The action of tragedy, after 472, always takes place entirely within a fictive setting in the heroic age; so too does the action of satyr-drama. The characters of comedy, on the other hand, even when they are enacting tales of heroic myth (as they often were), never wholly forget that they are also Athenians taking part in a performance, and that they and their audiences will soon be stepping back into a real world; and they are always free to address the audience as an audience, to refer to themselves as actors in a theatre, and to mention persons and events known to the audience regardless of whether they, the fictive characters, could possibly have known of them; frequently a dialogue will zigzag bewilderingly back and forth between language appropriate to the fictive and to the theatrical setting.

Old Comedy comprised several well-marked subgenres. One of the most important, though no complete example of it survives, was that of mythological burlesque. For one play of this type, Cratinus' *Dionysus as Paris* (*Dionysalexandros*), a papyrus gives us the greater part of a synopsis of the plot. The play (produced in 430 BC, in the first year of the Peloponnesian War) was based on the legend of the Judgement of Paris, but the role of Paris was largely usurped by Dionysus. Apparently Dionysus, escorted by the satyrs (who form the chorus), had arrived at Paris' rustic abode on Mount Ida and taken possession of it in Paris' temporary absence, Dionysus disguising himself as Paris; presumably Dionysus had heard that the three goddesses Hera, Athena and Aphrodite were coming to have Paris judge which of them was the most beautiful, and he and the satyrs wanted to put themselves in the way of any inducements (especially sexual ones) that they might offer. When our text of the papyrus synopsis begins, Hermes has just asked Dionysus–Paris to act as judge and is going off to summon the contestants. After an interlude during which the chorus 'talk to the audience . . . and make fun of Dionysus when he appears', the contest itself is staged, and Dionysus declares Aphrodite the winner after she has offered him 'stunning good

---

7 Or, *a fortiori*, actually do them harm (e.g. *sykophantai*, crooked politicians, excruciatingly bad poets and musicians, etc.).

looks and sex-appeal'. He then 'sails to Sparta, takes Helen away and returns to Ida'; presumably the time required for this to take place is covered by a choral interlude (there are parallels for this elsewhere in Old Comedy). Hearing that the Greeks are ravaging the country and demanding the surrender of Paris, Dionysus 'conceals Helen in a basket and turns himself into a ram' to await developments; but the real Paris now comes home, discovers them, and orders them both to be handed over to the Greeks. This, of course, threatens (so to speak) to prevent the Trojan War from taking place, but this mythological catastrophe is averted by Helen, who, fearing punishment for her adultery, begs to be allowed to stay, and Paris agrees to make her his wife; Dionysus he sends off to be handed over, accompanied by his ever-loyal satyrs. The play ends there. It has made fun of Dionysus, as did Aristophanes' *Frogs* and several other comedies, presenting him as selfish, lustful and cowardly. It has ingeniously reversed the traditional assumptions of the story: Paris and the Trojans are innocent of everything except taking pity on a woman in distress. But in contrast with the satyr-plays, which in some respects it so much resembles, it has also been commenting on contemporary Athenian affairs: the papyrus synopsis states quite specifically that the play satirized Pericles 'for having brought the war upon the Athenians', and its evidence is confirmed by a quoted fragment of a play by another dramatist, Hermippus (fr. 47), in which Pericles is apostrophized as 'king of the satyrs' – though we do not know precisely *how* it was made clear that Dionysus represented Pericles (perhaps, it has recently been suggested, it was done by giving him a mask/headpiece caricaturing the unusual shape of Pericles' cranium).

Another type of comedy, possibly stimulated by the repressive legislation of the early 430s, largely abandoned political topicality and concentrated on the world of the symposium and the *hetaira* (courtesan); one might call this the comedy of night-life. The leading figures in this development were Crates, a contemporary of Cratinus, and the somewhat younger Pherecrates. The surviving fragments of Crates include not one reference to any living contemporary, and food, drink and symposiac games are prominent themes. Pherecrates' fragments show his output to have been more varied, but at least three of his plays were actually named after *hetairai* and probably featured them as central characters. A fragment of *Corianno* (Pherecrates, fr. 77) clearly shows that we are here in the early stages of the development of the love-plots typical of New Comedy: a young man is telling an old one that 'it is natural for me to be in love right now, but *you* aren't in season for it any more', and it is plausible to suppose that the two are rivals for Corianno's affections. It was some time before this variety of comedy caught on again, but its influence can be seen in, for example, the scene in Aristophanes' *Wasps* where old Philocleon abducts a slave-*hetaira* from a symposium and vainly resists his son's attempt to take her away from him.

For the third major variety of Old Comic plot structure – the plot of predicament and rescue, found in all the surviving plays of Aristophanes – see pp. 67–8, where the formal structure and the social and intellectual attitudes of Old Comedy, as exemplified by Aristophanes, are also discussed.

The costume of Old Comedy appears to have been based on that of ordinary life (except of course for the numerous divine or fantastic characters), but most male characters had their garments cut short to reveal a large artificial phallus. In contrast with the satyric phallus, this was not normally shown erect except where there was dramatic significance to showing it thus; sometimes it was allowed to hang limp and loose, very often it was coiled into a loop and tied up to itself. Where convenient it could be concealed by outer garments of suitable length – an option of great importance in plays like *Women at the Thesmophoria* and *The Assemblywomen*, in which men disguise themselves as women or vice versa. For other physical aspects of Old Comic production see pp. 9–14.

MIDDLE AND NEW COMEDY

Beginning in the early fourth century, comedy moved fairly rapidly away from the public and political themes of Aristophanes' time; Aristophanes himself, and his contemporary Plato,[8] joined in this movement in their later plays. Ancient scholars conjectured that comic satire had again been restricted by legislation, or (contrary to clear contemporary evidence) that the institution of *chorēgoi* had been abolished so that comic choruses could no longer be properly trained; a more probable explanation, supported by a wealth of artistic evidence (mainly from southern Italy) and confirmed by the vast increase in dramatists' productivity from *c*.380 onwards, is that Athenian comedy, like Athenian tragedy, was now being composed with an eye to foreign as well as Athenian audiences. Whether a play was to be given its first production abroad, or whether it was to be produced first at Athens and taken abroad later, the dramatist could not afford to build it around issues and personalities that would mean nothing to its audience.

8 Not to be confused with the famous philosopher of the same name.

In this period, therefore, while themes of civic concern were not wholly abandoned, varieties of comedy that had been somewhat in the background in the late fifth century – the mythological burlesque, the comedy of night-life, and increasingly also the comedy of love-intrigue – came to the fore; it seems fairly certain, for example, that such stock character-types of later comedy as the cook, the parasite and the pimp were largely developed in the middle decades of the fourth century. The term 'Middle Comedy' is often applied to comedy of the period beginning, at latest, with the death or retirement of Aristophanes *c*.385 BC, and ending with the debut of Menander *c*.321. Such a division of a genre into periods is bound to be somewhat artificial; in particular, it is clear that the style we know as New Comedy was already fully established, not only by 321 but several years earlier when Aristotle was writing the *Poetics*, and H.G. Nesselrath, author of the standard study of Middle Comedy, allows it only one generation of relative stability (380–350) before it begins to metamorphose into New Comedy. It is significant that one source (the Suda lexicon) credits Anaxandrides – whose career coincides almost exactly with the central period of Middle Comedy – with being the first to introduce 'love affairs and the rape of virgins' into (non-mythological) comedy. This drama of love-intrigue, traces of which in Old Comedy are fairly exiguous, probably derived partly from the prominence of *hetairai* in some symposium-centred plays, partly from mythological dramas, especially those which (on the model of certain tragedies by Euripides and others) centred on the consequences of the many rapes and seductions perpetrated in myth by gods; indeed the ancient biography of Aristophanes ascribes to *him*, in his last two plays (both with plots based on myth, and both produced by his son Araros), the introduction into comedy of 'rape and recognition, and all the other things that Menander imitated'.

The evidence for Middle Comedy is inferior both in quantity and in quality to that for Old or New Comedy. No dramatist of this period was admitted to the canon of outstanding poets; papyrus fragments are very scanty and hard to identify; and a high proportion of ancient quotations come from a single author, Athenaeus, who has a very strong bias towards passages that bear on the world of the symposium.

Until 1844, Greek New Comedy was known only from ancient quotations (many of them ethical and sententious) and from the Roman adaptations of Plautus and Terence. In that year the first fragments of actual texts of Menander were found in St Catherine's monastery at Mount Sinai, sewn into the binding of another book; they were not even partially published until 1876, and made little impact. Papyrus fragments began to appear from 1898, but the true modern rebirth of Menander occurred in 1907, with the publication of a fifth-century codex ('the Cairo codex') whose preserved portions include parts of five plays; it was now possible to read whole scenes and sequences of scenes, and to get a fair idea of the plot of two or three entire plays. Of subsequent discoveries the most spectacular has been that of a codex of the third or fourth century, now in the Bodmer collection at Geneva, from which between 1958 and 1969 were published virtually the whole of *The Curmudgeon* and substantial parts of two other plays. Today we have significant papyrus evidence for about twenty of Menander's 108 plays, and at least seven are well enough preserved to make it possible to study them effectively as whole (if sometimes gappy) dramas. In addition there are sixty or seventy papyrus fragments whose style shows them to come from New Comedy, but whose authorship is at present unknown; most of these are likely to be by Menander also, but some may well be from plays by Philemon, Diphilus and others.

The typical plot patterns, character types and formal features of New Comedy are described in Chapter 2 (see pp. 72–5). Menander and his contemporaries gave the genre its definitive shape, which seems to have changed little as long as comedies continued to be written: one of the very few fragments of late Hellenistic comedy, by Athenion (mid-first century BC?), presents us with a boastful cook who could have stepped straight out of a comedy of 250 years earlier, dilating on the role of cooks in creating human civilization as we know it.

2

THE AUTHORS

AESCHYLUS

Life and works

Aeschylus, son of Euphorion, was born at Eleusis in western Attica, probably in 525/4 BC. He produced his first plays at the City Dionysia about 499, but gained his first victory only in 484. He fought in the battle of Marathon in 490 (where his brother Cynegeirus was killed) and probably also at Salamis and Plataea in 480/79. At least once, possibly twice, in the 470s he visited Sicily at the invitation of Hieron of Syracuse, for whom he produced *The Women of Aetna* (in honour of the new city of Aetna which Hieron had recently founded) and also restaged *The Persians*. By this time, with the death of Phrynichus *c*.473, he was the premier tragic dramatist in Athens, and was victorious almost every time he competed, though he is said to have been defeated by Sophocles in 468. After the production of the *Oresteia* in 458 he again visited Sicily; he died there, at Gela, in 456/5; his epitaph commemorated him, not as a poet, but as one who had fought at Marathon. At some date during the next thirty years a state decree permitted anyone who so wished to restage Aeschylus' plays at the dramatic festivals in competition with those of living dramatists. Two of Aeschylus' sons, Euphorion and Euaeon, themselves became tragic dramatists; so did a nephew, Philocles, who was the founder of a dynasty of tragic poets that spanned four generations and lasted until 340 or later.

Ancient sources give figures ranging from seventy to ninety for the number of plays Aeschylus composed. On the evidence available it is likely that ancient scholars knew of seventy-eight plays which they attributed to Aeschylus; two of these (*Prometheus Bound* and *Prometheus Unbound*) are probably to be regarded as spurious (see p. 36), leaving seventy-six genuine plays of which ten were certainly, and nine probably, satyric – exactly the right proportion to make up nineteen City Dionysia productions, of which thirteen won first prize. Six of these seventy-six plays, plus *Prometheus Bound*, survive complete or nearly so; in addition there are seven plays of which there survive substantial papyrus fragments[1] – namely, *The Carians or Europa*, *The Myrmidons*, *Niobe*, *Semele or The Water-carriers*, and the satyr-plays *The Isthmian Tourists* (*Theoroi or Isthmiastai*), *The Netfishers* (*Diktyoulkoi*) and *Prometheus the Firekindler*.

On many, perhaps most occasions, the first three plays of a suite of four dramatized successive episodes of the same myth and formed a higher-level artistic unity (now referred to as a *trilogy*), and the following satyr-play also presented a closely related story (making the whole complex a connected *tetralogy*). It is likely that the connected tetralogy was also popular with Aeschylus' contemporaries; after his time it remained an occasional option, though most productions came to consist of four unrelated plays. In all, as many as thirteen of Aeschylus' nineteen productions may have included connected sequences of two or three tragedies; in addition to the *Oresteia* (which survives almost complete) and the Theban and Danaid trilogies (from each of which one play survives), these included four further trilogies on subjects from the Trojan cycle (among them dramatizations of both the *Iliad* and the *Odyssey*) and two presenting the discomfiture of enemies of Dionysus (Lycurgus and Pentheus). On the other hand we know that the production of which *The Persians* was part was comprised of four unrelated plays.

Surviving plays (brief information about associated lost plays is given in square brackets)

The Persians (472; first prize)
News reaches the Persian capital that King Xerxes has been defeated at Salamis; the ghost of his father, Darius, called up to give advice, prophesies the further disaster at Plataea; Xerxes returns home to general lamentation.

Seven against Thebes (467; first prize)
[*Laius* told of the killing of Laius by his son Oedipus; *Oedipus* of Oedipus' discovery that he has killed his father and married his mother, and of his curse on his sons.] Eteocles, son of Oedipus, organizes the defences of Thebes against an impending assault by the besieging Argives under Adrastus; reserving himself to defend the seventh gate, he learns that it is being attacked by his brother Polyneices; when the brothers have met

---

1 Papyrus fragments of a play are here regarded as 'substantial' if they include at least twenty lines whose general purport can be understood.

and killed each other, their bodies are brought on, lamented, and escorted away for burial.[2]

The Suppliant Maidens (probably 463; first prize, defeating Sophocles)[3] [In *The Egyptians*, Aegyptus probably proposed to his brother Danaus, king of Egypt, that his sons should marry Danaus' daughters; Danaus refused, because he knew from an oracle that he would one day be killed by his daughter's bedfellow, and the dispute led to civil war.] Danaus and his daughters, who have fled from Egypt, seek and are granted asylum at Argos; the Argive king Pelasgus thwarts an attempt by an Egyptian herald to seize them, and accepts his declaration of war. [By the time *The Danaids* began, Pelasgus had been killed, and Danaus had made terms with the enemy, agreed to the marriages, and instructed his daughters to kill their husbands on the wedding-night. All but one, Hypermestra, did so; Danaus probably attempted to punish her, but her husband, Lynceus, saved her and himself, and it was Danaus who was killed. Aphrodite proclaimed the universal power of the sexual principle, Lynceus and Hypermestra became the founders of a new royal house in Argos, and the other Danaids were found acceptable husbands.]

Oresteia (458; first prize) *Agamemnon*: Agamemnon returns from Troy to Argos with his prize of war, the Trojan princess Cassandra; his wife Clytaemestra murders them both, and she and her lover Aegisthus set themselves up as rulers of Argos.

Choephoroi:[4] Agamemnon's son Orestes returns to Argos from exile, is reunited with his sister Electra, and, as commanded by Apollo, kills Aegisthus and Clytaemestra; he is then forced to flee again by his mother's avenging spirits (Erinyes).

Eumenides:[5] At Delphi, Apollo promises Orestes his protection. He flees on to Athens, pursued by the Erinyes; there Athena sets up a court to try

---

2 The transmitted text contains a further scene in which a herald announces that the Theban authorities have forbidden the burial of Polyneices, and his sister Antigone declares that she will bury him nevertheless; this scene, which ruins the finality of the trilogy's ending (and which requires a third actor), was probably added for a production in the late fifth or early fourth century.

3 It has usually been thought that *The Suppliant Maidens* came first in the trilogy and *The Egyptians* second, but Wolfgang Rösler demonstrated in 1993 ('Der Schluss der "Hiketiden" und die Danaiden-Trilogie des Aischylos', *Rheinisches Museum* 136:1–22) that the order was the reverse of this.

4 Literally 'Women bearing drink-offerings to the dead'; often translated as 'The Libation Bearers'.

5 Literally 'The Kindly Ones', a euphemistic name (nowhere actually used in the play) for goddesses sometimes identified with the Erinyes.

him for his mother's murder, and he is acquitted on a tied vote. In revenge the Erinyes threaten to blight Athens with sterility, but Athena promises them cultic honours and they become the *Semnai Theai* ('Awesome Goddesses') worshipped near the Acropolis.

Prometheus Bound

Prometheus is chained to a rock in the far north, by the order of Zeus, for having stolen fire and given it to mortals. He reveals that he possesses a secret vital to Zeus: Zeus will be overthrown if he mates with a certain female who is destined to have a son mightier than his father. He defiantly refuses to disclose this female's identity, and finally is swallowed up by the earth. [In *Prometheus Unbound*, Prometheus, back on the surface but still chained to his rock, is being tormented by an eagle that comes daily to gnaw his liver; Heracles shoots the eagle; eventually Prometheus reveals his secret (the fatal female is Thetis) and Zeus in gratitude releases him and decrees cultic honours for him.]

Since 1856 (though never in antiquity) the authenticity of the Prometheus plays has been increasingly doubted: sometimes because *Prometheus Bound* portrays Zeus as an evil tyrant; sometimes because the intellectual concerns of the play seem closer to those of the 430s than to those of Aeschylus' lifetime; sometimes (most cogently) because the language, metre, style and technique of the play (and, so far as we can judge, also of *Prometheus Unbound*) are in certain respects clearly divergent from those of Aeschylus. Echoes of *Prometheus Unbound* in Cratinus' comedy *The Wealth-gods* show that the two plays must predate 429; it is likely that they were written by Aeschylus' son Euphorion, and that he submitted them for production as his father's work, perhaps in 431 when he is known to have won first prize.

Profile

Aeschylus was the most innovative and imaginative of Greek dramatists. His extant plays, though covering a period of only fifteen years, show a great and evolving variety in structure and presentation.

The Persians, *Seven against Thebes* and *The Suppliant Maidens* are two-actor plays designed for the pre-*skēnē* theatre; the main interactions are less between character and character than between character and chorus (often expressed in epirrhematic form), and in two cases the chorus open the play in marching anapaests. There is a wide variety of structural patterns, some of them (like *Seven*, lines 375–676, with its seven pairs of speeches punctuated by short choral stanzas) probably unique experiments. The pace of the action is usually rather slow.

In the *Oresteia*, when Aeschylus had available to him a *skēnē*, an *ekkyklēma*, a *mēchanē* and a third actor, he makes imaginative, and once again very varied, use of the new opportunities. After composing the first half of *Agamemnon* entirely in his old style (with no actor–actor dialogue whatever), he centres the play on a verbal trial of strength between Agamemnon and Clytaemestra, meanwhile keeping Cassandra long silent and then, in an inversion of the familiar messenger-speech convention, making her narrate Agamemnon's death prophetically before it happens. The house and its entrance are firmly controlled throughout by the 'watchdog' Clytaemestra. In the second half of *Choephoroi* the action increasingly accelerates as the climax approaches, and then abruptly slows as Clytaemestra for a time staves off her doom with brilliant verbal fencing. In *Eumenides* a series of short scenes, full of surprises and changes of location, and including a trial-scene with some virtuoso four-sided dialogue, leads to a conclusion mainly in the old epirrhematic mode for one actor and chorus (with a second chorus at the very end).

Aeschylus' plots tend to be characterized, not by abrupt changes of direction (*peripeteiai* as Aristotle later called them), but by a build-up of tension and expectation towards a climax anticipated by the audience if not by the *dramatis personae*. He was quite capable of contriving *peripeteiai* when he wished, as witness *Seven against Thebes* where the whole action pivots on Eteocles' discovery that he has unwittingly brought about the fulfilment of his father's curse; the trilogy form, however, encourages sharp changes of direction and mood between plays rather than within them.

In general, the central interest in Aeschylean drama is in situation and event rather than in character. Even quite major figures in a play (like Pelasgus or Orestes) can be almost without distinctive character traits: if their situation gives them effectively no choice how to act, their personal qualities are irrelevant and are ignored. On the other hand, characters who make (or have previously made) decisions vitally affecting the action, when alternative choices were possible, are portrayed as far as is necessary for illuminating these decisions: Eteocles is usually calm and rational but can be carried away by strong emotions (such as his hatred of his brother), Agamemnon is one who values prestige above all other considerations (such as the life of his daughter). The character most fully drawn is Clytaemestra, because the plot requires her to be a unique individual, 'a woman with a man's mind'. In the *Oresteia* several minor characters (the watchman, the herald, the nurse) are drawn with marked vividness, less perhaps for their own sake than to focus special attention on what they have to say.

For similar reasons, Aeschylean choruses nearly always have a strong and distinctive personality. Their words are often of the utmost importance in drawing attention to the deeper principles underlying events (even when they do not themselves fully understand these principles or their implications) and, together with their music and dance, in establishing the mood and theme of a whole play. The women of *Seven*, dominated almost throughout by fear, contrast sharply with the Danaids, utterly determined in their rejection of marriage, and coercing Pelasgus by a cool threat of suicide; the Argive elders of *Agamemnon*, enunciators of profound moral principles yet unable to understand how these principles doom Agamemnon to death, share a trilogy with the Erinyes, hellish bloodsuckers yet also divine embodiments of these same principles. Aeschylus' choruses often have a substantial influence on the action; the Danaids and the Erinyes are virtually the protagonists of their plays, the women's panic in *Seven* causes Eteocles' promise to fight in person, while in *Choephoroi* it is the chorus who ensure that Aegisthus is delivered unguarded into Orestes' hands. Sometimes a chorus will surprise the audience near the end of a play (as when the Argive elders defy Aegisthus); it is a distinctly Aeschylean touch in *Prometheus Bound* when the hitherto submissive Oceanids resolve to stay with Prometheus despite Hermes' warning of apocalyptic destruction impending.

Aeschylus' lyric style is smooth, flexible and clear, though with a vocabulary that tends towards the archaic and the Homeric. In iambic dialogue, where he had fewer models to follow, he sometimes seems stiff compared with Sophocles or Euripides, though he can also create an impression of everyday speech through informal grammar and phraseology. He excels at devising patterns of language and imagery, elaborating them down to minute detail, and sustaining them all through a play or a trilogy.

Patterns of metre (and presumably of music) are likewise designed on a trilogic scale; in the *Oresteia* ode after ode ponders the workings of justice in syncopated iambic rhythms, with variations and deviations to suit particular contexts (epic-like dactyls for the departure of the expedition to Troy, ionics[6] for Helen's voyage and her welcome by the Trojans). Aeschylus' lyrics are mostly simple and perspicuous in structure, resembling Alcman or Stesichorus more than Pindar or Sophocles. He makes extensive use of marching anapaests as preludes to (and occasionally substitutes for) choral odes, and also in quasi-epirrhematic alternation with lyrics.

Aeschylus is consistently bold and imaginative in exploiting the visual aspects of drama. The contrast between the sumptuous dress of the Persian

---

6 Ionic metre is based on the unit $\cup\cup--$.

Queen at her first, carriage-borne entry and the return of Xerxes alone and in rags; the chaotic entry of the chorus in *Seven*; the African-looking, exotically dressed Danaids and their confrontation with brutal Egyptian soldiers; the purple cloth over which Agamemnon walks to his death, and the display of his corpse in the bathtub with Cassandra beside him and Clytaemestra 'standing where I struck' (a scene virtually repeated in *Choephoroi* with a different killer and different victims); the Erinyes presented anthropomorphically on stage (probably for the first time), yet tracking Orestes like hounds by the scent of blood; the procession that ends the *Oresteia*, modelled on that at the Great Panathenaea – these are far from exhausting the memorable visual images in only six or seven plays, quite apart from numerous careful touches of detail (for example, at the end of *Agamemnon* where Aegisthus, that 'woman' of a man, alone of those on stage has neither weapon nor staff in his right hand).

Aeschylus is well aware of, and vividly presents, the terrible suffering, often hard to justify in human terms, of which life is full; nevertheless he gives the impression of believing strongly in the ultimate justice of the gods. In his surviving genuine work, all human suffering is clearly traceable, directly or indirectly, to an origin in some evil or foolish action – Xerxes' ill-advised decision to attempt the conquest of Greece; Laius' defiance of an oracular warning to remain childless; the attempt by Danaus to keep his daughters permanently unmarried in order to save his own skin; the adultery of Thyestes with Atreus' wife; the abduction of Helen by Paris. The evil consequences of these actions, however, are never confined to the original guilty parties, but spread to involve their families and ultimately a whole community; some of these indirect victims have incurred more or less guilt on their own account, but many are completely innocent. In some of Aeschylus' dramas, like *The Persians* or the Theban trilogy, the action descends steadily towards a nadir of misery at the end. In the *Oresteia*, however, presumably also in the trilogy based on the *Odyssey*, and not improbably in the Danaid trilogy, it proves to be possible to draw a line under the record of suffering and reach a settlement that promises a better future; each time a key element in the final stages is the substitution of persuasion for violence, as when in the *Oresteia* a chain of retaliatory murders is ended by the judicial trial of Orestes, and the spirits of violent revenge, the Erinyes, are persuaded to accept an honoured dwelling in Athens.

In dramas of the darker type described above, the gods are stern and implacable, and mortals often find themselves helpless prisoners of their own or others' past decisions – though they may still have considerable freedom to choose how to face their fate (compare the clear-sighted courage of Pelasgus or Cassandra with Xerxes or Agamemnon). Elsewhere, especially perhaps in Aeschylus' latest work, a different concept of divinity may appear. In the *Oresteia* ethical advance on earth, as the virtuous Electra and an Orestes with no base motive succeed the myopic Agamemnon and the monstrous Clytaemestra, is presently answered by ethical advance on Olympus as the amoral gods of *Agamemnon* and *Choephoroi* turn in *Eumenides* into responsible and even loving protectors of deserving mortals. Something similar may well have happened in the Prometheus plays.

Aeschylus is intensely interested in the community life of the *polis*, and all his surviving genuine works have strong political aspects; he seems to be a strong supporter of democracy, a word whose elements first appear together in two passages of *The Suppliant Maidens*. In *The Persians*, for which the youthful Pericles was his *chorēgos*, he implicitly praised, though naming no names, the strategic acumen of Themistocles when in political danger. In the Danaid trilogy the actions of Pelasgus, who involves the Argives in a major war without ever telling his people of the risks they are running or of the dubious justice of their cause, are curiously reminiscent of a recent successful attempt by Cimon to persuade the Athenians to aid Sparta against the rebel Helots/ Messenians; it is significant that the outcome of Pelasgus' policy is that Argos becomes subject to a foreign tyrant (Danaus). In the *Oresteia*, produced at a time both of serious internal tension and of serious external conflict, war against foreign enemies is spoken of as a blessing, as is the alliance with (democratic) Argos against Sparta – though the overriding importance of avoiding civil conflict by conciliating rival interests is clearly recognized (*Eumenides*, lines 858–866, 976–987), and on the controversial issue of the powers of the Areopagus Council Athena's advice is couched in terms of studied ambiguity. Throughout all Aeschylus' plays runs the contrast between the powerful, self-interested individual in control of a state, whose irresponsible acts often threaten it with ruin, and the community which ought to be in control of itself and whose collective actions regularly secure the general safety; thus in *Seven against Thebes* Laius' wilful defiance of an oracle nearly leads to the destruction of Thebes, but the city is saved by six men, modest in word but resolute in action, who defeat the boastful leaders of the invading army. It has recently been suggested that Athenian tragedy in general regularly shows the triumph of the collective values of the *polis* over the self-promoting values of the family (*oikos*). It takes considerable ingenuity to justify this claim in the case of Sophocles and Euripides, but it applies perfectly to Aeschylus. He, more than any other fifth-century Athenian whose writings we possess, can deservedly be called the prophet of democracy.

SOPHOCLES

Life and works

Sophocles, son of Sophillus, was a native of the village of Colonus, then about 2 km north of Athens, and was born about 497/6 BC. He won his first victory at the City Dionysia in 468, possibly at the first attempt. There is some evidence that early in his career he was patronized by the statesman Cimon, but Cimon was ostracized in 461 and in later life Sophocles appears to have enjoyed reasonably good relations with Cimon's opponent Pericles, under whose supremacy he held high office at least twice (as a treasurer of the Athenian Alliance in 443/2, and as a general in 441/0) – though a contemporary who knew him personally, Ion of Chios,[7] thought that he had no great political ability, and quoted Sophocles himself as saying that Pericles did not think him fit to be a general. Originally, like Aeschylus, Sophocles acted in his own plays, but he is said to have given up doing so because he had a weak voice. Our sources associate Sophocles' name with various other developments in theatrical practice that took place in the 460s and 450s (the third actor, painted scenery, the increase in the chorus from twelve to fifteen, the general abandonment of the tetralogy form). After Aeschylus' death Sophocles dominated the Athenian tragic stage for half a century, winning eighteen first prizes at the City Dionysia and probably a further six at the Lenaea. He clearly came to be regarded as one of the great and wise men of Athens, and at the age of eighty-three he was elected as one of the ten *probouloi* who formed an emergency supervisory policy board after the Sicilian disaster of 413; he therefore shared some of the responsibility for the takeover of power by the Four Hundred two years later, but this does not seem to have damaged his popularity (he was victorious at the very first City Dionysia after the restoration of full democracy). Like Aeschylus and Euripides, he was invited by foreign rulers to visit their courts, but he never accepted any of these invitations. He died, aged ninety or ninety-one, in the winter of 406/5. At the Lenaea a month or two later, both Aristophanes (in *Frogs*) and Phrynichus (in *The Muses*) inserted warm compliments to him into their comedies. Putting these together with Ion's account of his geniality and wit in the symposiac circle, one can well believe the assertion of his ancient biographer that 'in his character there was so much charm that he was loved everywhere and by everyone'. Of Sophocles' five sons, one (Iophon) was himself a tragic poet; another

---

7 *FGrH* (= F. Jacoby *et al.*, *Die Fragmente der griechischen Historiker* [Leiden, 1923–]), 392 F 6.

(Ariston) became the father of the younger Sophocles, who produced his grandfather's last plays, including *Oedipus at Colonus*, in 401, and later became a prolific and successful dramatist on his own account. At some time Sophocles had written a paean for the god Asclepius, and it was later believed that he had given Asclepius hospitality when the god was introduced to Athens in 420/19 and that, partly for this service, Sophocles himself was later worshipped as a hero under the name Dexion; the first part of this story is known to be false, and the second is not much more probable.

Ancient scholars knew of 130 plays attributed to Sophocles, of which they judged seven (or, according to another source, seventeen) to be spurious. Seven plays survive (details follow); there are substantial papyrus fragments of the satyr-plays *The Trackers* (*Ichneutai*) and *Inachus* and the tragedies *Eurypylus* and *Niobe*, but neither papyri nor ancient quotations give us anything like as much material for Sophocles as they do for Euripides.

Surviving plays (the order of composition is uncertain, especially for the first three)

The Women of Trachis (*Trachiniai*) (perhaps *c.*451)
Deianeira, wife of Heracles, after having had no news from him for fifteen months, learns that he has won a great victory, but also that he is bringing home a young concubine. To win back his love, she sends him a robe smeared with what she thinks is a love-charm but discovers, too late, that it is a deadly venom; she commits suicide. Heracles, returning to Trachis in mortal agony, and recognizing in what has happened the fulfilment of old oracles, orders his son to have him burned alive on Mount Oeta.

Antigone (perhaps *c.*442)
After the defeat of the Seven against Thebes, Creon, the new ruler of the city, has forbidden the burial of the traitor Polyneices. Polyneices' sister Antigone defies this edict, is arrested, and (despite being betrothed to Creon's son Haemon) is ordered to be entombed alive. Creon changes his mind too late, and Antigone, Haemon and Creon's wife Eurydice all commit suicide.

Ajax (probably 440s or 430s)
Ajax, defeated by Odysseus in the contest for the armour of Achilles, has tried to take revenge for the slight, but has been driven mad by Athena and has tortured and killed some cattle and sheep. Returning to his senses and conscious of his deep disgrace, he commits suicide. Menelaus and

Agamemnon try to forbid his burial, but Odysseus persuades Agamemnon to allow it.

Oedipus the King (Oidipous Tyrannos) (between 436 and 426; did *not* win first prize)
The Thebans, in the grip of a terrible plague, are instructed by Delphi to kill or expel the murderer(s) of their former king, Laius. The present king, Oedipus, determined to uncover the truth, eventually discovers that he himself is the murderer and, moreover, that Laius was his father and the widowed queen, Iocaste, whom Oedipus had married, is his mother. Iocaste commits suicide; Oedipus blinds himself and begs, in vain, to be cast out of Thebes.

Electra (probably 418)
Orestes returns to Argos/Mycenae and kills Clytaemestra and Aegisthus (the basic story is the same as that of Aeschylus' *Choephoroi*, but it is so shaped as to give the major role to Electra, who is not reunited with Orestes until late in the play and is deceived by the false report of his own death which he has a messenger bring to Clytaemestra).

Philoctetes (409; first prize)
Odysseus, who ten years ago had abandoned the crippled Philoctetes on the island of Lemnos, comes back with Neoptolemus (son of Achilles) to bring Philoctetes (and/or his bow, once owned by Heracles) to Troy. Neoptolemus wins Philoctetes' confidence with lying tales and promises, and gets possession of the bow, but his better self revolts and eventually, defying Odysseus, he returns the bow to Philoctetes and yields to his insistence that he be taken home. Heracles, however, appears as *deus ex machina* and orders the pair to go to Troy where they will win glory.

Oedipus at Colonus (produced posthumously, 401; first prize)
Oedipus, old, blind and exiled, led by his daughter Antigone, comes to the grove of the Eumenides at Colonus. The Athenian king, Theseus, grants him asylum, and rescues Antigone and her sister Ismene when Creon has them seized as hostages to force Oedipus to surrender to Theban control. Polyneices comes to appeal for Oedipus' assistance in his war against Eteocles, but Oedipus refuses and curses both his sons. Oedipus then leads the way to where, after promising to be a blessing to Athens, he mysteriously disappears as if the gods had taken him to themselves. This is the longest of all surviving Greek dramas, and the only tragedy in which a role (that of Theseus) has to be split up if the play is to be performed by three actors.

Profile

Sophocles' surviving tragedies are more complex in plot, but more uniform in structure, than those of Aeschylus. Only one of them, *Electra*, proceeds in the Aeschylean manner directly to an end foreseeable in outline from the beginning – and even in *Electra* the dramatist teases his audience throughout with the possibility of a major change to the story (see p. 17). The other plays fall into two groups. In the three which are probably earlier (*The Women of Trachis*, *Antigone* and *Ajax*) the focus of interest changes about two-thirds of the way through (from Deianeira to Heracles; from Antigone to Creon; from the fate of Ajax to the question of his burial), and as a result all these plays have sometimes been seen as poorly constructed. The pattern, however, is so common (it reappears in Euripides) that Athenian audiences must have found it quite acceptable for a tragedy to be structured in this way – in other words, they were willing if necessary to revise their idea of what a play was about in the course of watching it. In all three of these plays the change of focus is marked by the final exit, to death, of the character who has hitherto been at the centre of interest; but the death of this character is never the end of the chain of events he or she has initiated. Indeed, the power of the dead over the living is an idea that perpetually haunts Sophocles; it is prominent in all his surviving plays except *Philoctetes*.

Oedipus the King and *Philoctetes* have (to the modern mind) a much tighter unity, centring throughout on the same person or persons. The sharp change of direction at about two-thirds distance is still apparent, but it is now more internal than external, as a key character comes to see the situation in a new light. In *Philoctetes* this occurs very suddenly, when Neoptolemus has the revulsion of feeling that forces him to reveal the truth;[8] in *Oedipus the King* it is brought about in three stages – the first when Oedipus begins to fear that he may be the killer of Laius (and Iocaste pooh-poohs his apprehensions), the second when Iocaste perceives the significance of the Corinthian messenger's revelations (and Oedipus pooh-poohs what he supposes to be *her* apprehensions), the last when Oedipus finally realizes the full truth. *Oedipus at Colonus* varies the pattern in a different way. The outcome is fairly clearly seen from the start, and is guaranteed quite early on when Theseus promises Oedipus his protection; the defeat of Creon, though achieved with much suspense and alarm, is

---

8 He is known to have had doubts throughout as to whether he was doing right by collaborating in Odysseus' scheme, but he has loyally continued to carry out his assigned task, and his breakdown, when that task is all but completed, comes, for the audience, out of the blue.

predictable; but as soon as it has been accomplished, there is another sharp and unexpected turn with the arrival of Polyneices, which casts over the otherwise peaceful and even glorious end of Oedipus the shadow of future troubles at Thebes and of what they will mean for his beloved Antigone.

With greater complexity of plot, character inevitably becomes more important; in the surviving plays one type of character is particularly prominent and is often called the 'Sophoclean hero'. The prime, almost the defining, characteristic of the Sophoclean hero is rigidity: he or she sticks to a principle, like a rock amid stormy waves (one of several images frequently applied to such characters), regardless of any consequences to themselves or to others. Heracles is inflexibly determined to have his will come what may, Antigone to honour her brother, Ajax never to accept disgrace nor to yield to the Atreidae, Oedipus to discover the truth, Electra to see that her father is avenged, Philoctetes and the aged Oedipus not to gratify those who have wronged them.

Other major characters often contrast with the hero in a range of ways. One is often a woman (e.g. Tecmessa, Deianeira, Antigone in *Oedipus at Colonus*) who is, or should be, close to the hero and tries to 'soften' him or her; usually she fails, and even when she succeeds it only makes things worse (Deianeira, meaning to melt Heracles' heart, melts his flesh and kills him; Antigone gets a hearing for Polyneices, and the result is a curse fatal in the end to Antigone herself). Another may be an antagonist (always male). The antagonist is never of the same mettle as the hero. Sometimes he tries to be, fails, and ends in ignominy (Creon in *Antigone* and *Oedipus at Colonus*, Odysseus in *Philoctetes*, and – even less impressive – the Atreidae in *Ajax*). Sometimes a subordinate, expected by his superior to be the hero's enemy, rebels out of pity and becomes his friend (Neoptolemus, Odysseus in *Ajax*). The only antagonists who are sure to get the better of a Sophoclean hero are the gods.

The Sophoclean hero is not necessarily the central character of a play. Indeed, the hero's very rigidity means that others (Deianeira, Creon in *Antigone*, Neoptolemus) often take more of the crucial decisions on which the action turns and which are the focus of suspense and tension.

Sophoclean choruses, though strongly and clearly characterized, and very much involved in the action (whose outcome is usually vital to them as a group), serve to comment on and illuminate the action rather than influencing its development. Six of the seven are closely attached to, and predisposed to sympathize with, a particular individual character – either the hero (Ajax, Oedipus, Electra) or the character who takes key decisions (Deianeira, Creon, Neoptolemus); the chorus of *Oedipus at Colonus*, at first hostile to Oedipus, later become his strong supporters. But the chorus never take any initiative of their own, and when a character asks them for advice (as Deianeira, Creon and Neoptolemus all do), it is a signal that the asker is at his or her wits' end. Like other tragic choruses, those of Sophocles are better at enunciating general principles than at perceiving their application to particular situations, and they are frequently made to sing an ode of joy or triumph just before the plot turns in a catastrophic direction (e.g. when they believe Ajax has renounced the idea of suicide, or when they speculate that Oedipus may be the son of a god).

Sophocles' language is less archaic than that of Aeschylus, nearer to fifth-century Attic, but he is fond of unusual, sometimes innovative syntactic constructions which must often, especially in lyric, have been hard for hearers to understand rapidly, and which may sometimes have been designed to be interpreted impressionistically rather than analytically. His lyric metres are more complex, with more variation within songs and strophes and less use of a persistent rhythm to shape a whole play or a large section of one; his later plays, like those of Euripides, make increasing use of actor lyrics.

Sophocles' exploitation of the visual aspects of drama is subtle and varied, and strongly oriented towards the arousing of emotion. Outstanding in his surviving work is the management of Oedipus' blindness, with all its implications for himself and others, throughout almost the whole of *Oedipus at Colonus*, when Oedipus not only cannot see but also, being polluted, cannot touch anyone except his daughters, so that he perceives and communicates almost exclusively by sound. In *Ajax* Sophocles comes as close as possible to presenting the suicide of Ajax onstage without actually doing so, and then creates a tableau consisting of his corpse and the silent, suppliant Tecmessa and Eurysaces which forms the backdrop to the whole second half of the play. In the second half of *Philoctetes* everything centres on the hero's bow, whose movements are the key moments of the action; in this phase of the play also, two lightning interventions by Odysseus suggest that Sophocles, uniquely so far as we know, has made him emerge from an unannounced concealment in the neighbourhood of the *skēnē*.

The universe that Sophocles portrays is one that has an awesome and far-reaching logic. This logic is perceptible in the regular, inexorable cycles of nature, of which Ajax speaks and the women of Trachis sing; in the equally inexorable fulfilment of prophecies and oracles, often by devious and unexpected paths; in the repeated motif, mentioned above, of the dead destroying the living; and in various small symmetries and coincidences – as when Ajax kills himself with the sword Hector had given him, after Hector had been dragged to his death by the belt Ajax had given *him*; or when the prayers of Iocaste and Clytaemestra to Apollo are each instantly answered by the arrival of a messenger with news which seems to be exactly what they had hoped for, but which in fact leads to the destruction of them both. In general, however, and in contrast with Aeschylus, it is not a logic that is agreeable either to our morality or to that of classical Athenians. For example, as Sophocles shapes the story of Oedipus, the actions of all those involved, from Oedipus himself to the two shepherds, which between them led to the catastrophe that happens in *Oedipus the King*, were all reasonable in the circumstances, and many of them were thoroughly praiseworthy. Again, Philoctetes suffers ten years of agony for a minor, and apparently inadvertent, act of sacrilege; it is true that the Atreidae and Odysseus, by abandoning him on Lemnos instead of taking him home, make his sufferings even worse, but we gather that whatever had happened his wound could be healed only at Troy and only in the tenth year. The gods, it seems, have their ways and their plans, and if human lives get in the way of these then human lives may be wrecked. The bleakness of this outlook is mitigated in three ways. In the first place, we are allowed to glimpse something of the grand logic by which these plans are governed: we cannot fully comprehend it, but we can at least see that it has its own cruel beauty. As a corollary of this, Sophocles never in the surviving plays shows gods in conflict with one another: either the gods are thought of as a collectivity, or else only one of them (Zeus, Apollo, Athena) is portrayed as active in a given story. Secondly, even if suffering is not always *caused* by wrongdoing, its major victims tend to be shown committing wrongs which for a theatre audience, if not for a philosophical observer, considerably mitigate any sense of injustice – the tyrannical behaviour of Creon and of Oedipus, the treatment by Heracles of the people of Oechalia, of Lichas, and of his wife; in *Philoctetes*, where the major victim is completely innocent, he is splendidly recompensed and his chief tormentor disgraced. And thirdly (and related to this), Sophocles' choruses and characters frequently encourage us to reflect on the uncertainties of life, the constant possibility of reversals of fortune, and the danger that success may lead to arrogance. Awareness of these things is one aspect of the virtue that Greeks called *sōphrosynē*. The trouble is that in general, he who is *sōphrōn* is not likely to be a person of great achievement, and vice versa; but such a combination is nevertheless possible, as witness Odysseus in *Ajax* and Theseus in *Oedipus at Colonus* – and indeed Neoptolemus, once he has shaken off the influence of his play's very different version of Odysseus.

Sophocles' plays do not normally bear any direct relation to specific contemporary events, but in a broader sense most of them are highly relevant to the public concerns of a *polis* community. *Antigone* explores the meaning and limits of the citizen's duty of obedience to law and authority and of the Athenian's oath of allegiance. The responsibilities of leaders, military and political, to those whom they lead, are as much a theme of *Ajax* or *Oedipus the King* as of *Seven against Thebes* or *The Persians*. *Philoctetes* taps into the great debates of the late fifth century on the social education of the young, and on whether political ends justify means. There are no easy answers; there never are. Communities need leaders of intelligence and resolution; yet to put all one's trust in one's intelligence, to persevere unshakably in one's resolution, are perilous for the individual and may themselves endanger the community. The contrast between the virtuous democratic community and the arrogant, selfish leader is much less prominent in Sophocles than in Aeschylus; the tendency in Sophocles is rather to emphasize the *dependence* of the community on their leader's guidance and protection. In his two Trojan War plays, the choruses are portrayed not as soldiers but as (unarmed, poor) sailors; the Thebans look to Oedipus almost as a god; in *Antigone* the public oppose Creon's edict but are apparently paralysed by fear; in *Oedipus at Colonus* the villagers of Colonus can take neither decision nor action without Theseus. Aeschylus died when the radical Athenian democracy was only five or six years old. Sophocles lived in it for another half century and came to know its weaknesses as well as its strengths: that while 'a *polis* that belongs to one man is no true *polis*' (*Antigone*, line 737), nevertheless 'the little without the great are a frail protection for a fortress: the small are best supported by the great, and the great by the lesser' (*Ajax*, lines 158–161).

EURIPIDES

Life and works

Euripides, son of Mnesarchides (or Mnesarchus), was probably born between 485 and 480; he belonged to the deme of Phlya (in what are now the eastern suburbs of Athens). It was alleged in his lifetime that he was of lowly origin and that his mother had been a vegetable-seller, but there is evidence of his participation, when a boy, in prestigious cultic activities, and it is likely that he belonged to one of the leading families of the deme. Ancient biographers purport to tell us a great deal about his adult life, hardly any of which shows any sign of being based on reliable evidence; but a story (Aristotle, *Rhetoric* 1416a29–35) that he was involved in a dispute over a 'liturgy' (see p. 8) shows that he was a wealthy man (the story is unlikely to be an invention, since Euripides' opponent in it is an otherwise unknown man named Hygiaenon). A revealing remark by one of his choruses (Euripides, fr. 369), describing leisure reading as one of the consolations of old age, tends to confirm the story (going back to Aristophanes, *Frogs* 943 and 1409) that he was a lover and collector of books.

In truth all we really know of Euripides' life is his dramatic career. He competed for the first time in 456/5 (the year of Aeschylus' death), and gained his first victory in 441. Altogether he won first prize five times (one of these victories was posthumous). His total output was reckoned by ancient scholars at ninety-two plays, of which four were judged to be of dubious authenticity (they were probably in fact by Critias, for whom see pp. 60–1); they seem to have had texts of seventy-four genuine plays, seven of which were satyr-plays, and probably most of the missing fourteen plays were satyric.

Nineteen Euripidean plays (including one satyr-play) survive complete, though one of these, *Rhesus*, is probably spurious, and another, *Iphigeneia at Aulis*, seems to have been left unfinished by Euripides at his death and patched up by another hand or hands. Ancient quotations give us substantial fragments of most of the other tragedies, and in many cases these have been supplemented by papyrus fragments either of the text or of ancient synopses. Moreover, Euripidean tragedy was a favourite source for ancient mythographers, and when a tale told by a Hyginus or a pseudo-Apollodorus corresponds with what is otherwise known of a Euripidean play and contains episodes clearly suitable for dramatic presentation, the chances are high that what we have is essentially a summary of Euripides' plot.

For many of Euripides' plays the dates of production are preserved, either in the ancient headnotes (Hypotheses) or in other sources, and when these are arranged in chronological order there appears a clear and consistent tendency towards greater freedom in the structure of the iambic trimeter, restriction after restriction being progressively relaxed or abandoned; it is thus possible to define fairly closely the chronology of all Euripides' surviving tragedies and most of the fragmentary ones (at least from the middle 420s when the tendency first becomes apparent), and in general the metrical evidence conforms well with other indications such as comic quotations and parodies (which must of course be later than the plays to which they refer).

In 408 or 407, when well into his seventies, Euripides accepted an invitation to the court of Archelaus, king of Macedon (413–399); he wrote *Archelaus* in honour of his host, and *The Bacchae* contains passages in praise of Macedonia. Euripides died in winter 407/6 (before the City Dionysia, if the story is true that Sophocles honoured his memory by dressing his chorus in mourning at the official preview or *proagōn*); probably he was killed by his first Macedonian winter, though ancient biographers spun various far-fetched tales about his death. He left three sons, one of whom, also named Euripides, was responsible for the posthumous production of his father's last plays.

The nineteen surviving plays ascribed to Euripides are summarized on the following pages. In addition there are substantial papyrus fragments of *Alexander* (415), *Antiope* (427–419), *Archelaus* (407), *Cresphontes* (427?–425), *The Cretans* (before 431?), *Erechtheus* (417?), *Hypsipyle* (410–408), *Melanippe the Captive* (*c*.420?), *Oedipus* (after 415), *Phaëthon* (*c*.420), and *Telephus* (438).

Surviving plays

Alcestis (438; substitute for satyr-play; second prize)
Admetus has been spared from death on condition that someone else accepts it in his stead, and his wife Alcestis lays down her life for him. Admetus' friend Heracles, arriving amid the mourning and learning its cause, goes off to wrestle with Death and rescue Alcestis, and brings her back to her husband.

Medea (431; third prize)
Medea, indignant that Jason, whom she helped win the Golden Fleece and who is the father of her two children, is abandoning her to marry the daughter of the king of Corinth, kills his bride and her father by means of a poisoned robe, and then kills her children; she escapes in the chariot of the Sun-god (her grandfather) to Athens, where King Aegeus has promised to take her in.

The Children of Heracles (*Hērakleidai*) (430–428)
Heracles' children, his mother Alcmene, and his nephew Iolaus petition the Athenians for protection against Heracles' old enemy Eurystheus, king of Argos. After one of Heracles' daughters has voluntarily offered herself as a sacrifice, the Athenians defeat Eurystheus in battle and take him prisoner; Alcmene insists, despite strong Athenian opposition, on putting him to death, and Eurystheus prophesies that after death, as a hero, he will defend Athens against Heracles' descendants (i.e. the kings of Sparta).

Hippolytus (428; first prize)
Aphrodite has made Phaedra, wife of Theseus, fall in love with her bastard stepson Hippolytus, who hates women and sex. She means to escape her passion by starving herself to death, but her nurse makes an unauthorized approach to Hippolytus, who denounces Phaedra so violently that, fearing for her reputation, she hangs herself but leaves a note accusing Hippolytus of rape. Theseus, believing this, curses his son, who is fatally injured when a monstrous bull makes his horses bolt; Hippolytus' favourite goddess, Artemis, reveals the truth before he dies.

Andromache (*c*.425)
Hermione, daughter of Menelaus and wife of Neoptolemus, plots in her husband's absence against his concubine Andromache (widow of Hector), whom she accuses of making her barren by witchcraft. She calls in her father, and Andromache and her son are about to be put to death but are saved by Neoptolemus' aged grandfather Peleus. Hermione contemplates suicide, but her ex-fiancé Orestes, who hates Neoptolemus for having robbed him of Hermione, opportunely arrives; she runs off with him, and he successfully plots to have Neoptolemus murdered at Delphi.

Hecuba (*c*.424)
After the destruction of Troy, Hecuba, the widowed queen, first loses her daughter Polyxene, sacrificed in honour of the ghost of Achilles, and then discovers the corpse of her last surviving son, Polydorus, who had been sent for safety to the Thracian king Polymestor who had murdered him for his gold. She secures Agamemnon's permission to take revenge and lures Polymestor into the captives' hut, where she and the other Trojan women kill his sons and then put out his eyes.

The Suppliant Women (Hiketides) (423–421)
At Eleusis, the mothers of the Seven against Thebes, together with Adrastus, king of Argos, who had led their expedition, beg Theseus to help secure for their sons the right of burial. Theseus agrees, defeats the Thebans in battle, and brings the bodies back to Eleusis where they are lamented and cremated (one of the widows, Euadne, throwing herself on the pyre). Athena as *dea ex machina* predicts that the sons of the Seven will one day destroy Thebes, and orders Adrastus to swear an eternal alliance between Argos and Athens.

Electra (417?)
Orestes returns from exile to find Electra living on a remote farm, married to a poor but virtuous peasant. At first incognito, he is recognized by a former slave of his living nearby. He and his friend Pylades treacherously kill Aegisthus at a sacrifice, and Clytaemestra, sent word that Electra has had a baby, comes to the farm where she is killed by Orestes with Electra's help. The killers are immediately stricken with remorse, and the *dei ex machina* tell them that Apollo's command to Orestes to take vengeance was unwise, and that he and Electra must leave Argos and part for ever.

The Madness of Heracles (Herakles Mainomenos) (417?)
With Heracles in Hades on the last of his labours, his family are threatened with death by Lycus, tyrant of Thebes. At the last moment Heracles returns and kills Lycus. But now his old divine enemy Hera sends Iris and Lyssa (the goddess of madness) to drive him insane, and he kills his

wife and children. Utterly broken, he determines on suicide, but his foster-father Amphitryon and his friend Theseus persuade him to go on living, and he leaves with Theseus for Athens.

The Trojan Women (Troades) (415; second prize)

As the Greeks prepare to leave Troy, Athena and Poseidon agree that in reprisal for their sacrileges their fleet shall be wrecked at sea. Meanwhile Hecuba learns that Polyxene has been sacrificed, and that Cassandra and Andromache are to be given as prizes to Greek leaders; Andromache's young son, Astyanax, is taken from her to be put to death; Menelaus spares the guilty Helen; finally, after Hecuba has prepared Astyanax for burial, the city is set on fire, and victors and captives make ready to leave, not knowing what the gods have planned.

Ion (c.414)

Ion, son of Apollo and the Athenian princess Creusa, has been brought up as a temple-servant at Delphi. Creusa and her husband Xuthus come to consult Apollo about their childlessness; a misleading response given to Xuthus leads to a complex series of intrigues in which Creusa and Ion in turn attempt to kill each other, until the Pythia intervenes, giving Ion the cradle in which he was once abandoned. Creusa recognizes the cradle, is reunited with her son, and tells him that Apollo is his father. Athena directs that Ion is to be taken to Athens and become its king, and ancestor of the Ionian people – but Xuthus is never to know that Ion is not his son.

Iphigeneia in Tauris (c.414)

Iphigeneia, spirited away by Artemis when about to be sacrificed by her father Agamemnon at Aulis, is now her priestess in the land of the Tauri (the Crimea), obliged to sacrifice every Greek who lands there. Orestes and Pylades arrive in quest of the image of Artemis Tauropolos; they are captured, but Iphigeneia spares Pylades on condition that he takes a message back to Greece for her. The message reveals her identity to Orestes, and after a joyful reunion they plan and execute a scheme to escape from the wicked King Thoas, taking the image with them (to be set up at Halaé in Attica).

Helen (412)

Helen has been seventeen years in Egypt, spirited there by Hermes while Greeks and Trojans fought over a phantom in her shape; the local king, Theoclymenus, is set on marrying her, but she is loyal to Menelaus. Menelaus is shipwrecked on the Egyptian coast, meets Helen, and after some natural early doubts is eventually convinced that this is his *real* wife; with the help of Theoclymenus' sister Theonoe, the couple successfully plot their escape from Egypt.

The Phoenician Maidens (Phoinissai) (410?)
Adrastus and the Seven are about to attack Thebes. A parley between Eteocles and Polyneices, arranged by their mother Iocaste, proves a failure. After Menoeceus, son of Creon, has made himself a sacrifice, against his father's will, to save the city, the Thebans get the better of a battle. Eteocles challenges his brother to single combat; Iocaste arrives too late to prevent it and kills herself over her sons' bodies. Oedipus, who is still in Thebes, is expelled by the new ruler, Creon; Antigone, renouncing marriage with Haemon, departs with her father.

Orestes (408)
After killing his mother, Orestes has been outlawed by the Argives, and is lying delirious tended by Electra, awaiting trial for his life. Orestes' uncle Menelaus, on whose help he had counted, proves a broken reed, and he and Electra are sentenced to death but given the option of suicide. With the help of Pylades they plot to save themselves by killing the much-hated Helen and taking Hermione hostage. They thus checkmate their enemies, but Apollo appears as *deus ex machina*, issues a set of instructions whose effect is to cancel everything that has happened (including Helen's death), and tells Orestes to go to Athens for trial and then marry Hermione.

The Cyclops (408?; satyr-play)
The satyrs have been enslaved by the Cyclops Polyphemus and set to tend his sheep. Odysseus arrives with his companions; the satyrs give him some of their master's food in exchange for wine, but thanks to their cowardice Polyphemus discovers the truth and declares he will kill and eat the intruders – Odysseus last. Odysseus plots with the satyrs to get Polyphemus drunk and put out his eye; Silenus helps do the former, but for the latter Odysseus has to rely on his own friends (offstage). When the blinded Cyclops comes out of his cave, the satyrs make fun of him and then depart, with Odysseus, to freedom.

The Bacchae (posthumous; first prize)
Dionysus returns to his birthplace, Thebes, to establish his worship there and punish those who deny his divinity, especially the young King Pentheus and his mother and aunts. Disguised as his own priest, he is imprisoned but miraculously escapes. Hearing reports of violent behaviour by female Bacchic devotees on Mount Cithaeron, Pentheus decides to attack them, but the disguised god persuades him instead to go and spy on them; once there, Pentheus is seized and torn to pieces by a band of bacchants led by his mother Agaue, who afterwards, restored to sanity, laments over her son (in a scene now lost).

Iphigeneia at Aulis (posthumous; first prize)

Told that Iphigeneia must be sacrificed to enable the Greek fleet to sail for Troy, Agamemnon has ordered her to be sent to Aulis, ostensibly to be married to Achilles; a later, countermanding letter never arrives. Clytaemestra herself comes to Aulis, uninvited, with Iphigeneia. Through a chance meeting with Achilles she learns she has been deceived. She and Iphigeneia plead with Agamemnon in vain; Achilles, who has sworn to save the maiden, finds himself facing the wrath of the whole army. At this Iphigeneia resolves to accept death for the good of the Greek people, vainly begging her mother not to hate Agamemnon.[9]

Rhesus

From the Trojan night-camp, on the plain outside the city, Hector sends Dolon to spy on the Greeks. The Thracian king, Rhesus, arrives to aid the Trojans, promising to destroy their enemies in a single day. Odysseus and Diomedes – who have killed Dolon – find Hector's bivouac empty, but Athena tells them about Rhesus. She decoys Paris away, the two Greeks deceive the Trojan guards by giving them the correct password (previously extracted from Dolon), and presently Rhesus' death is reported by his charioteer, who blames Hector; but Rhesus' divine mother, as *dea ex machina*, tells them Odysseus is responsible. As day breaks the Trojans prepare for battle. This is the shortest surviving tragedy, and the only one whose action takes place entirely at night.

Profile

The preservation of a large, and partly random, sample of Euripides' work gives the impression that his story-patterns are more varied than those of Aeschylus or Sophocles: the surviving plays exemplify all four of the basic tragic plot-structures discussed on pp. 17–19. As real-time experiences they can on the whole be divided into two broad categories. In some of them, the action moves inexorably towards a goal fairly clearly foreseeable from the start, and sometimes (as in *Hippolytus*, *Ion* and *The Bacchae*) announced by a divine prologue-speaker. In others there is a sharp change of direction in mid-play which – unlike the superficially comparable changes of direction in several Sophoclean plays – often seems to have little logical connection with anything that has gone before; examples

---

9 The play's ending has suffered massive alteration; the original ending apparently had Artemis, as *dea ex machina*, telling Clytaemestra that she would rescue Iphigeneia unknown to the army.

are the arrival of Orestes in *Andromache*, or the intervention of Iris and Lyssa in *The Madness of Heracles*. In such cases it may be only when the play is over, if then, that the spectator can perceive how it all hangs together: in *Andromache* that everything that has happened, both the near-murder of Andromache and the murder of Neoptolemus, springs from Neoptolemus' unwise acceptance, tempted by a large dowry, of Menelaus' unwise offer of a marriage alliance; in *The Madness of Heracles* that the bonds of true human *philia* are stronger than anything the universe, or malicious gods, can throw at us. Plots of this type did not appeal to Aristotle, and have not appealed to many modern critics, but their frequency in Euripides suggests that his audiences are unlikely to have objected to them seriously – indeed they probably enjoyed being surprised.

Despite the wide variety of their plot-patterns, Euripidean tragedies are remarkably uniform in many of their formal components. They all begin with a prologue delivered in soliloquy, situating the action of the play precisely in its mythical context, often with elaborate genealogical antecedents, and providing the audience with a 'story so far' recapitulation. Almost all of them contain a set-piece debate (often called an *agon*, though with none of the formal structures of the Old Comic *agon* – see p. 68) between two leading characters, in which each uses standard oratorical techniques and often far-fetched lines of argument to establish his or her case – and whose outcome, curiously, usually makes no difference to the action: thus the debate between Theseus and Hippolytus in *Hippolytus* occurs *after* Hippolytus has been irrevocably doomed to death by Theseus' curse, while after the debate between Helen and Hecuba in *The Trojan Women* the judge, Menelaus, decides to do exactly what he was meaning to do anyway (namely, take Helen to Greece and put her to death there). A long narrative by a messenger, which (like the debate) the audience are clearly expected to enjoy for its own sake almost independently of its relevance to the play's action, is also a regular feature in Euripides, whereas Aeschylus and Sophocles vary the form of this element greatly and often omit it altogether. At the end it becomes more and more the normal thing for the action to be wound up, and the future foretold, by a *deus ex machina*; and either this divinity, or some other character, almost invariably includes an aetiology of the origin of some fifth-century custom or place-name. Thus, however surprising the events of a Euripidean play might be, they were presented in a formal framework that had a comforting familiarity.

The world in which the characters lived and moved was in some ways a curious blend of the heroic age and the fifth century. By the conventions of tragedy, open reference to contemporary matters was impossible; but features of contemporary social and intellectual life could be and were backdated into the heroic age. Theseus in *The Suppliant Women* defends, and a Theban herald attacks, the democracy of Athens with arguments very probably taken from the speeches and pamphlets of the 420s. Hecuba prays to Zeus in the language of fifth-century philosophy; Phaedra frets over the same ethical questions that exercised Socrates. Poetry is repeatedly referred to as the source of knowledge of divine and heroic myth. Jason and Neoptolemus grapple unsuccessfully with the problems that could arise when a man who had lived for many years in a stable relationship with a woman of inferior status decided that he must now make a proper marriage with a wife of his own rank. Contemporaries felt that whereas Aeschylus and Sophocles made their major characters seem larger than life, Euripides made his seem very much like the people they met every day. This is one reason why so much fuss was made over Euripides' practice of presenting heroes in rags. He may not in fact have done this much more than Sophocles (*Philoctetes*, *Oedipus at Colonus*) or even Aeschylus (*The Persians*), but it was emblematic of his whole approach to the tales he presented. It was apt, whether or not it was true, when an anecdote reported Sophocles as saying that he made characters such as they ought to be made, whereas Euripides made them such as they were (Aristotle, *Poetics* 1460b33–34).

Euripides' characters, at any rate, usually fall well within the normal range of physical, mental and spiritual qualities. The commanding, self-sufficient hero is virtually unknown; or if he appears, like Heracles, he is brought low and learns to be dependent on the aid and support of others. If anything, Euripides agrees with comedy in tending to see special virtues in classes whom myth traditionally marginalized – old men, peasants, slaves; and Athenians are nearly always favourably presented. His presentation of women is ambivalent. Contemporaries accused him of being misogynistic, because he so often presented women committing atrocious acts such as adultery and child-murder. Since other dramatists did this too, this probably suggests that there was something about Euripides' presentation of such stories which deeply disturbed many people but which they could not quite specify. It is not, or not principally, that Euripides' wicked women escaped unpunished; indeed the two most often cited, Phaedra[10] and Stheneboea, both died in disgrace (one by suicide, one by execution). It is more likely, then, to be the fact that these women, like virtually all major characters in Euripides, were made eloquent *advocates* for the justice of their case. There is no crime so horrendous that Euripides cannot make a character speak persuasively in its defence. In *Aeolus* a brother admitted having raped his sister and justified

---

10 Not in the surviving *Hippolytus*, but in Euripides' earlier play of the same name.

himself by the argument that morality is purely relative and subjective ('What's shameful, if it seem not so to those who do it?'). Medea questions the institution of marriage and justifies her murder of her children; Phaedra's nurse argues, uncontradicted, that there is nothing wrong with adultery . . . The women of Sophocles, in contrast, when they argue, almost always argue for values with which women were traditionally associated, above all the values of caring and of family solidarity (this applies even to a 'rebel' like Antigone).

The most striking features of Euripides' choruses are their overwhelming femaleness (only two of Euripides' seventeen surviving tragic choruses are male) and their increasing irrelevance. In a few plays, such as *The Suppliant Women* and *The Bacchae*, their fate is closely tied up with the action, but in many they are mere spectators. The chorus remain useful, especially in the darker plays, for creating atmosphere and pathos; in *The Bacchae* their role is vital, representing in sight and sound the Dionysiac spirit that is the driving force of the play while its other representatives, the Theban bacchants, are away on Cithaeron. In light plays such as *Helen* and *Iphigeneia in Tauris*, the chorus have little function; their songs can be reduced in number, and occasionally have no bearing whatever on the action. The decline of the chorus is matched by an increase in actor lyrics, comprising solos (monodies), duets and actor-chorus ensembles, especially the *parodos*, in which an actor takes part in every surviving play from *Electra* to *Orestes* inclusive. In these respects Euripides' last plays to some extent revert to older patterns; thus in *The Bacchae* there are five full, and highly relevant, choral odes and no extended actor solos at all.

Euripides' language is closer than that of Sophocles to the vocabulary and syntax of ordinary speech, and in spoken verse he makes occasional but effective use of colloquial expressions. This stylistic tendency is accentuated, from the mid-420s onwards, by an increasing freedom and frequency of 'resolution' (replacement of a long syllable by two short ones) in the iambic trimeter; on the other hand, from a slightly later date, Euripides also more and more reintroduces into dialogue scenes the chanted (and musically accompanied) trochaic tetrameter. His lyrics, both choral and solo, show an increased and increasing variety both in the range of rhythms employed and in their combination within songs, no doubt associated with contemporary innovations in musical practice.

In visual effects, Euripides excelled in the portrayal of pathos: tableaux of women and children threatened with death, or as suppliants at altars, feature repeatedly in his plays. Like Sophocles, he could also present horror very effectively, most harrowingly perhaps at the end of *The Bacchae* when Agaue returns to Thebes with her son's head mounted on the end of her

Bacchic wand, after which Cadmus brings back his dismembered body and Agaue, once restored to her right mind, 'takes each separate limb in her hands and laments over it' (in a passage that has not survived) before laying it in its proper place on the bier; but he often found horror easier to narrate (in messenger-speeches) than to present onstage. He made full and enthusiastic use of the *mēchanē*, not only for divine interventions but also for flying scenes involving human heroes (Bellerophon, Perseus and, innovatively, Medea). A favourite device of his was to have an expected character make his or her entrance in an unexpected way, especially early in a play: Hypsipyle as an old slave-nurse, keeping a baby amused by clicking castanets; Electra as a farmer's wife, carrying a jar of water on her head; Clytaemestra, in contrast, arriving in a carriage, resplendently dressed, with a train of Trojan slaves; Ion with a broom, sweeping clean the precinct of Apollo; Theonoe accompanied by acolytes with torches and incense, Theoclymenus with hounds and hunting paraphernalia, both quite unnecessary from the point of view of dramatic relevance; the chorus of *The Bacchae* invading Thebes in Asian costume and providing their own percussion accompaniment.

Euripides' lighter plays are pure, often exhilarating entertainment, which find their true successors in New Comedy. In the darker ones he portrays a chaotic and cruel universe. Mortals may tell the gods they ought to be wise and just, but this the gods hardly ever are; the friendship of one god is no protection against the malice of another, and the schemes of gods to punish their enemies (who may or may not, by human standards, be guilty of any wrong) regularly involve terrible suffering for the innocent. The one abiding value is *philia*, both 'affection' and 'the solidarity of kin and friends', repeatedly shown in pairs and trios of individuals in shattering circumstances – Theseus and the dying Hippolytus; Euadne uniting herself with Capaneus in death; Heracles, Amphitryon (his real father, he declares, if not his biological one) and Theseus; Iocaste and Antigone desperately trying to save Eteocles and Polyneices from themselves and each other; or Cadmus and Agaue, clinging together before parting for ever. To trust in oneself alone is usually a sure recipe for coming to grief, as it is for Hippolytus, Heracles, Eteocles and Pentheus. The values of the *polis* community, as such, are not prominent; rarely does a *polis* take any action in a Euripidean play, and rarely is a community's well-being of major interest as it is in all the genuine plays of Aeschylus and most of those of Sophocles. The Argive assembly in *Orestes* is dramatically important, not because of anything it can do for Argos but because it has the power of life and death over Orestes and Electra. No one except the self-sacrificing Menoeceus speaks for Thebes in *The Phoenician Women*, no one except a herdsman in *The Bacchae*. Euripidean characters, including those with whom we are made to sympathize most, normally do not look to the *polis* as the focus of their lives.

Has Euripides, then, anything to say to his audiences in their capacity as citizens? On the one hand he makes a point of appealing, whenever possible, to Athenian patriotic and cultural pride; in line with the ideology voiced in Athenian public funeral oratory, Athens is particularly celebrated (e.g. in *The Children of Heracles* and *The Suppliant Women*) as the *polis* whose pride it is to help those in need. Within the *polis*, Euripides regularly and sometimes irrelevantly makes his characters praise the wisdom of the ordinary citizen (especially the independent peasant) and condemn the selfishness and dishonesty of generals, popular orators, and sometimes of townsmen generally; this attitude, very close to that of Old Comedy, is probably taken for the sake of its audience appeal. On the other hand, the plays encourage, almost enforce, a critical approach to almost all established values and institutions (which is not the same thing as saying Euripides rejected these values and condemned these institutions); even the glory of helping the helpless is implicitly brought into question. Athens saves the family of Heracles from Eurystheus, yet it is Eurystheus who becomes after death a hero-defender of Athens; Athens secures the burial of the Seven against Thebes and wins Argos as an eternal ally, but from what has been seen of the Argive leader Adrastus both the moral and the military value of this alliance may well seem dubious. Nothing is ever as simple as it seems.

Most of Euripides' surviving plays were produced during the long war (431–404) against Sparta and her allies, and again two different approaches can be discerned. The attitude to Sparta herself, as represented by characters who are themselves Spartan (or whose Spartan connections are stressed, as in the case of Alcmene, ancestress of Sparta's kings, in *The Children of Heracles*), is uniformly hostile. But also there is an increasing revulsion from war itself, when not fought in a plainly righteous cause. This is evident as early as *Andromache*, and climaxes in *The Trojan Women* – produced at a time when the Athenians were besieging Melos (having probably already resolved that should it be captured the adult male Melians would be put to death and the rest of the population enslaved) and considering whether they should send an expedition to conquer Syracuse, neither the Melians nor the Syracusans having done them any harm. In more than one passage in this play Euripides goes out of his way to include words that would strike home very directly to an audience thinking of these two campaigns – Poseidon condemning the destruction of cities, the chorus praising the valour of the people of Sicily; and in the behaviour of the Greeks throughout the action, many spectators who had themselves been members of conquering armies would have seen much that was familiar to them. Was that why the judges (influenced as usual by audience opinion) gave first prize to Xenocles?

MINOR TRAGIC POETS[11]

Of the work of **Thespis**, the founder of Athenian tragedy (*fl. c.*533), nothing survives, and of **Choerilus** (*fl.* 523/0–499/6) very little. **Pratinas** of Phlius (*fl.* 520?–468) is said to have introduced satyr-drama to Athens, but a long satyric fragment ascribed to him may actually be from a dithyramb by his grandson of the same name. **Phrynichus** (*fl.* 511/508–476) is reported to have been the first dramatist to use female characters, was almost certainly the first to experiment with drama on contemporary topics, and was noted for the sweetness of his lyrics and the inventiveness of his choreography; in 476 he won a victory, perhaps with his Persian Wars play(s), with Themistocles as his *chorēgos*.

Among the numerous tragic dramatists contemporary with Sophocles and Euripides, four are outstanding – apart of course from the author of *Prometheus Bound*, who may have been **Euphorion** (*fl.* 431), son of Aeschylus. **Ion** of Chios (*fl.* 451/48–428) and **Achaeus** of Eretria (*fl.* 447/4) were regarded by Hellenistic scholars as almost fit to rank with the Big Three. Ion was perhaps the most versatile literary figure of the fifth century; no fragment of more than five lines has survived, but quotations give us some idea of a scene from a satyr-play, *Omphale*, in which Omphale prepared a sumptuous banquet for her temporary slave Heracles. **Agathon** (*fl.* 416–405) was noted for his distinctive style, full of antitheses, and for his lifelong homosexual relationship with one Pausanias, who accompanied him to the court of Archelaus of Macedon; he was the first to write choral odes with no pretence of relevance to the subject of the play, and the first to compose a tragedy (*Antheus*) whose plot and characters were freely invented (but see p. 20). He is criticized by Aristotle (*Poetics* 1456a15–19) for trying to fit too much plot material into a single play. There is a lively portrayal of him in Plato's *Symposium*. **Critias** (d. 403), uncle of Plato and leader of the 'Thirty Tyrants', seems to have written only four plays, but more is known of them than of the

---

11 Dates given with '*fl.*' are the earliest and latest at which an individual's dramatic activity is attested or reasonably deducible. Where two dates three years apart are paired in the form '499/6', the reference is to an Olympiad (the four-year period between one Olympic Games and the next, used by later Greek scholars as the unit of their standard reference chronology).

work of any other minor tragedian of the fifth century, doubtless because they were ascribed by many to Euripides. There survive substantial papyrus fragments of his *Peirithous*, which with its underworld setting and its chorus of Eleusinian initiates seems to have been in several respects a model for Aristophanes' *Frogs*; his *Sisyphus* contained a famous speech, evidently of sophistic inspiration, claiming that religion was a human invention designed to deter wrongdoing which human law-enforcers could not detect or punish.

In the early part of the fourth century there were few outstanding tragic dramatists; the most popular may have been **Sophocles the Younger** (*fl.* 401–375) who won a total of twelve first prizes, but not one word of his plays survives. The genre strikingly revived from the 370s onwards, when four dramatists in particular attained near-classic status, as references by Aristotle and Menander indicate. **Carcinus** (*fl.* 380–*c*.350), son of the Xenocles who had once defeated Euripides, wrote 160 plays (many of which must have been produced abroad, notably at Syracuse where he spent much time) and won eleven first prizes at the City Dionysia; only ten or eleven titles of his plays are known, one of them a *Medea* in which Medea was *falsely accused* of killing her children. **Chaeremon** (*fl. c*.355) was thought by Aristotle (*Rhetoric* 1413b12–13) to have a style more suitable for reading than acting (the surviving fragments suggest this refers to his precision in detailed description); his *Achilles Kills Thersites* was still being performed in the mid-third century, and he is cited twice in a series of tragic quotations, on the theme of the frailty of human existence, trotted out by a character in Menander's *Shield*. **Theodectas** of Phaselis (*fl. c*.370–353), a professional orator as well as a dramatist, wrote fifty plays and won seven or eight first prizes; his *Lynceus*, which reworked the ending of Aeschylus' Danaid trilogy, was so famous for its diametrical reversal of fortune (first Danaus had Lynceus sentenced to death, then vice versa) that Aristotle could cite it without author's name. But perhaps the outstanding figure in fourth-century Athenian tragedy was **Astydamas (the Younger)** (*fl.* 372–340), great-grandson of Aeschylus' nephew Philocles, who in the reconstructed theatre of the 330s was honoured with a bronze statue (and criticized for writing its laudatory inscription himself). He wrote 240 plays and won fifteen victories at the Dionysia and Lenaea combined. A papyrus fragment in which the climax of the *Iliad* is presented from the Trojan side may or may not come from his *Hector*. Towards the end of Astydamas' career the breakdown of the old generic distinctions was heralded when **Timocles** (*fl.* 340–*c*.325) began competing successfully in tragedy, satyr-drama and comedy alike.

Until now all aspiring tragedians had thought above all of competing at Athens; given his principles, it is perhaps not surprising that **Diogenes** of Sinope, the famous Cynic philosopher (d. 324/1), so far as we know did not. His tragedies (ascribed by some to his associate **Philiscus**, who was certainly a dramatist in his own right) promoted his principles so forthrightly that six centuries later the emperor Julian said that not even a prostitute could have surpassed their obscenity.[12] In *Atreus* (or *Thyestes*: very likely the two plays were one) he used the physical theories of Anaxagoras to demonstrate that we are all cannibals all the time, in *Oedipus* he argued that there was nothing evil in parricide or incest; and it is unlikely that anyone had spoken before, in a tragedy, of 'shit-spattered luxury'! Meanwhile the conquests of Alexander were changing the world, and in 324 **Python** of Catana presented at his court a one-off satyr-play called *Agen* in which Alexander's rebel treasurer Harpalus was extensively lampooned.

The last Athenian tragic dramatist of any significance was **Moschion** (*fl.* 310?), from whom there survive a brief but stirring defence of Athenian freedom of speech, an account of the origin of civilization, and a narrative of the arrival of a former king of Argos (Adrastus?) as a suppliant in a foreign city. One of his three known plays (*Themistocles*) and possibly another (*The Pheraeans*, which may have been about the tyrant Jason of Pherae) were on historical themes. The main centre of activity in tragedy, as in all other forms of poetry except comedy, was now Alexandria, where in the reign of Ptolemy II there were seven poets of considerable repute, known from their number as the Pleiad: **Homer** of Byzantium (*fl.* 284/1), who probably won the Dionysia competition at Athens some time in the 280s; **Sositheus** of Alexandria Troas (*fl.* 284/1), who appears to have specialized in satyr-plays; **Lycophron** of Chalcis (*fl.* c.270), **Alexander Aetolus** of Pleuron (*fl.* 279/6), whose one known play dealt with the childhood killing for which, according to the *Iliad*, Patroclus was exiled; **Aeantides** (for whom some sources substitute **Dionysiades** of Mallos); **Sosiphanes** (b. 306/5); and **Philicus** of Corcyra. Later tragic dramatists are mostly little more than names to us, sometimes with the date of a victory or two; from the second century BC to the end of antiquity we possess just seventeen lines of tragic verse by named, datable poets.

With one remarkable exception. There survive fragments, totalling 269 lines, of a tragedy called *The Exodus* (*Exagoge*) by a Jew of (probably) Alexandria named **Ezechiel**. It is based on the Septuagint version of the book of Exodus (chapters 1–15), with some expansions; the action moves freely from place to place and covers a period of many years, and God

---

12 Julian, *Against Heraclius the Cynic* 6.

himself is among the *dramatis personae* (though he is not seen, only heard). Since Christian writers refer to Ezechiel as 'the poet of Jewish *tragedies*', he must have written other works of the same kind; they cannot have been performed, or ever meant to be, and should be regarded as part of the attempt to provide Jewish Alexandria with a Greek literary heritage more Hellenically respectable than the often uncouth Septuagint.

ARISTOPHANES

Life and works

Aristophanes, son of Philippus, was born in the early 440s; he belonged to the city deme of Cydathenaeum, but had some connection (it is not known of what kind) with the island of Aegina. Probably after a period of unofficial collaboration with other poets, he competed at a major festival for the first time with *The Banqueters* (*Daitalês*) in 427, winning second prize; on this occasion, and often again, he had one of two colleagues, Philonides and Callistratus, undertake the production on his behalf and be entered as *didaskalos* in the festival records. After the production of *The Babylonians* at the Dionysia of 426, which probably gained first prize, Aristophanes was threatened with prosecution by Cleon, the most powerful politician of the day, for 'slandering the City in the presence of foreigners'; according to a passage in *The Acharnians*, produced a few months later, Cleon denounced him before the Council (*Acharnians*, lines 377–382), but there is no mention of the case being taken to court, and Aristophanes was not deterred from devoting *The Knights*, the first play he produced himself (424), almost entirely to a vicious assault on Cleon. *The Knights* won first prize, but this did not affect Cleon's political popularity (he was elected to a generalship a few weeks later).

The Clouds, produced at the City Dionysia of 423, was a failure, and this setback was followed by a further clash with Cleon. By renewed threats of prosecution, perhaps for exercising citizen rights when not entitled to them, Cleon forced Aristophanes to agree to moderate his satire in future, a promise which the dramatist gleefully broke in *The Wasps* at the very next festival (Lenaea 422). He later revised *The Clouds* with a view to restaging it, but apparently was not granted a chorus; eventually the incompletely revised script went into circulation in book form alongside the original one (and, unlike the original, it has survived to the present day).

Aristophanes' feud with Cleon ended when the latter was killed in action in 422, and our subsequent biographical information is scantier. He received extraordinary public honours in (probably) the autumn of

405, when he was commended by the Assembly and awarded a crown of sacred olive for the political advice he had offered in the *parabasis* of *The Frogs*, and the play was ordered to be restaged; this was probably a political manoeuvre by anti-democratic intriguers, to which Aristophanes may or may not have been knowingly a party. At any rate, after the fall of the Thirty (403), he was able to work his way back into public favour, and in or about 390 his name appears on an inscribed list of members of the Council (who were chosen by lot, but had to be approved as fit and proper persons before they could serve).

Wealth (388) was the last play Aristophanes produced in his own name; his two later plays, *Cocalus* and *Aeolosicon*, were produced for him by his son Araros, one of them winning first prize. Both of these plays reflected, much more strongly even than *Wealth*, the innovative trends affecting comedy in the 380s; *Aeolosicon* was described in Antiquity as a typical Middle Comedy play, while *Cocalus* is said to have contained 'rape, recognition, and all the other elements that Menander imitated', and to have had its plot taken over with little change by the New Comedy poet Philemon. Aristophanes probably died between 386 and 380. Araros and his brother Philippus both later became comic dramatists in their own right.

Ancient scholars knew of forty-four plays ascribed to Aristophanes, of which they judged four to be spurious. The total number of victories he gained is not known, but he won at least twice at the City Dionysia and at least four times at the Lenaea; an inscription also records what seems to be a victory in a local festival at Eleusis. There are several papyrus fragments of lost Aristophanic comedies, but no substantial one that can be assigned with confidence to a specific play.

Surviving plays

The Acharnians (Lenaea 425; first prize)
An elderly countryman, Dicaeopolis ('Honest Citizen'), annoyed that the Assembly is prevented from discussing peace, arranges a private peace treaty with the Peloponnesians for his own family, and persuades the bellicose men of Acharnae that he was right to do so. He trades profitably with ex-enemies in a private market from which *sykophantai* (and the fire-eating officer Lamachus) are excluded; at the festival of the Choes he is invited to the party given by the priest of Dionysus, while Lamachus is sent to defend the snowy frontier passes where he is badly wounded.

The Knights (Lenaea 424; first prize)
The household of Demos (i.e. the Athenian people) is dominated by the tyrannical slave Paphlagon (i.e. Cleon). Two fellow-slaves recruit a sausage-

seller to overthrow Paphlagon by outdoing him in vileness and vulgarity. With the help of the chorus of aristocratic young cavalrymen the plan succeeds, and Demos, magically rejuvenated by the sausage-seller, regains his political intelligence and is hailed as king of the Greeks.

The Clouds II (419/18; abortive revision of the unsuccessful *Clouds I* of Dionysia 423)
Strepsiades ('Twister'), a farmer plunged into debt by an extravagant wife and son, goes to the school run by Socrates in order to learn rhetoric so that he can cheat his creditors. Proving a poor learner, he sends his son Pheidippides to the school in his place, and afterwards the creditors are duly routed; but Pheidippides has learnt 'unjust argument' so well that he beats up his father and 'proves' that he was justified in doing so. Strepsiades complains to Socrates' patron goddesses, the Clouds, but they tell him he has brought his fate on himself; repentant, he burns down Socrates' school.

The Wasps (Lenaea 422; first or second prize)
Philocleon ('Cleon-lover'), an old man addicted to jury service, is imprisoned in his house by his rich son Bdelycleon ('Cleon-makes-me-puke') to prevent him from going to court; an attempt by his waspish fellow-jurors to rescue him fails. Bdelycleon sets up a private court in which one of his dogs prosecutes another, and tricks his father into acquitting the accused. He then takes Philocleon to an upper-class symposium, at and after which Philocleon becomes gloriously drunk, assaults all and sundry, and finally leads the company in a grotesque display of mock-tragic dancing.

Peace I (Dionysia 421; second prize)
Trygaeus ('Vintager'), a wine-grower, flies to heaven on a dung-beetle to ask Zeus why he is making the Greeks ruin themselves by war. He finds that War has taken over the gods' palace and imprisoned Peace in a deep cave. With the help of Hermes and the peasants of Greece he rescues the goddess, and celebrations, culminating in Trygaeus' marriage to Peace's beautiful companion Opora ('Fruit-harvest'), occupy the rest of the play.

The Birds (Dionysia 414; second prize)
Two old Athenians, Peisetaerus ('Persuasive Comrade') and Euelpides ('Optimist'), who have left Athens in quest of a lawsuit-free place to live, come to the land of the birds. The birds are initially hostile to these human intruders, but Peisetaerus promises to win back for them the rulership of the universe which was theirs (he says) before the gods usurped it. He founds the bird-city of Cloudcuckooville, starves the gods into submission by an aerial blockade, and forces Zeus to give him (not the birds!) the

sceptre of kingship and the beautiful Basileia ('Princess') whose possession is the key to universal power.

Lysistrata (Lenaea 411)
An Athenian woman named Lysistrata ('Disbander of Armies') persuades the women of all Greece to force their menfolk, by means of a sexual boycott, to end the war; meanwhile the women of Athens occupy the Acropolis to cut off funding for war purposes. The action is entirely successful, and the men, reduced to helpless appendages of their own phalli, make peace, experience the pleasures of the symposium together, and are reunited with their wives.

Women at the Thesmophoria (Thesmophoriazousai) I (Dionysia 411)
At the all-women festival of the Thesmophoria, the women of Athens have decided to punish Euripides for his alleged slanders against them. A relative of his, infiltrated into the meeting disguised as a woman to plead his cause, is discovered and sentenced to death for sacrilege. Euripides tries unsuccessfully to rescue him by adopting roles from various recent plays of his; eventually he succeeds by disguising himself as an old bawd, promising the women not to slander them any more, and using a dancing-girl to decoy the Scythian archer guarding the condemned man.

The Frogs (Lenaea 405; first prize; restaged Lenaea 404)
Dionysus, feeling acutely the lack of good tragic poets in Athens, goes down to Hades to bring back his beloved Euripides, who had died about a year before. Reaching Pluto's palace after various misadventures, he finds that Euripides has challenged Aeschylus for the tragic laureateship of the underworld, and is asked to judge the contest. After long hesitation he decides for Aeschylus, whom he takes back to earth to 'save' Athens with his good advice.

The Assemblywomen (Ekklēsiazousai) (391?)
Since male politicians are leading Athens to ruin, Praxagora ('Effective Speaker') organizes the women to pack the Assembly, disguised as men, and take control of the state. Once this is achieved, she announces the foundation of a new society based on communism both in property and in sex. The effects of this double revolution are explored in the second half of the play, at the end of which all depart for a mouth-watering feast.

Wealth (Ploutos) (388)
Guided by a Delphic oracle, Chremylus, an honest man who has been poor all his life, meets the blind god of Wealth, brings him home (thus becoming rich), and decides to have him cured at the temple of Asclepius

so that he can recognize the virtuous and live exclusively with them instead of, as hitherto, with the wicked. The goddess of Poverty denounces this as folly, but is not listened to. The healing is performed, the virtuous prosper at the expense of sykophants[13] and grasping *hetairai*, and Hermes and even Zeus become humble followers of Wealth, the new supreme god.

Profile

In most respects it is not easy to distinguish what is typical of Aristophanes from what is typical of Old Comedy generally, and therefore much of what is said in this section applies as much, or nearly as much, to Aristophanes' contemporaries as to Aristophanes himself. In his surviving plays at least, however, Aristophanes shows a very strong liking for one particular plot-pattern, a pattern, moreover, for whose previous existence there is no clear evidence. This pattern may have been invented by Aristophanes himself, or by one of his slightly senior contemporaries such as Hermippus, Eupolis or Phrynichus. It certainly was not confined to Aristophanes, for its pattern is clearly discernible in the fairly extensive papyrus fragments of Eupolis' *Demes* (412?), but it fits well with the one feature that does appear from our evidence to be uniquely Aristophanic, the dramatist's insistence on presenting himself as an adviser and benefactor of the community. The pattern is what may be called the *plot of predicament and rescue* – or, in one Greek word, of *sōtēriā*.

It begins with a situation that is extremely unsatisfactory, sometimes in the eyes of any objective observer, sometimes only in the eyes of a particular character; the predicament always has an important bearing on political, economic, artistic or intellectual issues of public concern. A character then devises a scheme, often with a high degree of fantasy, for putting things right and rescuing himself, or his family, or Athens, or the whole Greek world. Usually he or she[14] personally attempts to implement this scheme, but sometimes another person is persuaded to do so instead. The plot can normally be divided into four parts. In the *Conception* phase we learn about the initial situation and the hero's project; sometimes the project leaps into the hero's mind as we watch, but in most cases (s)he is already, at the outset, in the course of implementing

---

13 'Sykophants' is used in the ancient sense ('malicious accusers').
14 Two of Aristophanes' heroes are female, and in what follows 'hero' should be taken to include 'heroine'. The masculine pronouns used above ('himself or his family') are deliberate; Aristophanes' *selfish* heroes are all male.

it, though it is always some time before the audience learn what it is. There follows a *Struggle* as the hero encounters difficulties, usually taking the form of the opposition (at first often violent) of some person or group; these are always in the end overcome, resulting in the *Realization* of the project, whose *Consequences* are displayed in the succeeding scenes. The consequences are usually very much to the good, not only for the hero but for a wider public as well; a frequent element in them is rejuvenation, including the restoration of sexual potency (the leading male character is often presented with one or two nude females for his personal enjoyment, and in *Peace* and *The Birds* he is married to a beautiful divine or semi-divine maiden). In two plays, however, *The Clouds* and *Women at the Thesmophoria*, in which the hero's project was blatantly selfish and anti-social, it ends in failure and humiliation, though (this being comedy) there is no profound disaster. In these two plays the ending is abrupt and austere, the chorus simply walking out with a few perfunctory words; most other Aristophanic plays end with some form of triumphal procession or revel-rout, with the chorus taking a prominent part.

This functional story pattern is to be distinguished from the formal structural pattern of Aristophanic comedy, which is probably a good deal older, being already, to judge by the surviving fragments, well established in Cratinus' time. This formal pattern is an elaboration of the basic alternation of dialogue scenes and choral interludes characteristic of all Greek drama. No two plays have an identical structure, but normally one of the dialogue scenes, usually but not always in the first half of the play, contains as its central feature a set debate (*agōn*) between two characters on an issue crucial to the play, with a distinctive, bipartite structure and marked off by short choral songs at its beginning and midpoint. And the first true choral interlude after the *parodos* – sometimes also the second – is expanded into an elaborate structure known as a *parabasis*, containing not only songs but also speeches, addressed directly and openly to the audience and often, especially in the earlier plays, including explicit self-promotion by the author or by the chorus on his behalf. The speeches in the *agōn* and *parabasis*, and often in other scenes in their vicinity, are not in spoken iambic trimeters but in various longer, chanted metres (usually iambic, trochaic or anapaestic tetrameters); in all these scenes there is a strong tendency to favour the 'epirrhematic' structure (of matching songs followed by matching spoken or chanted sections) already mentioned in connection with early tragedy.

The second half of Aristophanes' career witnesses a progressive simplification of this elaborate and variable structure. After 414 no surviving play has a second *parabasis*, while the first *parabasis* loses some of its traditional components and in the two fourth-century plays disappears entirely. In the two late plays as well, the *agōn* is also drastically simplified, the duplication of its components being abandoned; by now epirrhematic structure has disappeared from other parts of the play too, and most of the choral interludes are of so little dramatic importance that their words are no longer included in the script, their occurrence simply being marked by the word *chorou* (see p. 11). In Aristophanes' last surviving play, *Wealth*, all that remains of the formal pattern of Old Comedy is a half-chanted, half-sung *parodos* (lines 257–321) and an *agōn* (lines 487–618) entirely in chanted anapaests with no lyrics at all.

Aristophanes, along with almost all his rivals, not only dealt regularly with specific issues of public importance, but also promoted specific attitudes on those issues – attitudes not unfairly characterized by Dover[15] as 'reactionary and philistine'. Politically, as already observed (see p. 27), the comic dramatists are uniformly hostile to those leaders who relied mainly on the support of the poor, and, while they never explicitly advocate the abandonment of the democratic constitution, they are also hostile to some of that constitution's vital safeguards, above all to the payment of jurors which guaranteed that the courts would not be dominated by the rich.[16] Artistically and intellectually, they consistently favour the old ways against the new – Aeschylus against Euripides, traditional against sophistic education. These attitudes are so uniform across the whole genre in the last four decades of the fifth century that they can hardly be explained by supposing that all the comic dramatists just happened to hold these opinions; indeed Cratinus' coinage of a verb 'to Euripidaristophanize' (Cratinus, fr. 342) shows that many people felt that Aristophanes at least had much in common with Euripides intellectually. Rather, the right-wing, traditionalist bias of so much Old Comedy was the dramatists' considered view of what would appeal to their audience (whose socioeconomic make-up may well have differed considerably from that of the average Assembly meeting).

Aristophanes' comedy is characterized, within the fairly well-defined structural framework described above, by extreme inventiveness in language and theatrical presentation, and by a carefree disregard of the physical and even the logical constraints of the everyday world if they interfere with the requirements of the plot or even of a momentary joke. The plot of almost all of his plays is full of events which a moment's

---

15 K.J. Dover, *Aristophanes: Clouds* (Oxford, 1968), p. liii.
16 In the fourth century Aristophanes seems much more sympathetic to the poor, probably because of changes in the socioeconomic composition of his audience resulting directly or indirectly from the defeat of 404.

thought will show to be impossible; their impossibility is never of any significance unless the dramatist chooses to draw the audience's attention to it.

MENANDER

Life and works

Menander, son of Diopeithes, was born between 343 and 341, and died while swimming off Peiraeus at the age of fifty-one or fifty-two. Between the ages of eighteen and twenty he underwent the two-year course of training in civic virtue and soldiership (the *ephebeia*) which had been made compulsory in 334; the philosopher Epicurus was an ephebe at the same time. He is said to have produced his first play, *Anger* (*Orge*), while still an ephebe, probably in 321; he won first prize at the Lenaea with *The Curmudgeon* (*Dyskolos*) in 316 (this may or may not have been his first Lenaean victory), and at the City Dionysia for the first time a year later. In all he won eight victories, which seemed surprisingly few to later generations who regarded him as by far the greatest representative of New Comedy. Possibly he was unpopular for a time because of his friendship with Demetrius of Phalerum, who had been virtually dictator of Athens from 317 to 307; he is said to have been prosecuted, or threatened with prosecution, after Demetrius fell from power. He is reported to have written some 108 plays, many of which must have been produced abroad, but unlike most of his rivals he did not himself visit the courts of foreign monarchs, although there is evidence that he did receive invitations from Ptolemy I of Egypt and Demetrius Poliorcetes of Macedon. Like Euripides, he enjoyed his greatest success posthumously.

There are nineteen identified plays of Menander of which substantial fragments survive on papyri. The seven best preserved are summarized below; the others are *The Double Deception* (*Dis Exapatôn*) (adapted by Plautus as *Bacchides*), *The Dagger* (*Encheiridion*), *The Farmer* (*Georgos*), *The Hero* (*Heros*), *The Carthaginian* (*Karchedonios*), *The Lyre Player* (*Kitharistes*), *The Flatterer* (*Kolax*), *The Women who Drank Hemlock* (*Koneiazomenai*), *The Girl from Leucas* (*Leukadia*), *The Girl from Perinthus* (*Perinthia*), *The Apparition* (*Phasma*) and *Possessed* (*Theophoroumene*). Other plays of Menander known to be the source of surviving Roman comedies are *The Brothers* (*Adelphoi*) I and II (Plautus, *Stichus* and Terence, *Adelphoe* respectively), *The Ladies' Lunch* (*Synaristosai*) (Plautus, *Cistellaria*) and three further plays adapted by Terence under unchanged titles, *The Girl from Andros* (*Andria*), *The Eunuch* (*Eunouchos*) and *The Man who Punished Himself* (*Hauton Timoroumenos*).

Surviving plays
(of which at least half is preserved)

The Shield (*Aspis*)

Cleostratus is thought to have been killed while serving abroad as a mercenary, leaving his sister as an heiress (*epiklēros*) who must marry the nearest relative who claims her. To prevent her being claimed by her grasping old uncle Smicrines, the rest of the family fake the illness and death of Smicrines' brother Chaerestratus in the hope that Smicrines will want to marry *his* daughter and so claim a much larger estate. Then Cleostratus unexpectedly returns alive; Chaerestratus is able to come back to life, and Cleostratus is able to give his sister to Chaereas who has long loved her.

The Curmudgeon (*Dyskolos*) (Lenaea 316)

The wealthy young Sostratus, while hunting at Phyle, has fallen in love with a beautiful girl, but her father Cnemon proves to be a misanthropic curmudgeon. On the advice of Cnemon's stepson Gorgias, Sostratus tries to impress Cnemon by working in the fields, but to no avail. Then Cnemon falls down his own well and is rescued by Gorgias; impressed with Gorgias' selflessness, he adopts him as his son and makes him the girl's guardian; Gorgias forthwith gives her to Sostratus, who then persuades his own father to take Gorgias as a son-in-law. Cnemon is eventually dragged kicking and screaming to the betrothal feast.

The Arbitration (*Epitrepontes*)

Charisius has left home after learning that his wife Pamphile has given birth to, and exposed, a baby five months after their wedding. By a series of happy accidents the baby is discovered and Charisius himself is proved to be its father. Pamphile, who had resisted the efforts of her father Smicrines to break up the marriage even when there seemed to be clear evidence that Charisius had had a child by a mistress, is reunited with her husband, and Charisius' slave Onesimus and the harp-girl Habrotonon, who had done much to make the discovery possible, are probably both given their freedom.

Hated (*Misoumenos*) (before 307)

The soldier Thrasonides has bought as his slave a girl prisoner of war from Cyprus, Crateia, and made her his mistress, but she now hates him (because, unknown to Thrasonides, she mistakenly believes he had killed her brother). The middle portion of the play is very scrappy, but Crateia's father Demeas, who has come from Cyprus, discovers her in Thrasonides' house and ransoms her. Thrasonides asks him for Crateia's hand in marriage and is refused; he perhaps attempts or pretends to attempt suicide, but Crateia's brother returns alive and the marriage is quickly agreed to by all.

Shorn (*Perikeiromene*) (313 or 312?)
The scene is Corinth. The soldier Polemon, who is living with a girl named Glycera, has cut off her hair in a rage after seeing her embracing her young neighbour Moschion (actually her twin brother, though only she knows this). Glycera leaves his house. Remorseful and lovesick, he asks his friend Pataecus to intercede with her. Glycera refuses to return, but she shows Pataecus the trinkets that were left with her when she and her brother were exposed as infants, and these prove that she and Moschion are Pataecus' children. Glycera forgives Polemon and is betrothed to him; Pataecus arranges another marriage for Moschion.

The Girl from Samos (*Samia*)
Demeas is living with the Samian *hetaira* Chrysis. His adopted son Moschion has raped the daughter of his neighbour Niceratus; her baby is being cared for by Chrysis. Independently Demeas and Niceratus, just back from abroad, decide to arrange a marriage between their children. Demeas then discovers the baby, overhears that Moschion is its father, and throws Chrysis out of his house. Moschion, to his embarrassment, is asked to intercede for Chrysis with his father, and eventually is forced to confess the truth. This reconciles Chrysis and Demeas; Niceratus is berserk with rage, but eventually calms down and agrees to the marriage.

The Sicyonian(s) (*Sikyonios/-oi*)
Stratophanes, a soldier brought up at Sicyon, is the owner of an Athenian girl named Philumene, sold to him by pirates when she was four. Fearing he wants to make her his mistress, Philumene takes refuge at a temple, but Stratophanes, who has just learned that he too is an Athenian citizen, readily allows her to stay there while he seeks her father. An old man, bribed by the soldier's 'parasite' Theron to say he is Philumene's father, proves to *be* Philumene's father, and happily betroths her to Stratophanes (to the chagrin of a youth named Moschion, who was in love with Philumene and who now finds Stratophanes is his brother).

Profile

The crucial plot elements of Menandrian comedy are love, deception and discovery. Virtually every play contains a young man in love (sometimes more than one) who meets and overcomes, usually with considerable assistance from good fortune, the obstacles posed to his desires by parents, pimps, rich soldiers or other hostile agencies. Nearly always many, sometimes all, of the characters, during much of the action, are kept in ignorance of vital facts, either through circumstances or through the machinations of others, and much of the action usually springs from such misapprehensions; the truth is generally known to the audience, being imparted to them if necessary by a god early in the play, and its discovery by the characters tends to be a climactic moment in the action. Very often the truth that is discovered relates to the parentage of a child – sometimes a recently born infant, sometimes a young woman who unexpectedly proves to be of citizen status and therefore marriageable. Almost always the play ends with one or more betrothals, or with the reconciliation of a married couple, or with the winning of a desirable *hetaira* by an impecunious youth. A surprising and indeed shocking feature to modern minds is the frequency with which rape is exploited as a plot-device. Partly this is a legacy from Euripidean tragedy and myth-based comedy (see pp. 52, 64), partly it is a dramaturgical contrivance to enable a child to be born out of wedlock without destroying the reputation and marriageability of the mother; nevertheless, the underlying assumption is clearly that rape is little more than an excessive display of youthful male energy, for which marriage atones completely, and that rapist and victim can be expected to live together happily ever after.

The characters tend to be drawn from a limited repertoire of semi-stock types: young lovers, old men (severe or mild, mean or generous), 'parasites' (men who live by sponging on rich friends), mercenary soldiers, pimps, slaves (who are often crafty schemers), cooks (usually garrulous and boastful), mothers, old nurses, *hetairai* (slave or free, young or experienced, poor or rich) and marriageable maidens (who, however, often remain wholly silent, and sometimes remain offstage throughout). Character names likewise tend to come from a limited repertoire and to be attached to particular types (e.g. Moschion for a young lover, Demeas or Smicrines for an old man, Daos or Getas for a male slave, Sophrone for an old nurse). Menander often surprises his audiences by making characters behave in a manner not normal for their type, but the surprise effect itself obviously depends on there being expectations as to how each character-type will normally behave. He was rightly admired in antiquity for the human credibility of his characters and their behaviour, and he particularly excels at constructing plots that depend crucially on specific character traits, plots that would not work if the personalities of the individuals involved were not exactly as they are. Thus, in order for the happy ending of *Epitrepontes* to come about, it is necessary not only for Pamphile to be a loyal wife and Charisius a fundamentally decent young man (and hence conscience-stricken when he comes to believe that he has fathered a bastard child), but also for the slave Syrus to be a more persuasive speaker than his rival Daos (so that he is awarded custody of the baby); for Smicrines to have a concern for justice in matters that do not impinge on his own interests (so that he agrees to judge the dispute between the two slaves, and judges it fairly) while in matters that *do* affect his own interests he thinks only of money (so that he drives his daughter to despair – but for which she would never have met Habrotonon and learned the truth about her baby); for Charisius' slave, Onesimus, to be a busybody (so that he discovers, by eavesdropping, that the trinkets left with the baby include a ring that once belonged to Charisius); for Habrotonon to be both extremely clever and passionately eager to gain her freedom (so that she devises the ingenious ploy of pretending to be the mother of the baby, in order to establish whether Charisius really is its father); even for the cook Carion to be (after the manner of many comic cooks) both talkative and self-important (so that by venting in public his resentment at being slighted, he becomes the means by which Smicrines learns of the supposed birth of a bastard to Charisius). The audience, of course, know from the start, because of the nature of the genre, that the ending *will* be a happy one, and in any case they were probably told by a god, in a 'delayed prologue' midway through the first act,[17] that the baby's parents were none other than Charisius and Pamphile; suspense and tension are created, not by any uncertainty on the audience's part about what the ending is to be, but by their acute uncertainty, or rather bewilderment, as to how on earth this ending is going to be reached from the given starting-point.

The structure of Menander's comedy, in sharpest contrast to that of Aristophanes', is extremely simple. A play comprises five acts, of roughly equal length though the last is sometimes shorter, separated by choral performances whose words, if any, were not included in the scripts that went into circulation. The action within each act is not necessarily continuous; the stage may be left empty at any point before the entry of a new character or characters. The dialogue is mostly in spoken iambic trimeters; the structure of these is very flexible, and line-rhythm and sentence-rhythm are often largely independent of one another. In several plays one scene – sometimes in the middle, sometimes at or near the end – is performed to musical accompaniment, in chanted iambic or trochaic tetrameters; in some there are set-piece musical solos (a song in dactylic hexameters by the 'possessed' girl who is the title-character of *Possessed* [*Theophoroumene*]; an anapaestic chant by a temple servant in *The Girl from Leucas* [*Leukadia*]). Many plays have a formal prologue

---

17 This portion of Act I has been lost, but such delayed prologues are regularly used by Menander to give the audience essential information not known to the characters.

delivered by a god; sometimes, as in *Dyskolos*, this begins the play, but more often it follows an initial scene which serves to arouse both interest and mystification. Every play, so far as we know, ends with a request for applause and a prayer for the blessing of the goddess Victory.

MINOR COMIC POETS

The first official victor in comedy at Athens, **Chionides**, is little more than a name. We know much more of his Syracusan contemporary **Epicharmus** (*fl. c.*500–465), and we have papyrus fragments of text or commentary from several of his plays, especially *Prometheus or Pyrrha* (on the Flood myth) and *Odysseus the Deserter*. **Magnes** dominated Athenian comedy in the 470s and 460s (his record of eleven City Dionysia victories was never surpassed), but the artistic level of his work does not seem to have been high.

The real founders of Athenian Old Comedy were **Cratinus** (*fl. c.*453–423) and his contemporaries **Ecphantides, Teclecleides, Callias** and **Crates**. Cratinus, who frequently satirized Pericles at the height of his power, was regarded by Aristophanes as the greatest comedian before himself; he was notoriously fond of wine, and in his last comedy, *The Bottle (Pytine)*, which defeated Aristophanes' *Clouds*, he made himself a character (in a love-triangle with the feminine personifications Comedy and Drunkenness). Papyri preserve substantial fragments of *The Wealth-gods (Ploutoi)* (429 or 428?) and most of a synopsis of *Dionysalexandros* (see pp. 28–9). Crates, who avoided personal and political satire, is important in the history of comedy for having pioneered types of plot that became the norm in Middle and New Comedy. In the mid-430s these established figures were joined by **Pherecrates** (*fl.* 437 to after 415), the first known writer of *hetaira* comedies and also fond of utopian fantasy, and **Hermippus** (*fl. c.*435 to after 420), who also wrote non-dramatic iambic poetry.

In the 420s a galaxy of new talent came to the fore, including **Eupolis** (*fl.* 429–412), **Phrynichus** (*fl.* 429–405), **Aristophanes, Ameipsias** (*fl.* 423–*c.*395) and **Plato Comicus** (*fl.* 422–*c.*380). Eupolis, the third of the canonical trio of Old Comedians, won seven first prizes in (at most) seventeen attempts before his death on naval service *c.*411; in 418–415 he fought a war of words with Aristophanes over allegations of plagiarism. Papyri show he was read down to the early fifth century AD, and preserve substantial portions of *The Prospaltians* (429) and *The Demes* (412?; a resurrection-play foreshadowing Aristophanes' *Frogs*) and a commentary on *Maricas* (421). Plato, spanning the transition from Old to Middle

Comedy, specialized at first in political plays, later in mythological ones; with about thirty known plays he was the most productive Old Comedian after Aristophanes. In the latter part of their careers Aristophanes' and Plato's rivals included **Strattis** (*fl. c.*410–*c.*385), **Theopompus** (*fl. c.*410–*c.*370), **Archippus** (*fl.* 403–400) who continued the tradition of satire on political leaders (*Rhinon*) and of animal fantasies (*The Fishes*), and **Philiscus** (*fl. c.*400–380), four of whose eight known plays were about gods' birth-legends (a fourteen-line papyrus fragment describing Cronus' child-eating habits may well come from his *Birth of Zeus*).

The period of Middle Comedy (see pp. 30–1) sees an extraordinary increase in the leading dramatists' productivity. The major figures are **Anaxandrides** of Rhodes (*fl. c.*385–348; sixty-five plays), **Eubulus** (*fl.* 375/2–*c.*335; 104 plays), **Antiphanes** (*fl.* 387/4–306; at least 260 plays), and the equally long-lived **Alexis** of Thurii (*fl. c.*350–*c.*275; 245 plays, of which *The Carthaginian* may well have been the model for Plautus' *Poenulus*). **Timocles** (*fl. c.*345–*c.*315), who also wrote tragedies and satyr-plays, attempted to revive aspects of Old Comedy (many of his titles clearly suggest imitation of Cratinus or Aristophanes) and satirized Demosthenes, Hypereides and other political leaders.

Later Antiquity identified the three outstanding New Comic drama-tists as **Menander, Diphilus** of Sinope (*fl. c.*320–*c.*285; 100 plays), and **Philemon** of Syracuse (*fl.* 327–*c.*263; ninety-seven plays); plays by all three were adapted by Plautus and/or Terence, as were two by **Apollodorus** of Carystus. It is highly probable that we possess papyrus fragments of plays by Diphilus and Philemon, but we cannot identify any. Philemon was honoured with Athenian citizenship, as was Diphilus' brother **Diodorus** (*fl. c.*300–*c.*280). **Philippides** (*fl.* 311–282) was not only a dramatist but an active and partisan politician and diplomat, who sometimes made his views clear in his plays (e.g. denouncing Demetrius Poliorcetes and his Athenian supporters). Only one play by **Straton** (*fl.* 302) is known, but a speech in it (about an eccentric cook who insisted on talking Homeric Greek) became famous independently of the play, survives by itself on a papyrus, and is quoted in an expanded form by Athenaeus. Meanwhile the western Greek tradition of light drama had been revived in the genre of *phlyakes* or *hilarotragōidiai* (mostly low-life farces, or burlesques of Euripidean tragedy) by poets such as **Rhinthon** of Syracuse or Taras (*fl. c.*300). After Philemon's time no comic dramatist acquired a lasting reputation.

3
CHRONOLOGY OF GREEK DRAMA

Period	Authors, works and developments		Contemporary events	
BC 600–575	600–570	'Tragic choruses' at Sicyon transferred from Adrastus to Dionysus cult	600–570	Cleisthenes tyrant of Sicyon
			594	Solon codifies and reforms Athenian laws
575–550	570	Susarion composing comedies at Megara?	560	Peisistratus becomes tyrant of Athens
550–525	c.550	Epicharmus born at Megara Hyblaea	545	Greeks of Asia Minor conquered by Cyrus of Persia
	c.533	City Dionysia founded at Athens; first tragic competition, won by Thespis	535–523	Polycrates tyrant of Samos
			527	Peisistratus succeeded by his son Hippias
525–500	510	Choerilus (tr) floruit	510	Hippias expelled from Athens

Period	Authors, works and developments		Contemporary events	
525–500	525/4?	Aeschylus born at Eleusis	508	Athenian democracy established by Cleisthenes
	c.520?	Pratinas brings satyr-drama to Athens		
	511/8	Phrynichus' first victory		
	501	Reorganization of City Dionysia; start of official record of contests		
500–475	c.499	Epicharmus (com) *floruit* at Syracuse; Aeschylus' first production	499–494	Asian Greeks unsuccessfully revolt against Persian rule
	497/6?	Sophocles born at Colonus	490	Athenians defeat Persians at Marathon
	493	Phrynichus' *Fall of Miletus*	487	First ostracism vote at Athens
	486	First official performances of comedy at Athens	487/6	Athens' chief magistrates first chosen by lot
	485–480	Euripides born	485	Gelon becomes tyrant of Syracuse
	484	Aeschylus' first victory	480–479	Persian invaders defeated in Greece, Carthaginians in Sicily
	476?	Phrynichus' Persian Wars drama(s), sponsored by Themistocles	478	Foundation of naval alliance ('Delian League') headed by Athens
	473?	Death of Phrynichus	478	Hieron becomes tyrant of Syracuse
475–450	472	Magnes (com) *floruit*; Aeschylus' *Persians*, sponsored by Pericles	c.470	Ostracism of Themistocles
	c.470	Aeschylus' first visit to Sicily	466	Death of Hieron; Syracuse becomes a democracy

468	Sophocles' first victory; death of Pratinas	
467	Aeschylus' *Seven against Thebes*	
463?	Aeschylus' *Suppliant Maidens*	
c.462	Athenian theatre redesigned, with new *skēnē* (and probably *ekkyklēma* and *mēchanē*); third actor introduced in tragedy	
		462/1 — Athenian democracy radicalized by Ephialtes; ostracism of Cimon
		461–429 — Ascendancy of Pericles at Athens
		460–446 — Athens at war with Sparta and allies
		454 — Treasury of Delian League moved to Athens
458	Aeschylus' *Oresteia*	
456/5	Aeschylus dies at Gela; Euripides' first production	
c.451??	Sophocles' *Women of Trachis*	
	Ion, Achaeus (tr), Cratinus, Callias, Crates, Ecphantides, Hermippus, Pherecrates, Telecleides (com) *floruerunt*	
		447–432 — Building of Parthenon
		443/2 — Sophocles a treasurer of the Delian League
c.450	Institution of prize for best tragic actor at City Dionysia	
		441/0 — Samos revolts against Athenian rule; Sophocles serves as a general
c.449	Birth of Aristophanes	
440s	Comedy becomes politicized	
440s/430s	Sophocles' *Ajax*	
c.442	Start of comic contests at Lenaea	
c.442?	Sophocles' *Antigone*	
441	Euripides' first victory	
440/39	Decree restricting comic satire (repealed 437/6)	
		431 — Outbreak of 'the' Peloponnesian War (Athens v. Sparta)
		430 — Pericles temporarily suspended from office
		429 — Death of Pericles

450–425

Period	Authors, works and developments	Contemporary events
450–425	438 Euripides' *Telephus* and *Alcestis*	
	436–426 Sophocles' *Oedipus the King*	
	c.432 Start of tragic contests at Lenaea	
	431 Euphorion wins first prize (with the *Prometheus* plays?), defeating Euripides' *Medea*	
	430 Cratinus' *Dionysalexandros*	
	430–428 Euripides' *Children of Heracles*	
	429 Eupolis' first production	
	429? Cratinus' *Wealth-gods*	
	428 Euripides' *Hippolytus*	
	427 Aristophanes' first production	
	426 Cleon's first attempt to prosecute Aristophanes (after *Babylonians*)	
	425 Aristophanes' *Acharnians*	
	c.425 Euripides' *Andromache*	
425–400	Ameipsias, Phrynichus, Plato (com) *floruerunt*	422 Cleon killed at battle of Amphipolis
	424 Aristophanes' *Knights*	421 Athens and Sparta make peace
	c.424 Euripides' *Hecuba*	415 Athenian invasion of Sicily
	423 Aristophanes' *Clouds* defeated by Cratinus' *Bottle*	413 Sparta renews war on Athens; Athenian force in Sicily destroyed; Sophocles elected a *proboulos*

425–400	422 Aristophanes' *Wasps*	411 Athenian democracy overthrown (restored 410)
	c.422 Euripides' *Suppliant Women*	404 Athens surrenders; Sparta supreme in Greece; junta of Thirty take power at Athens
	421 Eupolis' *Maricas*; Aristophanes' *Peace*	403 Thirty overthrown; Critias killed in battle; Athenian democracy restored
	c.419/18 Aristophanes revising *Clouds*	
	c.418 Stage platform raised to height of about 1 metre	
	418? Sophocles' *Electra*	
	c.417 Euripides' *Electra*	
	c.417 Euripides' *Madness of Heracles*	
	416 Agathon's first victory	
	415 Euripides' *Trojan Women*	
	414 Aristophanes' *Birds*	
	c.414 Euripides' *Ion* and *Iphigeneia in Tauris*	
	412? Eupolis' *Demes*	
	412 Euripides' *Helen*	
	411 Aristophanes' *Lysistrata* and *Women at the Thesmophoria*	
	411? Death of Eupolis, on naval service	
	410? Euripides' *Phoenician Maidens*	
	409 Sophocles' *Philoctetes*	
	408 Euripides' *Orestes* and (?) *Cyclops*	
	408/7 Euripides goes to Macedonia	
	407/6 Death of Euripides	
	406/5 Death of Sophocles	

Period	Authors, works and developments	Contemporary events	
425–400			
	405	Aristophanes' *Frogs*	
	405?	Euripides' *Bacchae* and *Iphigeneia at Aulis* produced posthumously	
	405/4	Public honours for Aristophanes; *Frogs* restaged	
	403–400	Archippus (com) *floruit*	
	401	Sophocles' *Oedipus at Colonus* produced posthumously	
400–375			399	Death of Socrates
		Sophocles the Younger (tr), Philiscus, Strattis, Theopompus (com) *floruerunt*	396–394	Agesilaus of Sparta campaigns in Asia Minor
	391	Aristophanes' *Assemblywomen*	395–387	Sparta at war with other leading states
	388	Aristophanes' *Wealth*	386	Persia imposes peace on Sparta's terms
	c.385	Aristophanes' last production	378	Athens founds a second naval league
375–350			late 370s	Plato's *Republic* completed
		Astydamas, Carcinus, Chaeremon, Theodectas (tr) *floruerunt*	371	Spartans defeated by Thebans at Leuctra
		Middle Comedy fully developed; Anaxandrides, Antiphanes, Eubulus *floruerunt*	369	Messenia (SW Peloponnese) becomes independent of Sparta
			362	End of Theban supremacy
			359	Philip II becomes king of Macedon

350–325		Diogenes, Philiscus (tr), Timocles (tr/com) *floruerunt*	346	Philip gains control of northern and central Greece
	c.350	Start of Alexis' long career	338	Philip defeats Athens and Thebes at Chaeroneia
	c.342	Birth of Menander	338–326	Lycurgus in charge of Athenian financial administration
	330s	Official Athenian text canonized for Aeschylus, Sophocles and Euripides	336	Philip assassinated, succeeded by Alexander
	330s	Athenian theatre reconstructed in stone	334	Alexander invades Asia
	330s/320s	Aristotle's *Poetics*	334	Official institution of *ephebeia* at Athens
	c.327	Philemon's first known production	331–330	Alexander overthrows Persian Empire
325–300		Moschion (tr), Diphilus, Straton (com) *floruerunt*	323	Death of Alexander at Babylon
	324	Python's satyr-play *Agen*	322	After unsuccessful Greek revolt, Macedonian general Antipater ends democracy at Athens
	321	Menander's first production		
	316	Menander's *Dyskolos*	317–307	Athens ruled by Demetrius of Phalerum
	313/2?	Menander's *Perikeiromene*		
	c.307	Abolition of *choregia*		
	c.300	Rhinthon (*phlyakes*, Syracuse) *floruit*		
300–275		The Alexandrian 'Pleiad' (tr) become prominent	283–246	Reign of Ptolemy II (Philadelphus) of Egypt

Period	Authors, works and developments		Contemporary events	
300–275		Apollodorus, Diodorus, Philippides (com) *floruerunt*		
		Earliest surviving dramatic papyri		
	c.291	Death of Menander		
	c.275	Alexis' last production		
275–250	c.263	Death of Philemon		
250–225	240	First Greek-type dramas produced at Rome		
225–200	c.205–184	Career of Plautus		
200–100	c.166–159	Career of Terence	196	Rome becomes dominant power in Greece
		Ezechiel *floruit*?		
100–101	c.50	Athenion *floruit*	86	Athens sacked by Sulla
	c.18?	Horace's *Ars Poetica*	30	Death of Antony and Cleopatra; Octavian (later Augustus) becomes sole master of the Empire

Period	Date	Literary event	Date	Historical event
AD 1–200	125–175	Revival of new drama writing in eastern provinces	117–138	Reign of Hadrian
200–400	c.300	Works of minor dramatists almost cease to be copied	306–337	Reign of Constantine; the Empire becomes Christian
	360s	Apollinaris' biblical dramas	361–363	Pagan revival under Julian
	c.400	Latest known papyrus of Eupolis	395	Final separation of Eastern (Byzantine) from Western Empire
400–800	700–800	Eclipse of pagan poetry; Menander's plays apparently lost	632–640	Arab conquests; Byzantine Empire loses Egypt and Syria
800–1200	c.850	Revival of interest in pagan poetry in Byzantine Empire		
	c.950	Earliest surviving medieval manuscripts of tragedy and Aristophanes		
1200–1400			1204	Constantinople sacked by Crusaders; many manuscripts destroyed
1400–1600	1494	Four plays of Euripides printed at Florence	1453	Constantinople captured by Turks
	1498	First printed edition of Aristophanes		
	1502	First printed edition of Sophocles		

Period	Authors, works and developments		Contemporary events	
1400–1600	1503	First full printed edition of Euripides		
	1518	First printed edition of Aeschylus		
	1521	Aristophanes' *Wealth* performed in Germany		
	1597	First known opera, *Dafne*, produced at Florence		
1600–1800	1607	Monteverdi's opera *Orfeo*		
	1667–77	Racine's *Andromaque*, *Iphigénie* and *Phèdre*		
	1671	Milton's *Samson Agonistes*		
1800–2000	1844	First fragments of a Menander manuscript found at Mount Sinai (published 1876)	1821	Restoration of Greek independence
	1881	Inauguration of the Cambridge Greek Play		
	1907	Publication of Cairo codex of Menander		
	1958	Publication of Menander's *Dyskolos*		

4

ANTHOLOGY OF TEXTS

PRODUCTION RECORDS

Records of the productions at the Athenian dramatic festivals, the City Dionysia and
Lenaea, have survived in various forms. Here we present extracts from three different
records, all now fragmentary, originally inscribed for public display at Athens in the
fourth and third centuries BC.[1]

Fasti

The so-called *Fasti* (*IG* ii² 2318) recorded the results of the four artistic competitions
at the City Dionysia (boys' dithyramb, men's dithyramb, comedy and tragedy), giving
the names of the winning tribe (for dithyramb), *chorēgos* (for all contests), and producer
(for comedy and tragedy; the producer was normally, but not always, the author of
the play). We present the entry for 459/8 BC, the year when Aeschylus produced the
Oresteia.

[In the archonship of Philo]cles.
[Oe]neis of boys:
Demodocus was *chorēgos*
Hippothontis of men:
Euctemon of Eleu(sis) was *chorēgos*
Of comedians:
Eurycleides was *chorēgos*

---

1 In these and other translations of inscriptions and papyri, [square brackets]
  enclose words, or parts of words, lost owing to damage to the original document
  and restored by conjecture; (round brackets) enclose parts of words which the writer
  of the original document omitted for the sake of abbreviation; and <angled
  brackets> enclose explanatory additions by the translator. All translations are my
  own.

Euphronius was producer
Of tragedians:
Xenocles of Aphidna was *chorēgos*
Aeschylus was producer

IG ii² 2318.41–51

Didaskaliai

The *Didaskaliai* (*IG* ii² 2319–23) comprised four separate listings giving particulars of all comedies and tragedies produced at the City Dionysia and Lenaea, naming the producers at each festival in the order of their success in the competition, together with the titles of their plays and the names of their leading actors (protagonists), and also the winner of the festival's acting prize if any. The entry printed here is for the tragic contest at the City Dionysia of 341/0 BC. By that time satyr-drama had ceased to be part of the actual competition; instead, a single satyr-play was presented at the start of the programme, followed by a single 'old' tragedy (on this occasion the *Orestes* of Euripides). Each of the three competing poets then presented two 'new' tragedies (not three as in the fifth century), and to ensure the fairness of the acting contest each contender for the acting prize had to appear in plays by all three poets.

In the archonship of Nicomachus. With a satyr-play:
Timocles with *Lycurgus*.
With an old <tragedy>: Neoptolem[us]
with Euripides' *Orestes*.
Of poe(ts): Astydamas
with *Parthenopaeus*, ac(ted by) Thet[talus],
<and> [*Lyca*]*on*, ac. Neoptole[mus];
[Timo]cles sec(ond) with *Phrixus*,
[ac.] Thettalus,
<and> [*Oedi*]*pus*, ac. Neoptol[emus];
[Euar]etus thi(rd)
[with *Alc*]*me*[*on*], ac. Thetta[lus],
<and> [. . . *l*]*e*, ac. Neopto[lemus].
[Of ac(tors) Th]ettalus was victorious

IG ii² 2320.16–29

Nikai

The third record, sometimes called the *Nikai* (*IG* ii² 2325), consisted of eight listings recording the names of the victorious poets (not producers) and actors, in comedy and tragedy, at each of the two festivals, with the number of victories each obtained. The best preserved list, reproduced in translation on p. 90, is that for comic poets at the Lenaea, from which there survive four separate sections covering, with some gaps, a period from the inauguration of the contest around 440 BC to a point near the end of the fourth century; during these 140 years, sixty-five different comic poets were victorious at the Lenaea, of whom the inscription preserves, in whole or in part, the names of forty-nine. The name of Aristophanes, who is known to have won at least three Lenaean victories, has been lost in the gap in the lower part of the first column.

The names are to be read down the columns; i.e. Xenophilus was the first victorious poet, Telecleides the next, and so on. The numerals are shown in the Greek form (Π = 5, I = 1). Where a number is followed or preceded by — , it means that the number is or may be incompletely preserved. Where a name is not followed by a number at all, it means that the number which must once have been shown on the stone is totally lost.

DIDASCALIC HYPOTHESES

In manuscripts both ancient and medieval, the text of a play is regularly prefaced by various kinds of introductory material. Frequently this includes information about the production similar to that found in the various inscriptional records. Two such 'didascalic hypotheses' are presented here. The first, from a papyrus published in 1952 (*P.Oxy.* 2256 fr. 3), provided crucial evidence that Aeschylus' *Danaid* trilogy, including the surviving *Suppliant Maidens*, was not (as had usually been thought) one of his earliest productions, but dated from the 460s when Sophocles was already active. The second, preserved in the medieval manuscripts of Aristophanes' *Frogs*, records that the play was given the unusual honour of a second production.

Aeschylus' *Suppliants* and companion plays

In the year of *ar*[²
victorious, [Ae]schylu[s with *Egyptians, Suppliants,*]³
Dan[ai]ds, Amy[mone a satyr-play;]
sec[o]n[d], Sophocle[s; third,]
Mesatus **with N[, ,]
Bacchae, Mute[s a satyr-play**]⁴
[with She]pherds, Cyc[⁵
a saty(r-play).

2 These letters could be the beginning of the word *archon* or of a name; the only archon's name beginning with these letters in the relevant period is that of Archedemides, archon in 464/3.
3 The sequencing of these two plays is disputed; see p. 35.
4 The words between double asterisks were placed in parenthesis by the scribe, probably to indicate that they were out of place; they are most likely the plays produced by Sophocles.
5 If the view taken in the previous note is correct, these will be the plays produced by Mesatus (two further titles may have appeared in the now lost latter part of the line); the last surviving title may be *Cycnus* or *Cyclops*.

[Lenae]a[n, of comic poe]ts
[X]enophilus I
[T]elecleides II
Aristomenes II
Cratinus III
Pherecrates II
Hermippus IIII
Phrynichus II
Myrtilus I
[Eu]polis III
[   ]
[   ]
[   ]
[   ]
[   ]
[   ]

Po[liochus] I
Me[tagene]s II
Theo[pomp]us II
Pol[yzelu]s IIII
Nicoph[on]
Apo[llophane]s I
Am[eipsias]
Ni[cochares]
Xeno[ph]on I
Philyllius I
Philonicus I
[. . . . .]s I
[   ]
[   ]
[   ]
[   ]
[   ]
[   ]

Phili[ppus —]II
Chore[gus]
Anaxa[ndri]des III
Phileta[eru]s II
Eubulus III
Ephippus I—
[A]ntiphan[es] IIIII
[M]nesim[achus] I
Nau[sicrat]es III
Euphane[s]
Alexis II—
[Ar]ist[ophon]
[   ]
[   ]
[   ]
[   ]
[Asclepiodo]rus I

[   ]
Dio[nysi]us I
Cle[arch]us
Athenocles
Pyr[rhen] I
Alcenor I
Timocles I
Procleides I
M[en]ander I—
Ph[i]lemon III
Apollodoru[s]
Diphilus III
Philippides II—
Nicostratus
Calliades I
Ameinias I

Aristophanes' *Frogs*

It was produced in the archonship of Callias[6] (the one who followed Antigenes), through Philonides, at the Lenaea. He was first; Phrynichus second with *Muses*; Plato third with *Cleophon*. The play was so much admired because of the *parabasis* in it that it was actually produced again, as Dicaearchus says.

SYNOPSES OF LOST PLAYS

Another type of prefatory information often found preceding a play-text is a synopsis of the plot. These synopses, of unknown authorship, are not always accurate when they can be checked against the text; but when a synopsis survives, in whole or in part, for a play whose text is mostly lost, it can be a vital aid to attempts at reconstructing the play. Two such synopses are reproduced below.

Euripides' *Stheneboea*

Euripides' *Stheneboea* was notorious in his own time for its portrayal of the adulterous and treacherous wife who was its central character. A complete synopsis of the play has been preserved by two Byzantine writers, Johannes Logothetes and Gregory of Corinth; scraps of it, in a slightly different form, also survive in two much earlier papyri.

Proetus was the son of Abas, brother of Acrisius, and king of Tiryns; he married Stheneboea and had children by her. When Bellerophon fled from Corinth because of a homicide, Proetus purified him from his pollution, but his wife fell in love with the visitor. Being unable to fulfil her desires, she accused Bellerophon of having assaulted her; Proetus, believing her, sent him to Caria in order to have him done away with – he gave him a written tablet and ordered him to convey it to Iobates <the Carian king>. He, acting in accordance with what was written, ordered Bellerophon to venture against the Chimaera; Bellerophon fought and killed the beast. He then returned to Tiryns, laid blame on Proetus, and excited Stheneboea with the promise to take her off to Caria. He learned from someone of a second plot against him by Proetus, and forestalled him by departing. He set Stheneboea upon <the winged horse> Pegasus, and flew aloft over the sea; then,

6 That is, in 406/5 BC. The archon Callias is called 'the one who followed Antigenes' to distinguish him from other archons of the same name who held office in other years.

when he was near the island of Melos, he threw her off. Her dead body was picked up by fishermen, who brought it to Tiryns. Bellerophon again returned to Proetus, and himself confessed to having done the deed; he had (he said) been twice plotted against and had taken appropriate revenge upon both parties – from the one, her life; for the other, his grief.

Cratinus' *Dionysalexandros*

For Cratinus' comedy *Dionysalexandros*, probably produced in 430 BC, a papyrus (*P.Oxy.* 663) preserves the second half of a synopsis, revealing that the play was built around the story of the Judgement of Paris (or Alexandros as he is usually called in Greek) but with the god Dionysus usurping the role of Paris as in Aristophanes' *Frogs* he usurps the role of Heracles. The last sentence of the synopsis implies that the play was designed as a political allegory, with Dionysus representing Pericles; confirmation of this view comes from a fragment of a comedy produced in 430 or 429 by Hermippus (fr. 47) in which Pericles is addressed as 'King of the Satyrs'. See also pp. 28–9. Many words in the papyrus are abbreviated; these abbreviations are not marked in the translation unless they make the sense uncertain.

. . . j]udgement Hermes [go]es [away]; and they[7] say some things to the spectators about the procreation of sons,[8] and when Dionysus appears they mock him and make fun of him. And he, on the arrival of <the goddesses, when there is offered>[9] to him by Hera unshakeable despotic rulership, by Athena courage in war, and by Aphrodite supreme beauty and sexual desirability, judges the latter to be victorious. After this he sails to Sparta, abducts Helen and returns to Mount Ida. Shortly afterwards he hears that the Achaeans are ra[vag]ing the country and [seeking] Alexan[dros], so he has[tily] conceals Helen in a basket, disguises himself as a ra[m] and awaits developments. <The real> Alexandros arrives, discovers the two intruders, and orders both to be taken to the ships, intending to hand them over to the Achaeans. Helen is reluctant, and he takes pity on her and keeps her to have as his wife; but he sends off Dionysus to be handed over, and the satyrs accompany him, encouraging him and saying they will never forsake him. In this play Pericles is very

---

7 That is, the chorus of satyrs.
8 Or 'about the adoption of sons', or 'about the poets' (there is uncertainty about the identification of one letter, and about the correct expansion of an abbreviation).
9 The words between angled brackets, or their equivalent, are required by the sense but are omitted (not lost) in the papyrus, evidently through a copying error.

persuasively satirized by innuendo[10] as having brought the war upon
the Athenians.

AESCHYLUS

The Persians, ll. 796–831

In this extract from *The Persians*, the ghost of King Darius, summoned from the
underworld to advise the Queen and counsellors after news has arrived of the Persian
defeat at Salamis, prophesies the further disaster that will soon befall the Persian army
at Plataea.

DARIUS: But not even the army that has now remained
  in the land of Hellas will have a safe return home.
CHORUS-LEADER: What do you say? Is not the whole army of the
    barbarians[11]
  crossing the strait of Helle back from Europe?
DARIUS: But few of many, if any trust is to be placed   800
  in the oracles of the gods which bear
  on what has now occurred – for oracles are not fulfilled by halves.
  And if that is so, he[12] is leaving behind a large, chosen portion
  of the army, persuaded by vain hopes.
  They abide where the Asopus waters the plain   805
  with its stream, bringing welcome enrichment to the Boeotians'
    soil;
  where they are destined to suffer a supreme disaster
  as punishment for their *hybris* and godless thoughts.
  For when they went to the land of Hellas they did not scruple
  to plunder the images of the gods and burn their temples: 810
  altars have vanished, and the dwellings of the gods
  have been overturned in chaos and uprooted from their
    foundations.
  Therefore, having done evil, no less evil
  are they suffering and have still to suffer, and there is no bottom
    yet

10 The Greek word *emphasis* indicates that while Dionysus is not directly identified
   as Pericles in the text, it is made clear in other ways that the former represents
   the latter.
11 Aeschylus' Persians regularly use the word *barbaros*, properly 'non-Greek', in
   reference to themselves and to the peoples of Asia generally.
12 Xerxes.

to the pit of troubles – they are still welling up: 815
so great will be the mass of clotted blood
shed by the Dorian spear in the land of the Plataeans.
The heaps of corpses will signify wordlessly
to the eyes of men even to the third generation
that one who is mortal should not pride himself to excess.   820
For *hybris* has blossomed and has produced a crop
of ruin, whence it is reaping a harvest full of woe.
Such is the punishment of these deeds; look on it
and remember Athens[13] and Hellas, and let no one
despise the good fortune he possesses   825
and, through lust for more, shatter his great prosperity.
Zeus, remember, stands over you, a punisher
of over-boastful thoughts, a stern auditor.
Accordingly you should warn that man[14] to learn wisdom
and admonish him with well-argued advice   830
to cease offending the gods with excessive arrogance.

Seven against Thebes, ll. 631–676

Our second extract includes the decisive turning point of *Seven against Thebes*. The
scout who had been sent to ascertain details of the enemy dispositions tells Eteocles
that his brother Polyneices is attacking the last of the city's seven gates. Eteocles,
who had reserved himself to defend this gate, recognizes in this stroke of fate the
fulfilment of Oedipus' curse on his sons, and declares his resolve to fight his brother.

SCOUT: Now of the seventh, the one at the seventh gate,
       I shall speak, your own brother, what a fate
       he invokes and denounces upon this city:
       to mount the walls, be proclaimed ruler of the land,
       raise a loud paean for the city's capture,   635
       confront you, kill you, and die by your side,
       or, if you live, to pay back in your own coin,
       with banishment, the man who dishonoured and banished him.
       Such words he shouts forth, the mighty Polyneices,

---

13 Probably an allusion to the story, told later by Herodotus (5.105), that after the
    rebellious Ionians had sacked Sardis, with Athenian help, in 499 BC, Darius,
    determined to take revenge, ordered a slave to say to him three times every day
    before dinner, 'Master, remember the Athenians.' Earlier in this play (285) the
    messenger who reported the disaster of Salamis had said, 'How I groan when I
    remember Athens!'
14 Xerxes.

and calls on the gods of his family and fatherland 640
to be in the full sense watchers over his prayers.[15]
He has a newly made, well-rounded shield
with a twofold emblem cunningly worked upon it;
for a man in armour, conspicuously made of gold,
is led by a woman walking with modest gait. 645
She names herself as Justice, so the letters
read; 'and I shall bring this man home, and he shall have
his father's city and the right to dwell in his house'.
Such are the devices of those men out there; 649
you will never, I tell you, have cause to criticize me 651
for my reports; but *you* must decide how to captain the city.
ETEOCLES: O race the gods drive mad, race the gods so much hate,
my race so full of tears, race of Oedipus!
Ah me, my father's curse has indeed come true now! 655
But it is not proper to cry or lament,
lest that give birth to grief even harder to bear.
For this man so well named – Polyneices,[16] I mean –
we shall soon know where that shield-device will end up,
whether those letters worked in gold, 660
blethering balderdash on his shield, are really going to bring
    him home.
If Justice, the virgin daughter of Zeus, *were* the companion
of his actions and his mind, that might have been the case;
but in fact, neither when he escaped the darkness of the womb,
nor when he was growing, nor when he reached adolescence, 665
nor when his chin was gathering hair,
did Justice ever set eyes on him or hold him in any honour;
nor now, surely, when he does harm to his own native land,
is she standing close by him, I imagine.
Truly Justice would be utterly false to her name 670
if she consorted with a man with so utterly audacious a mind.
Trusting in this, I will go and stand against him
myself: who else has a better right to do so?
Ruler against ruler, brother against brother,
enemy against enemy I will stand. Give me at once 675
my greaves, protection against spear and stone.[17]

---

15 That is, to see to it that they are fulfilled.
16 This name means 'Much-strife'.
17 Greaves would be the first piece of armour a soldier put on and the last he took
off.

Agamemnon, ll. 160–217

At the beginning of *Agamemnon*, the chorus of Argive elders recall the departure of the Greek host to Troy, ten years before. In this extract from their first song (*parodos*) they pass from reflections on the power of Zeus, and the principles by which he governs the world, to a narrative recounting how Agamemnon reacted to the demand that he sacrifice his daughter to Artemis to enable the fleet to sail, after it had been windbound for a long time at Aulis.

> Zeus – whoever he may be,   160
> if it pleases him to be so called,
> then so I address him.
> I have nothing that can compare,
> weighing all things on the scale,
> except Zeus, if one is truly to cast aside   165
> the profitless burden of worry.
>
> And the one who was great before,[18]
> swollen by the assurance he could fight all comers,
> will not even be spoken of as 'the previous one';   170
> and he who was born next[19]
> has gone, having met his conqueror.
> One who enthusiastically voices a victory-song for Zeus
> will thoroughly hit the mark of good sense –   175
>
> Zeus who set mortals on the road to wisdom,
> who laid down the rule
> 'learning by suffering' to hold good.
> Instead of sleep there drips near the heart
> anxiety, a reminder of pain; and good sense comes   180
> to those reluctant to have it.
> The favour of the gods, who sit on the august
> bench of command, comes somehow by force.
>
> And at that time the senior leader
> of the Achaean ships,   185
> blaming no prophet,
> swimming with the sudden tide[20] of fortune,

18 Uranus, grandfather of Zeus.
19 Cronus, father of Zeus.
20 Literally 'blowing together with sudden fortunes'.

when the Achaean host was afflicted
with foul sailing weather that emptied their food stores,
when he was on the coast facing Chalcis   190
at Aulis, the place where the waves strike both ways;

and winds came from the Strymon[21]
bringing unwelcome idleness, hunger, bad anchorage,
making men wander about, merciless   195
to ships and their ropes,
making delay longer and longer
and painfully wearing the bloom off the Argives;[22]
and when another remedy
for the bitter storm,
even more grievous for the leaders,   200
was proclaimed by the prophet, who mentioned
the name of Artemis, so that the sons
of Atreus struck the ground with their sceptres
and could not restrain their tears;

and the elder king spoke and said: 205
'It is a grievous fate not to comply,
and grievous too if I slaughter
my child, the ornament of my house,
polluting a father's hands
with streams of maiden blood   210
by the altar. Which of these two is free of evil?
How can I become a deserter from the fleet
and so lose my alliance?
A sacrifice to stop the winds,
the blood of a maiden –   215
they desire it with fierce passion
and rightly. May all be well.'

21 That is, from the north.
22 'Argos' and 'Argives' in the *Oresteia* refer sometimes to the city of Argos (of which
    Agamemnon and Menelaus are assumed to be joint kings) and sometimes, as often
    in Homer, to Greece in general.

Choephoroi, ll. 869–930

The last of our Aeschylean extracts is the climactic scene of *Choephoroi*, the second part of the *Oresteia*. It begins with the dying scream of Aegisthus, and ends with Orestes and Pylades driving Clytaemestra indoors to her death. The three lines spoken by Pylades are the only words he utters in the play; it has often been said that this sudden break into speech by a character long silent has almost the effect of a divine voice. Note that all 'stage directions', in this and subsequent extracts, are added by the translator and are not part of the transmitted text. In this scene, the performing area seems to represent, not as usual the area in front of the outer door of the palace, but its inner courtyard, with doors leading to the men's and women's quarters respectively.

AEGISTHUS [*within*]: E-e! Otototoi!
CHORUS [*singing*]: Ah, ah, listen!   870
    How goes it? What fate has befallen the house?
CHORUS-LEADER [*speaking*]: Let us stand away from the business that
    is coming to a climax,
    so that we may not be thought to be complicit
    in these grim deeds; for the battle has really come to its final
    decision.

[*As the chorus move well away from the doors, a servant bursts out of the men's quarters*]

SERVANT: Help, help indeed – master is done for!   875
    Help, I say it again, for the third time!
    Aegisthus is no more!

[*He begins to knock frantically on the door of the women's quarters*]

               Open up,
    as fast as you can; undo the bolts
    on the women's doors! It needs someone really in his prime –

[*With a sudden change of tone*]

    not to help someone who's finished with, though, what's the point?

[*At the top of his voice again*]

    Hey, hey!   881
    I'm shouting to the deaf and crying out uselessly
    to people asleep, for nothing. Where's Clytaemestra? What's she
    doing?
[*Aside*] It looks as though her head is now on the block
    to be chopped and fall – and quite right too.
CLYTAEMESTRA [*coming to her door*]: What's the matter? What's this
    noise you're raising in the house?

SERVANT: I say the dead[23] are killing the living.   886
CLYTAEMESTRA: Ah me, I understand these riddling words!
   We will perish by deception, just as we killed by deception.
   Can someone give me, right away, an axe that will kill a man!

[*The servant runs off*]

   Let's know if we win or if we're beaten –   890
   because that's where I've got to in this wretched business.

[*Orestes and Pylades come out of the men's quarters*]

ORESTES [*to Clytaemestra*]: It's *you* I'm after; *he's* been satisfactorily
   dealt with.
CLYTAEMESTRA: Ah me, you are dead, my dearest, mighty Aegisthus!
ORESTES: You love the man? Then you shall lie with him –
   in the same tomb! Now he's dead you'll never betray him!   895
CLYTAEMESTRA [*baring one breast to him*]: Stop, my son! Respect this
   breast, my child,
   at which many times, while you were half asleep,
   you sucked with your gums the nurturing milk!
ORESTES: Pylades, what shall I do? Shall I respect my mother and not
   kill her?
PYLADES: Then where from now on are Loxias' oracles   900
   which he proclaimed at Pytho, and the faithful oath you pledged?
   Hold anyone an enemy rather than the gods!
ORESTES: I judge you the winner; you give me good advice.
[*To Clytaemestra*] Follow me; I want to slaughter you right beside this
   man;
   in life, after all, you thought him better than my father.   905
   Sleep with him in death, since he's the man
   you love, while hating the man you should have loved.
CLYTAEMESTRA: I nurtured you; I want to grow old with you!
ORESTES: You killed my father, and you expect to live with me?
CLYTAEMESTRA: Destiny, my child, shares the responsibility for
   these events.   910
ORESTES: Then your death, too, has been caused by Destiny.
CLYTAEMESTRA: Have you no respect for a mother's curse, my child?
ORESTES: You gave birth to me – and then cast me out into misery.
CLYTAEMESTRA: I did not cast you out; I sent you to the home of a
   friend and ally.

---

23 Orestes, disguised as a pedlar from Phocis, had brought Clytaemestra the 'news'
   of his own death.

ORESTES: I was insultingly sold, when I was the son of a
    free father.   915

CLYTAEMESTRA: Then where is the price that I received for you?

ORESTES: I am ashamed to reproach you with *that* in plain terms.

CLYTAEMESTRA: But you should say the same thing about your
    father's strayings.[24]

ORESTES: Don't criticize him, when he was toiling and you were
    sitting at home.

CLYTAEMESTRA: It is painful for women, my child, to be shut
    off from a man.   920

ORESTES: But it's the man's labour that feeds the women sitting at
    home.

CLYTAEMESTRA: It seems, my child, that you mean to kill your
    mother.

ORESTES: Not I, I tell you, but you yourself will be your killer.

CLYTAEMESTRA: Take care, beware your mother's wrathful hounds![25]

ORESTES: And how shall I escape my father's, if I fail to do this
    deed?   925

CLYTAEMESTRA: It looks as if I'm talking to a tomb, lamenting to no
    purpose.

ORESTES: Yes, because my father's destiny is determining this death
    for you.

CLYTAEMESTRA: Ah me, this is the serpent that I bore and
    nurtured![26]

ORESTES: Very prophetic, that fear from your dreams!   929
    You killed whom you ought not; now suffer what you ought not!

SOPHOCLES

Ajax, ll. 646–692

Ajax, deeply ashamed by his defeat in the contest for the arms of Achilles and his
subsequent insane attack on the army's flocks and herds, has declared his resolve to
end his life, in spite of all the pleas of his concubine Tecmessa and of the men under
his command. In this speech he seems to relent; but the next time we see him he has

---

24 That is, his keeping of concubines both during the war (Chryseis) and after it
    (Cassandra).

25 The Erinyes.

26 Clytaemestra had dreamed the previous night that she gave birth to a snake,
    wrapped it in baby-clothes and put it to her breast, where it sucked out a clot of
    blood. Orestes, told of the dream, had identified the snake as himself.

planted the sword, of which he here speaks, point upwards in the ground and is preparing to fall upon it. Is this speech, then, sincere, deceptive, or both at once?

> Long, uncountable Time brings all things
> to light from obscurity and, having done so, hides them again;
> and no event is inconceivable – anything can be defeated,
> even the most fearsome oath or the most robust heart.
> For even I, who once endured such terrible trials,   650
> have had my edge softened, as iron is softened by dipping,
> by this woman: I pity her,
> to leave her a widow among enemies and our child an orphan.
> Now I am going to the bathing-places and to the meadows
> by the sea, so that I can cleanse my pollutions   655
> and escape the heavy wrath of the goddess:[27]
> I shall go where I can find an untrodden place
> and hide this sword of mine, most hateful of weapons,
> digging it into the ground where no one will see.
> Let Night and Hades keep it safe below.   660
> For since my hand first received this sword
> as a gift from my greatest enemy, Hector,[28]
> nothing good has ever come to me from the Argives.
> The proverb men speak is a true one:
> 'An enemy's gifts are no gifts, and bring no good.'   665
> Therefore for the future we shall know to yield
> to the gods, and we shall learn to revere the sons of Atreus.
> They are the rulers, so of course one ought to yield to them.
> Even the most awesome and powerful things
> yield to the privilege of others: snowy Winter, for one,   670
> yields place to fruitful Summer;
> the sinister sphere of Night stands aside
> so that Day with her white steeds may bring flaming light;
> the breath of fearsome winds lulls to rest
> the groaning sea;[29] and among the rest, all-powerful Sleep   675
> releases those he has chained, and does not hold them for ever.
> How then can *we* not learn good sense?
> For I have lately come to understand

---

27 Athena.
28 After the indecisive duel described in book VII of the *Iliad*.
29 That is, apparently, the previously 'fearsome' winds fall light, and thus calm the waves; but it is possible that a line or so has been lost from the text.

that an enemy should not be hated so much
that it becomes impossible to be his friend afterwards;
and to a friend   680
I will aim to give the aid and service appropriate
to one who will not always remain so – for most mortals
find the harbour of friendship a treacherous one.
But regarding these things, it will be well. You, woman,
go inside at once and pray to the gods   685
that what my heart desires may be fulfilled.
And you, my friends, respect these wishes of mine
just as she does, and if Teucer[30] comes, tell him
to take care of us and also be loyal to you.
For I am going where I have to go;   690
do what I tell you, and perhaps you will learn later
that whatever my present misfortunes, I am safe.

Antigone, ll. 332–375

This choral ode from *Antigone* is perhaps the most famous lyric in Greek tragedy. The
chorus of Theban counsellors has just heard that an unknown person has defied Creon's
decree forbidding the burial of Polyneices; immediately after the end of the song the
violator is brought before Creon under arrest and proves to be Polyneices' young
sister Antigone.

Many things are awesome, but nothing
is more awesome than man.
He journeys beyond the grey sea
on the wings of the stormy south wind,   335
travelling amid
the waves of the deep; the most ancient
of divinities, Earth
the imperishable, the untiring, he wears away,
as ploughs go this way and that, year after year,   340
and he plies the ground with horses' brood.[31]

The tribe of flighty headed fowl
he snares and catches,
likewise the races of wild beasts

30 Ajax's half-brother (who at just about this time, we later learn, is all but lynched
   by the army simply for being kin to Ajax).
31 Presumably meaning mules (horses were not normally used for ploughing).

and the marine creatures of the sea, 345
in the toils of fine-spun nets,
man the skilful: by his devices
he conquers the beasts
that dwell in the wild mountains, and can bring 350
the shaggy necked, double-maned horse under the yoke
and the tireless mountain bull.

He has taught himself speech, and thought
swift as the wind, and the impulse
to give laws to cities, and the means 355
to escape the cold misery of lodging under the sky
and the wretched driving rain;
he has resources for everything, and he faces the future 360
baffled by nothing: only against Death
will he not find a means of escape to apply,
but he has contrived remedies
for sicknesses that seemed beyond cure.

Having this cleverness in contriving crafts 365
to a degree beyond all imagining,
he goes now to the bad, now to the good.
When he carries out the law of the land
and the oath-sanctioned justice of the gods
he stands high in his city;[32] but a man without a city is he 370
who, thanks to audacity, consorts with wrong.
May he never share my hearth,
may he never think my thoughts,
who can do these things! 375

Oedipus the King, ll. 1119–1185

Our next extract is the scene from *Oedipus the King* in which Oedipus finally discovers the terrible truth about himself. The Corinthian shepherd who had brought the abandoned baby Oedipus from Mount Cithaeron to King Polybus at Corinth is confronted with the Theban shepherd who had given the baby to him. Initially the Theban shepherd (who is also the sole survivor of the incident in which Laius was killed) is very reluctant to give any information; the Corinthian, on the other hand, is eager to assist the inquiry, in order to convince Oedipus that he is not the son of

---

32 Or 'he makes his city great'.

the Corinthian queen Merope and can therefore safely return to Corinth despite having
been told by an oracle that he would marry his mother.

OEDIPUS: I ask you first, stranger from Corinth:
    is this the person you mean?
CORINTHIAN: The same that you see.   1120
OEDIPUS: You there, old man, look at me here and answer
    whatever I ask you. Did you once belong to Laius?
THEBAN: I did; not a bought slave, but brought up in the house.
OEDIPUS: What work or way of life were you involved with?
THEBAN: For most of my life I followed the flocks.   1125
OEDIPUS: What regions did you mostly frequent?
THEBAN: There was Mount Cithaeron, and there were the parts
    nearby.
OEDIPUS: Well then, do you know this man here? Did you make his
    acquaintance at all?
THEBAN: What was he doing? What man might you be talking
    about?
OEDIPUS: This man who is here. Did you ever meet him at all?   1130
THEBAN: Not so as to say straight away from memory.
CORINTHIAN: No wonder, master. But since he doesn't know,
    I'll remind him clearly. I know very well
    that he knows of the time when we were together,
    this man and I – he with two flocks, I with one –   1135
    in the region of Cithaeron for three whole spells
    of six months, from spring to Arcturus;[33]
    when winter came, I would drive my flocks
    to their folds, and he to those of Laius.
    Is what I say the true fact, or is it not?   1140
THEBAN: What you say is true, though it's a long time ago.
CORINTHIAN: Well, tell me now, do you remember having given
    me then
    a baby, for me to bring up as a child of my own?
THEBAN: What is all this? Why are you asking that question?
CORINTHIAN: My friend, *this* is the man who was then that baby.   1145
THEBAN [*shaking his fist at him*]: To hell with you! Why can't you keep
    quiet?
OEDIPUS: Here, old man, don't hit him; your words
    rather than his are deserving of chastisement.

---

33 The time (in early autumn) when the star Arcturus begins to rise before daybreak.

THEBAN: Best of masters, what am I doing wrong?
OEDIPUS: Not answering about the baby that he is asking you
about.   1150
THEBAN: Because he's wasting his time talking about things he knows
nothing of.
OEDIPUS: If you're not going to speak the easy way, you'll speak the
hard way.[34]
THEBAN: No, in the gods' name, don't ill-treat an old man like me!
OEDIPUS: Twist back his arms, somebody, at once!
THEBAN: Wretched me, what for? What else do you want to
know?   1155
OEDIPUS: Did you give this man the baby he has spoken of?
THEBAN: I did, and I wish I had died that day.
OEDIPUS: Well, that's what you *will* come to if you don't tell the
truth.
THEBAN: It'll be worse ruin still for me if I do!
OEDIPUS: This man seems bent on spinning things out.   1160
THEBAN: No, I'm not. I've already said I did give it him.
OEDIPUS: Where did you get it from? From someone else, or was it
your own?
THEBAN: No, it wasn't mine. I received it from someone.
OEDIPUS: From which of these citizens, and from what house?
THEBAN: In the gods' name, master, don't, don't ask any more
questions!   1165
OEDIPUS: You're a dead man if I have to ask you this again.
THEBAN: Well then, it was one of the offspring of Laius' people.
OEDIPUS: Was it a slave, or a member of his family?
THEBAN: Help, I've come right to the thing that's most fearful to say!
OEDIPUS: And I to hear; but still, hear I must.   1170
THEBAN: Well, you know, it was actually *said* to be his own child; but
she, inside,
your wife, would best be able to speak the truth of the matter.
OEDIPUS: What, *she* gave it to you?
THEBAN: Exactly, my lord.
OEDIPUS: For what purpose?
THEBAN: To dispose of it.
OEDIPUS: Its mother, poor woman?
THEBAN: She was in dread of a terrible oracle. 1175

34 Literally 'you will not speak to your pleasure, but you will speak howling', a threat
of torture.

OEDIPUS: What oracle?

THEBAN: It was said that it would kill its parents.

OEDIPUS: Why did you let it go to this old man?

THEBAN: I took pity on it, master. I thought he would take it
to another land, where he came from. And he
saved it, for the greatest of catastrophes. For if you are
the man   1180
he says you are, then, I tell you, you were born to an evil fate.

OEDIPUS: Ah, ah! It is all coming out clear!
Light, may I look on you now for the last time,
I that am revealed to have been born to those I should not, to
have slept
with those I should not, and to have slain those I should not!

Electra, ll. 1126–1170

Electra makes the following speech while holding in her hands the urn that she believes
to contain the ashes of her brother Orestes, supposedly killed in a chariot-racing
accident. Listening to it are the two young men who brought the urn from Phocis –
one of whom is Orestes himself.

All that is left to remind me of Orestes,
the dearest soul on earth to me! How far you are, now I receive
you back,
from the hopes with which I sent you forth!
For now, when I hold you in my hands, you are nothing,
but when I sent you from this house, child, you were
glorious.   1130
How I wish I had departed this life
before with these hands I stole you and saved you
from murder and sent you to a foreign land!
Then you would have been lying dead that day,
and gained your allotted share of your ancestral tomb.   1135
Now you have died wretchedly, far from home, an exile
in another land, separated from your sister;
and, wretched that I am, I did not honour you by washing you
with these loving hands, nor take up, as is proper,
your sad burden from the all-consuming fire,   1140
but you, poor boy, were cared for by strangers' hands
and now come here as a small pile in a small urn.
Ah, miserable that I am, for my care for you back then,
given to no avail, which I so often provided for you

with toil that was a delight. For you were never   1145
more your mother's baby than you were mine,
and I was your nurse, not the household staff,
and you always addressed me as sister.[35]
And now all this has vanished in one day
with your death. You have passed like a whirlwind,   1150
blowing everything away. Father is gone;[36]
you have killed me; you are dead and gone yourself;
our enemies are laughing; and our most unmotherlike mother
is mad with joy, she of whom you often
sent me secret word that you would be appearing   1155
to take revenge on her in person. All this your evil fate
and mine has taken away from us,
sending you to me not in your own beloved shape
but as dust and a useless shadow.
[*Singing*] Ah, me, me!   1160
O pitiable corpse, alas, alas!
O most dreadful journey, ah me, me,
[*Speaking*] that you were sent on, dearest! How you have
    destroyed me,
yes, destroyed me, my own dear brother!
Receive me, then, into this house of yours,   1165
a nothing coming to nothing, that I may live henceforth
with you in the world below. For when you were above ground,
I shared the same fortune as you; and now I long
to die, and not to miss sharing your tomb;
because I see that the dead suffer no pain.   1170

EURIPIDES

Medea, ll. 465–519

Medea denounces Jason who has deserted her and her children to marry the daughter of the Corinthian king. This speech seems to have been in part the model for Dido's denunciations of Aeneas in Virgil's *Aeneid* (IV 305–330, 365–387).

35 Meaning, presumably, that Electra was the only one of his three surviving sisters whom he addressed in this way.
36 Agamemnon had been killed long before, but Electra means that he has lost the hope of regaining honour now that he no longer has a son to avenge his death. Electra's own 'death', mentioned immediately afterwards, likewise means the ruin of her hopes.

You utter villain – for that is the only thing I can call you,   465
the worst insult my tongue can find for your unmanliness!
You come to us, you come, you loathsome creature?
This is not courage or boldness,
to ill-treat one's friends and then look them in the face,   470
but the greatest of all the evils among humanity,
shamelessness! But you have done well to come:
I shall get some relief for my soul
by reviling you, and you'll be hurt by hearing it.
I will begin what I have to say from the beginning.   475
I saved your life, as is known to all the Greeks[37]
who embarked on that same ship *Argo*,
when you were sent to take charge of the fire-breathing bulls,
put them to the yoke, and sow that deadly field.[38]
And the never-sleeping serpent, which surrounded and
    protected   480
the golden fleece amid its intricate coils,
I slew it, and made the light of safety shine on you.
I myself abandoned my father and my home
and, more ardent than wise,
came to Iolcus under Pelion with you.   485
I caused the death of Pelias, the most harrowing kind of death,
at the hands of his own children, and destroyed the whole family.[39]
That is what I did for you, most villainous of men,
and you have betrayed us and got yourself a new wife,
when you already had children! If you were still childless,   490
your desire for this marriage would have been forgivable.
Your faithful oaths are gone and vanished. I cannot tell
if you believe that the gods of that time are no longer in power
or that they have now laid down new laws for mortals –
because you are well aware that you have broken your oath
    to me!   495
Alas for my right hand, which you clasped so often,

---

37 In the original Greek this line is literally hissed out, the first six consonants all
    being 's'.
38 Jason was ordered, by Medea's father Aeetes, to sow the field with dragon's teeth,
    from which armed men would spring up; on Medea's advice Jason threw stones
    among these men, whereupon they fought and killed each other.
39 Medea persuaded the daughters of Jason's enemy Pelias that her magic could enable
    them to restore their father to youth by cutting him up and boiling him in a
    cauldron.

as you did these knees,[40] how empty and defiling was the touch
of this wicked man, and how vain have been our hopes!
Come on, I'll discuss this with you as friend to friend –
why? because I expect you to do me some good?   500
I will all the same, because the questions will make your
   disgracefulness even plainer –
where should I turn now? Back to my father's house,
which I betrayed, as I did my country, to come here for you?
Or to the wretched daughters of Pelias? Oh, they'd give me
   a *fine* reception
in their house, when I killed their father!   505
Because this is how it is: to my kin at home
I have become an enemy, and those whom I should not have
   harmed
I have made into foes to do favours to you.
That is why, in return for this, you have made me so happy
in the eyes of many Greek women![41] I have in you   510
(poor me!) a marvellously faithful husband,
if I'm going to be cast out and banished from this land,[42]
bereft of friends, all alone with my children!
A fine reproach, that, to the new bridegroom,
that your children, and the woman who saved you, are
   vagrant beggars!   515
O Zeus, you have given men clear signs
to judge when gold is counterfeit;
why is there no token stamped on *men's* bodies
whereby one can tell which of them is bad stuff?

The Trojan Women, ll. 308–340

In this monody from *The Trojan Women* Cassandra, who has been allotted to
Agamemnon as his slave and concubine, joyfully anticipates her 'wedding' in
seemingly insane ecstasy, brandishing a torch. The real reason for her joy, which she
will later reveal (though, as usual, she will not be understood or believed), is that
through her prophetic gifts she knows that when Agamemnon brings her home it
will be the final insult that provokes his wife to murder him.

40 To clasp hands was a powerful pledge of faithfulness; to clasp a person's knees
   was an act of supplication.
41 This is, of course, said sarcastically.
42 Medea has just been ordered by Creon, king of Corinth and soon to be Jason's
   father-in-law, to leave the country at a day's notice.

Stop! Make way! Bear the light! Look, look,
I honour this temple,
I make it blaze with torches, Lord Hymenaeus![43]   310
Happy is the bridegroom,
and happy am I to be wedded
in a royal union in Argos!
O Hymen, O Lord Hymenaeus!
For while you, mother, with tears and wailing   315
continually bemoan
the death of my father and of my fatherland,
I, in honour of my wedding,
make the light of fire blaze up high   320
up to the bright sky, up to the sunshine,
giving light to you, Hymenaeus,
giving light to you, Hecate,
in honour of the bedding of a virgin,
as custom ordains.

Raise a leg skywards, lead on, lead on the dance –   325
euhan, euhoi! –
for the most happy fortune
of my father! The dance is sacred!
Lead it, Phoebus! I sacrifice in your temple,
crowned with laurel!   330
O Hymen, O Hymen Hymenaeus!
Dance, mother, lead on the dance, twirl your foot
this way, that way, treading your steps with delight
together with mine!
Shout Hymenaeus, hey!   335
for the bride, in songs
and cries of blessing!
Come, Phrygian maidens
in your fair robes, celebrate in song
the husband who is to marry me,   340
whom destiny has assigned to my bed!

43 Hymen, or Hymenaeus, was the god of weddings.

Helen, ll. 437–482

This is a semi-comic scene from the light drama *Helen*. Menelaus, shipwrecked on the Egyptian coast on his way home from Troy, arrives at King Proteus' palace to be confronted by a formidable slave-doorkeeper (a woman – but in Egypt, so Greeks believed, women did men's work and vice versa, see Herodotus II 35) and learns, to his bewilderment, that the Spartan Helen, daughter of Zeus, is in the building. Having just left Helen in a cave by the seashore, he concludes (in a soliloquy directly following this extract) that the woman must be speaking of another person with the same name, with another father of the same name, from another city of the same name . . . In fact, as he will discover, the Helen in the palace is his real wife; the Helen he brought from Troy was a phantom.

DOORKEEPER: Who is at the door? Won't you get away from the
    house
    instead of standing at the front door
    and being a nuisance to my masters? Or else you'll die,
    because you're a Greek; there's no admission for them.   440
MENELAUS: Yes, yes, old lady, you're quite right;
    you're entitled to complain, I'll do what you say; only don't be
    so cross!
DOORKEEPER: Go away. Those are my instructions,
    that no Greek is to approach this house.
MENELAUS: Here, don't raise your hand to me, don't start shoving
    me away!   445
DOORKEEPER: It's your fault; you're taking no notice of anything I say.
MENELAUS: Go in and tell your masters –
DOORKEEPER: I think I'd be asking for trouble, telling them anything
    from *you*.
MENELAUS: I come here a shipwrecked stranger, and therefore immune
    from molestation.
DOORKEEPER: Then go to some other house, not this one.   450
MENELAUS: No, I'm going to come inside; you should do what I say.
DOORKEEPER: You're a nuisance, do you know, and you're just about
    to be removed by force.
MENELAUS: Alas, where is my glorious expedition?
DOORKEEPER: Well, you may have been high and mighty there, but
    here you're not!
MENELAUS: O my god, how unworthy is this humiliation!   455
DOORKEEPER: Why are there tears in your eyes? What are you so
    sorrowful about?
MENELAUS: My happy fortunes in the past.
DOORKEEPER: Well, go away, won't you, and give your tears to your
    friends!

MENELAUS: What country is this, and whose is this royal abode?

DOORKEEPER: This is the house of Proteus, and this land is
    Egypt.   460

MENELAUS: Egypt? Wretched me, what a place to have landed!

DOORKEEPER: What have you got against the life-giving waters
    of the Nile?

MENELAUS: I've nothing against them; I'm lamenting my own
    misfortune.

DOORKEEPER: Plenty of people are unfortunate, not only you.

MENELAUS: Is the king you mentioned at home?   465

DOORKEEPER: This is his tomb; his son now rules the land.

MENELAUS: Where might he be? Is he at home, or out?

DOORKEEPER: He's not at home, and he's bitterly hostile to Greeks.

MENELAUS: What reason has he, of which I get the benefit?

DOORKEEPER: Helen, daughter of Zeus, is in this house.   470

MENELAUS: What are you saying? What was that you said? Tell me
    again.

DOORKEEPER: The daughter of Tyndareos,[44] who was formerly at
    Sparta.

MENELAUS: Where has she come from? What is the meaning of all
    this?

DOORKEEPER: She travelled here from Lacedaemon.[45]

MENELAUS: When? [*Aside*] My wife hasn't been kidnapped from the
    cave, has she?

DOORKEEPER: Before the Achaeans went to Troy, stranger.   476
    Now go away from the palace. There's a situation in there
    that has caused disturbance in this royal house.
    You've come at a bad time, and if master
    catches you, you'll get death as your guest-gift.   480
    I'm really friendly to Greeks, not like the harsh words
    I uttered in fear of my master.

The Bacchae, ll. 370–430

In this song from *The Bacchae*, the chorus, female Asiatic devotees of Dionysus, celebrate
the joys of Dionysiac worship, with only brief and oblique reference to the doom
awaiting those who resist the god, such as Pentheus who has just ordered the arrest
of all Dionysiac worshippers in and around Thebes. The mainly ionic rhythm of the

44 Helen's father was actually Zeus, but she was brought up by Tyndareos, who had
    married her mother Leda.
45 Another name for Sparta (or the region centred on it).

song helps to characterize both song and singers as Asian, feminine and orgiastic. The praise of Pieria (lines 409–416) may have been designed by Euripides to compliment his patron and host Archelaus, king of Macedon, in whose realm Pieria lay.

Piety, honoured among the gods,   370
Piety who flies over the earth
on golden wings,
do you hear these words of Pentheus?
Do you hear his impious
arrogance towards Bromius,[46] the son   375
of Semele, the god who is present
at garlanded rejoicings
as the first of the Blest Ones, the god to whom belong
dancing in bands of worshippers,
laughing with the music of the pipes   380
and banishing cares,
when the juice of the grape comes
in the feasting of the gods, and when
in banquets crowned with ivy
the mixing-bowl casts sleep over men?   385

Of unbridled lips
and of lawless folly
the end is misfortune;
but the life of quiet
and of wisdom   390
keeps its head above water
and keeps families safe; for the sons of heaven,
though they dwell far off in the skies,
watch the doings of men.
Cleverness is not wisdom,   395
and to think thoughts beyond mortal bounds
means a short life; this being so,
who would pursue great things
rather than accept what he has?
To my mind these are the ways   400
of mad, ill-counselled men.

Would I could come to Cyprus,
Aphrodite's island,

---

46 'The Noisy One', a common designation for Dionysus, used at least nineteen times
in *The Bacchae*.

where the spirits of love
that charm mortal hearts   405
dwell in Paphos, which is made fertile
by the hundred-mouthed stream
of the barbarian, rainless river;[47]
or where Pieria lies, said to be
of supreme beauty, the home of the Muses,   410
the awe-inspiring slopes of Olympus!
Lead me there, Bromius, Bromius,
chief of the bacchants, god hailed with cries of *euhoi*!
There are the Graces, there is Desire, there is the proper place   415
for the bacchants to perform their rites.

The god, the son of Zeus,
delights in feasting
and loves Peace, bringer of prosperity,
the goddess who nurtures young men;[48]   420
to the wealthy and to the lower orders
he gives to possess in equal measure
the painless delight of wine;
and he hates the man who does not care for this –
by day and through the lovely night   425
to lead a happy life,
and wisely to keep his heart and mind apart
from men who are too clever.
The norms and customs of the modest majority,
these would I accept.

The Cyclops, ll. 519–589

This is a scene from *The Cyclops*, the only satyr-drama that survives complete. The
Cyclops, just introduced to wine for the first time, is treated to a symposium by
Odysseus and Silenus, and enters into the spirit of the occasion rather too fully for
Silenus' comfort – though Silenus at least knows that the Cyclops will soon be blinded,
and he and the satyrs will be released from their captivity.

ODYSSEUS: Listen to me, Cyclops, because I'm an expert
      about this Bacchus[49] that I've given you to drink.   520

47 The Nile, whose current was believed to be so strong that it reached the south
    coast of Cyprus (Manilius, *Astronomica* 4.635).
48 The point is the contrast between Peace and War, which *destroys* young men.
49 Often used as a metonym for 'wine'.

CYCLOPS: And who's Bacchus? Is he regarded as a god?

ODYSSEUS: The greatest of gods for bringing joy to mortals' life.

CYCLOPS: I certainly enjoy belching him up!

ODYSSEUS: That's what the god is like: he harms no mortal.

CYCLOPS: And how can a god enjoy making his home in a leather
　　　bottle?　　　　　　　　　　　　　　　　　　　　　　525

ODYSSEUS: He's happy to go wherever anyone puts him.

CYCLOPS: Gods ought not to enclose their bodies in skins.

ODYSSEUS: What does it matter if he gives you pleasure? Or do you
　　　have a dislike for leather?

CYCLOPS: I hate the flask – but I like this drink!

ODYSSEUS: Well, stay here, Cyclops, drink and enjoy yourself.　　530

CYCLOPS: Shouldn't I give some of this drink to my brothers?

ODYSSEUS: Your prestige will be greater if you keep it to yourself.

CYCLOPS: But if I share it, I'll be of more service to my friends.

ODYSSEUS: Revelling in company[50] tends to mean quarrelling, strife
　　　and fists.

CYCLOPS: I'm drunk, but all the same no one would dare touch
　　　me!　　　　　　　　　　　　　　　　　　　　　　535

ODYSSEUS: My dear fellow, when you're drunk you should stay at
　　　home.

CYCLOPS: He who's drunk, and doesn't enjoy group revelling, is a fool.

ODYSSEUS: No, he who's drunk and stays at home is wise.

CYCLOPS: What shall we do, Silenus? Do you think we should stay
　　　here?

SILENUS: Yes, I do. Why should we need others to drink with,
　　　Cyclops?　　　　　　　　　　　　　　　　　　　540

CYCLOPS: The ground is certainly lush with grass and flowers.

SILENUS: And it's nice to drink in the sunshine.

　　　Now recline, please, laying your side on the ground.

CYCLOPS [*doing so*] There you are.

　　　Why are you putting the mixing-bowl behind me?　　　545

SILENUS: So that no passer-by will knock it over.

---

50 'Revelling in company' (and 'group revelling', line 537) translates *kōmos*, an
irregular procession of drunken (usually young) men, typically going from house
to house in search of free drink. Throughout this dialogue Odysseus is
systematically and deliberately giving the Cyclops *wrong*, anti-social advice in
order to encourage him to drink alone instead of in company (because, of course,
he does not want the Cyclops to have his friends with him when he eventually
falls into a stupor); the Cyclops left to himself, paradoxically enough, would have
had sound instincts on this subject!

CYCLOPS: No, you want to drink from it
on the sly! Put it down between us. [*Silenus does so*]
And you, stranger, tell me what name I should call you by.

ODYSSEUS: Nobody. What favour will I have to thank you for in
return?

CYCLOPS: I'll eat you last after all your companions.   550

SILENUS: A very fine present you're giving your guest, Cyclops!

[*He raises the bowl to his lips*]

CYCLOPS: Hey, you, what are you doing? Drinking up the wine
on the sly?

SILENUS: No, this god just kissed me because I look so lovely.

CYCLOPS: You'll catch it,[51] kissing Wine[52] when he doesn't love you.

SILENUS: Yes, he does; he says he adores me for my beauty.   555

CYCLOPS: Just pour it and give me the cup – full.

SILENUS: So what's its strength? Come on, let's check.

CYCLOPS: You'll be the death of me! Just hand it over.

SILENUS: I will, but not till I see
that you've taken a garland – and till I've had another taste.

CYCLOPS: This wine-steward's a crook!

[*He tries to seize the cup, but only succeeds in spattering himself*]

SILENUS: No, by Zeus – but the wine *is* sweet!
But you must wipe yourself clean if you want to take a drink.

CYCLOPS [*hastily wiping his face with his arm*]: Look, my lips and beard [560]
are clean.

SILENUS: So put your elbow to the floor, in the proper style, and
drink, like you see me drinking – and like you don't see me
drinking!

CYCLOPS: Hey, hey, what are you trying to do?

SILENUS [*presenting him with an empty cup*]: I drank it at one go.
Lovely!

CYCLOPS [*passing the mixing-bowl to Odysseus*]: Take it yourself, stranger, [565]
and you be my wine-steward.

ODYSSEUS: At least the vine is known to my hand.[53]

CYCLOPS: Come on then, pour it.

---

51 Literally 'you'll howl'.

52 The Cyclops follows Odysseus in personifying wine – but instead of calling it
'Bacchus' he calls it 'Wine'.

53 That is, Odysseus, unlike both the Cyclops and Silenus, has actually *grown*
grapes.

ODYSSEUS: I'm pouring it; just keep quiet.

CYCLOPS: A hard thing to ask of any big drinker!

ODYSSEUS [*giving him a cup*]: There you are; drink it off, and
  don't leave any.   570
  You should quaff it so that when it runs out, you *pass* out!⁵⁴

CYCLOPS [*tasting the wine for the first time*]: Wow, that vine-wood is
  clever!⁵⁵

ODYSSEUS [*as the Cyclops drinks the cup off*]: And if you drink a lot of it
  on top of your large meal,
  wetting a stomach that isn't thirsty, you will fall asleep;
  but if you leave any, Bacchus will make you wither.   575

CYCLOPS: Whee-whew!
  I just survived! Thank you, a hundred per cent!
  The sky seems to me to have come down and merged
  with the earth, and I can see the throne of Zeus
  and all the revered holiness of the gods!   580
  The Graces are wooing me; should I not kiss them?
  No, enough! [*Seizing Silenus*] I shall take my rest with this
  Ganymede⁵⁶
  rather than with the Graces. Somehow I enjoy
  pretty boys more than I do females.

SILENUS [*alarmed and incredulous*]: You think, Cyclops, that I'm Zeus'
  boy Ganymede?!   585

CYCLOPS: Yes, by Zeus, and I'm abducting you from Dardanus!

SILENUS [*crying out to the other satyrs*]: I'm done for, lads! I'm going to
  be dreadfully abused!

CYCLOPS: Do you object to your lover, are you playing hard to get
  with him, just because he's drunk?

SILENUS [*as he is carried off*]: Help, I'm shortly going to regret I ever
  heard of wine!⁵⁷

---

54 Literally 'you should die together with the drink, quaffing it'.
55 That is, if it can generate a drink like this.
56 The beautiful youth, son of a king of Troy (here Dardanus; elsewhere usually
  Tros or Laomedon), who was taken up to heaven to be Zeus' cupbearer and catamite
  (a word derived, via Etruscan, from his name).
57 Literally 'to see very bitter wine'.

MINOR TRAGEDIANS

Euphorion (?), *Prometheus Bound*, ll. 907–940

Prometheus Bound, traditionally ascribed to Aeschylus, may well in fact have been written by his son **Euphorion**, probably in the 430s. In this extract Prometheus, chained and impaled on a rock by order of Zeus, anticipates with satisfaction the destined overthrow of Zeus at the hands of a son Zeus himself will beget, and brushes aside the cautionary advice of the chorus of Ocean nymphs.

PROMETHEUS: I tell you that Zeus, arrogant though his thoughts are,
    will yet be brought low: such a union
    he is preparing to make,[58] which will cast him from his tyrannical
    throne into oblivion. Then at last   910
    the curse of his father Cronus will be entirely fulfilled,
    which he uttered when he fell from his ancient throne.
    How to turn aside this peril, no god
    except myself can show him truly.
    I know it all, and how it will happen. In the light of that,   915
    let him, for now, sit there secure, trusting
    in his atmospheric noises, and brandishing his fiery weapon in
      his hands;[59]
    for none of that will help him to avoid
    falling into humiliating, unendurable ruin.
    Such an opponent[60] he is now himself preparing   920
    to pit against himself, a monster impossible to fight,
    who will find himself a fire mightier than the lightning-bolt
    and a sound whose power surpasses the thunder;
    and the plague from the sea that shakes the earth,
    the trident, the weapon of Poseidon, he will shatter.   925
    When he stumbles into that disaster, he will learn
    how different servitude is from rulership.
CHORUS-LEADER: You are surely only saying against Zeus what you
    wish were true.
PROMETHEUS: I am saying what will happen, and *also* what I wish.
CHORUS-LEADER: Is it really to be expected that another will lord
    it over Zeus?   930

---

58 With a female (actually Thetis) who is destined to bear a son mightier than his
    father.
59 Referring, respectively, to thunder and the lightning-bolt.
60 Literally 'wrestler'.

PROMETHEUS: Yes, and he will have even more crowning agonies
than that.
CHORUS-LEADER: How can you not be afraid to utter such words?
PROMETHEUS: What should I be afraid of, when my destiny is never
to die?
CHORUS-LEADER: But he can give you trials even more painful than
that.
PROMETHEUS: Then let him; there is nothing I have not
foreseen.   935
CHORUS-LEADER: Those who bow to the inevitable are wise.
PROMETHEUS: Go on, revere and worship and fawn on the current
holder of power!
I care less than nothing for Zeus!
Let him rule, let him act as he pleases
for this short time; he will not long be king of the gods.   940

Critias, *Sisyphus*, fr. 19.1–40

Critias, leader of the Thirty Tyrants who ruled Athens in 404–403, was a versatile
intellectual who among other things wrote several tragic dramas (his nephew Plato,
we are told, at one time aspired to a dramatic career also). The philosophical writer
Sextus Empiricus has preserved this extract from his play *Sisyphus* in which Sisyphus
presents a sceptical, sophistic account of the origin, or rather invention, of religion
as a device for social control. There are a few short gaps in the text.

There was once a time when human life was unorganized,
beastlike, subservient to brute force,
when there was no reward for good men
and no punishment for the wicked.
And then, I think, men laid down laws   5
to inflict punishment, so that Justice might be queen
. . . . and keep violence in subjection;
and anyone who did wrong would suffer a penalty.
Then, when the laws were preventing them
from committing deeds of open violence,   10
but they still did wrong in secret, then, I think,
some crafty and intelligent man
invented among mortals the fear <of gods>, in order
that there should be something for the wicked to be afraid of,
even when they were acting or speaking or thinking in secret.   15
Hence he introduced the concept of divinity, the idea   16
that there is a god, enjoying immortal life,   17

who can hear everything that is said among mortals   20[61] 20[61]
and see everything that is done.
So if you are quietly planning something evil,
it will not go unperceived by the gods; for <to all>
who had sense in them, by saying these things
he introduced a most salutary piece of instruction,   25
concealing the truth under false words.
He said that the gods dwelt in that place where
he could frighten men most by locating them,
the place from which he knew there came to mortals
their fears and their blessings in their wretched life,   30
up in the outer rim of the world, where they saw
the lightning flash, the terrible noise
of the thunder, and the starry firmament of heaven,
craftily fashioned by Time, that skilled artificer,
from whence come the blazing starlike lumps of matter[62]   35
and the moist rain that falls to earth.
With such fears did he surround mankind,
through which he persuaded them effectively
that the god dwelt in an appropriate place,
and quenched lawlessness by law.   40

Chaeremon, *Oeneus*, fr. 14

Chaeremon was one of the leading tragic dramatists of the mid-fourth century;
Aristotle thought his style more suitable for the reader than for the theatre spectator,
but some of his lines had evidently become famous quotations by the time of Menander
(see *Aspis*, lines 425–428). His longest surviving fragment is this one from *Oeneus* in
which Oeneus describes a group of young women whom he has seen sleeping in the
open air.

One of them was lying down, displaying to the light of the moon
a white breast, for her upper garment had come loose,
and another's left flank had been bared
in the dance, and unclad she showed to the watching stars[63]
a living painting, and the white colour of her skin   5
shone to the eye in opposition to the dark shadows.

61   Lines 18 and 19 of the transmitted text are a spurious addition.
62   Probably meteorites are meant; a famous one fell at Aegospotami on the Hellespont
      in 467 BC (Plutarch, *Lysander* 12).
63   Literally 'to the watchings of the sky'.

Another had bared her beautiful arms
which embraced another's feminine neck.
Another again was displaying a thigh
through the folds of a torn garment, and the seal of desire   10
was set, beyond all expectation, on her radiant youth.
They had fallen in sleep upon the calamint flowers,
crushing the dark violet petals
and the crocus, which rubbed off a shadowy sun-coloured image
on the fabric of their clothes;   15
and the full-grown marjoram, glistening with dew,
stretched its soft neck across the meadow.

Theodectas (unknown play), fr. 8

Theodectas of Phaselis was a contemporary of Chaeremon who seems to have been
rather more successful in the theatre, with seven victories at the City Dionysia; he is
said to have studied rhetoric under Isocrates. In the following fragment, from an
unknown play, an ingenious explanation is offered for the notorious tendency of the
gods to be tardy in punishing the wicked.

Let any mortal who blames divinity because
it pursues the unjust not immediately
but a long time afterwards, listen to this explanation.
If punishments came straight away,
many would exalt the gods not through pious character   5
but through fear; but in fact, with punishment
being distant, men behave according to their nature,
and when they are unmasked as being evil,
they pay the penalty at a later time.[64]

Moschion (unknown play), fr. 9

Moschion, who lived near the end of the fourth century, was the last Athenian tragic
dramatist of any note; of his three known plays, probably two, but at least one
(*Themistocles*), were on historical themes. Here a speaker in an unknown play describes

---

64 This argument, it will be noted, presupposes (1) that persons of a wicked
    disposition *deserve* to be punished but (2) that only actions, not dispositions,
    actually *can* be punished; on these assumptions, justice will be served if those of
    a wicked disposition are given the fullest opportunity to make their character
    manifest by wicked actions. This of course takes no account of the interest of
    society in the prevention of crime.

an Argive king or noble who has 'entered the country' as a humble suppliant; it is not clear whether 'the country' is Argos (in which case the person might be, say, Thyestes returning from exile) or some other land (in which case one might think of Adrastus entering Attica after the failure of his expedition against Thebes).

> . . . with which he, once a lord of Argos, great
> in descent and reputation, now fallen from a kingly throne
> to poverty, entered the country
> clutching a suppliant-branch to his bosom, with a look that
> aroused compassion,
> and showing to all that the glory of good fortune   5
> does not grant men a secure possession of itself.
> Every citizen pitied him on sight,
> every citizen extended to him a hand and a word of greeting,
> and their eyes melted with tears
> as they grieved with him in his distress; for the decay of former
> rank   10
> arouses pity in many men.

Anonymous, *Candaules and Gyges*, fr. 664.18–32 from *Tragica Adespota*

A papyrus of the second or third century AD (*P.Oxy.* 2382) preserves all or part of forty-seven lines of a play about the story of Candaules and Gyges as told by Herodotus (I 8–12). We reproduce the best preserved section. King Candaules of Lydia, wishing to impress his friend Gyges with the beauty of his wife, has arranged for him to see her naked without her knowledge, but she has caught sight of Gyges and, ashamed and enraged, has decided to confront him with the choice of accepting death or plotting with her to kill Candaules. Here she is telling her story to a chorus of women. The play was known to two writers of the imperial period (Ptolemaeus Chennus and Achilles Tatius) who give the queen's name as Nysia (Herodotus leaves her nameless); some linguistic details that are alien to Attic and/or to classical tragedy make it likely that it was written in the Hellenistic age.

> [For whe]n I saw Gy[ges, n]ot some vague shape,
> I fea[red] there might be some murderous amb[u]sh,
> su[ch as] are often attempted against tyrants;   20
> but w[he]n I saw that Candaules was still awake,
> I knew what had been done an[d] what man had done it;
> but pretending ignorance, though my hear[t] was pounding,
> I restrained in si[lence . . . . . .] a cry of sham[e].
> In bed, tossed about by my [though]ts,   25
> I had an inter[minable] night [of] sleeplessness;

but when the [splen]did Morning Star ros[e],
the har[b]inger of the first li[ght of d]ay,
I rouse[d] him[65] from bed and sent him out
to dispense justice to his people: I had read[y]   30
words of persuasion [. . . . .]
that the king slept all [night. . . . .]
and [I sent] a man to summon Gyges to me . . .

Ezechiel, *Exagoge*, ll. 1–58

From the biblical drama *Exagoge* by the (probably Alexandrian) Jew **Ezechiel** we print
the prologue, in which Moses, who has fled from Egypt to Ethiopia, tells the story of
his early life (corresponding to the first two chapters of Exodus); the pattern of the
prologue is clearly modelled on Euripidean practice.

Since Jacob left the land of Chanan
and went down to Egypt, having seventy
souls with him, and became the ancestor of a numerous
people, who were oppressed and crushed,
ill-treated down to the present time   5
by wicked men and the hand of rulers.[66]
For seeing our race increasing greatly,
king Pharao contrived a great plot
against us, abusing some of our men
in brickmaking and heavy building,   10
and he built fortified cities thanks to these wretched slaves.
Then he proclaimed to the Hebrew race
that the males should be thrown into the deep river.
Thereupon the mother who bore me hid me
for three months, as she said; but not being able to keep me
    concealed,   15
she exposed me, putting clothes around me,
in a dense reed-marsh by the river's edge,
with Mariam, my sister, watching from close by.
Then the king's daughter, together with her maids,
came down to bathe her young flesh in the stream.   20
As soon as she saw me, she took me and picked me up,
and knew that I was a Hebrew. And my sister Mariam
ran up to the princess and said this:

---

65 Candaules.
66 This sentence is equally ungrammatical in the original Greek.

'Do you want me to find you quickly a nurse for this boy
from among the Hebrews?' And she urged the girl to hurry.   25
She went and told my mother, and quickly was back,
and my mother herself was with her, and took me in her arms.
The king's daughter said: 'Woman, nurse this child,
and I will pay your wages.'
And she named me Moses, because   30
she had taken me up from the bank of the watery river.[67]
When my time of infancy had passed,
my mother brought me to the princess's house,
telling and explaining to me everything about
my ancestral race and what God had given them.   35
While I remained in the age of childhood,
she[68] provided me with a royal upbringing and education
in every way, as if I were of her own blood.
But when I had arrived at full age,
I went out of the royal palace; for the spirit   40
and cunning of the King[69] were urging me to action.[70]
The first thing I saw was two men at blows,
one a Hebrew by race, the other Egyptian.
Seeing that they were alone and no one else present,
I defended my brother, killed the other man,   45
and hid him in the sand, so that no one else
might see us and uncover the murder.
Next day I again saw two men
fighting, both very much my kinsmen,
and said, 'Why are you hitting a man weaker than you?'   50
But he said, 'Who appointed you a judge
or overseer here? Are you perhaps going to kill me,
as you killed that man yesterday?' And I was afraid,
and said, 'How did this become known?'
And he quickly reported all this to the king,   55
and Pharao sought to take my life;
and I, hearing of this, departed out of the way,
and now I am wandering in a foreign land.

---

67 This etymology of Moses' name is based on the Hebrew verb *mashah* ('to draw
    up') and would be meaningless to any monolingual Greek-speaker not acquainted
    with the relevant biblical text (Exodus 2.10).
68 This must refer to the king's daughter, not to Moses' mother.
69 Presumably God rather than the Egyptian monarch.
70 Or 'to visit the work-sites' (cf. Exodus 2.11).

ARISTOPHANES

The Acharnians, ll. 43–133

Aristophanes' earliest surviving play, *The Acharnians*, begins with a meeting of the Athenian Assembly at which the hero, Dicaeopolis, is exasperated by the persistent refusal of the presiding officials to allow the question of peace to be raised, even when a certain Amphitheus ('Godschild' in this translation) claims that he has been commissioned by the gods to end the war. In this extract, the main business of the Assembly is to hear a report by an Athenian embassy returning from the Persian court; the ambassadors are accompanied by a cyclops-like individual who according to them is the high Persian official known as 'the King's Eye'.

HERALD: Move forward!
　　Move, to be inside the purified area!
GODSCHILD [*arriving late; aside to Dicaeopolis*]:　Has anyone spoken
　　yet?
HERALD: Who wishes to speak?　　　　　　　　　　　　　　　　45
GODSCHILD: I do.
HERALD:　　　　　Who are you?
GODSCHILD:　　　　　　　　　Godschild.
HERALD:　　　　　　　　　　　　　You are not human?
GODSCHILD:　　　　　　　　　　　　　　　　No,
　　I am an immortal. The original Godschild was son of Demeter
　　and Triptolemus, and to him was born Celeus;
　　and Celeus married my grandmother Phaenarete,
　　of whom was born Lycinus; and as the son of the latter,　　50
　　I am immortal.[71] And the gods have entrusted the making of
　　　peace
　　with Sparta to me, myself alone.
　　But though I am immortal, gentlemen, I have no journey-money;
　　the Prytaneis[72] refuse to provide it.
HERALD [*at a signal from the chairman of the Prytaneis*]: Archers!

[*Two Scythian archer-policemen seize hold of Godschild*]

GODSCHILD [*desperately*]: Triptolemus and Celeus, will you stand idle
　　while I'm –　　　　　　　　　　　　　　　　　　　　55

71　The names in this genealogy derive in part from Eleusinian mythology (in a wildly confused form; Triptolemus was Celeus' son, not his grandfather, and was Demeter's nursling and pupil, not her lover) and in part are pure invention.
72　The fifty-man committee who presided over the Assembly.

[*He is dragged off*]

DICAEOPOLIS: Prytaneis, you wrong the Assembly
 by arresting the man who was ready
 to make peace for us and let us hang up our shields.
HERALD: Stay seated and keep silence.
DICAEOPOLIS: By Apollo, not I,   60
 unless you initiate a debate about peace.
HERALD: The ambassadors from the King![73]
DICAEOPOLIS: You and your King! I'm tired of ambassadors
 and their peacocks[74] and their bragging.
HERALD: Silence!

[*Enter a party of Ambassadors, richly attired*]

DICAEOPOLIS: Whew! Ecbatana,[75] what a get-up!
AMBASSADOR [*to the assembled people*]:   You sent us to the Great
    King,   65
 drawing a salary of two drachmas a day,
 in the archonship of Euthymenes[76] –
DICAEOPOLIS: Alas for the drachmas!
AMBASSADOR: And we wore ourselves out wandering
 through Caystrian plains under awnings,
 softly bedded down in carriages –   70
 we were practically dying.
DICAEOPOLIS: *I* must have been absolutely
    thriving, then,
 bedded in rubbish by the ramparts![77]
AMBASSADOR: And when we were entertained, we were compelled to
    drink
 unmixed sweet wine from cups
 of glass and gold –

73 In classical Greek, 'the King' *par excellence* was the King of Persia (usually referred
   to, as here, simply as *basileus*, 'King', with no definite article).
74 Probably alluding to a gift of peacocks made by the Persian King to the Athenian
   ambassador Pyrilampes (Plutarch, *Pericles* 13.15; Antiphon, fr. 57).
75 The capital of Media; to a Greek the name had connotations of oriental luxury.
76 In 437/6 BC, eleven years before *Acharnians* was produced! Each of the ambassadors
   would thus have 'earned' some 8,000 drachmas, or more than a talent, quite
   apart from any presents he received from the King.
77 Either as a refugee from the countryside unable to find accommodation in the city,
   or as a reservist on guard duty.

DICAEOPOLIS: City of Cranaus![78]   75
Are you aware how these ambassadors mock you?
AMBASSADOR: Because the barbarians regard as real men
only those who can eat and drink vast quantities.
DICAEOPOLIS: As we do pathics and male prostitutes.
AMBASSADOR: After three years we arrived at the King's
   residence;   80
but he had gone off with an army to a bog,
and stayed shitting for eight months on the Golden Hills –
DICAEOPOLIS: And how long did he take to close up his arse?
Was it at the full moon?
AMBASSADOR: – and then he went off home.
Then he entertained us, and served us up oxen   85
baked whole in the oven –
DICAEOPOLIS: And who's ever seen
oven-baked oxen?[79] What bragging balderdash!
AMBASSADOR: And also, I swear it, he served us a bird
three times the size of Cleonymus;[80] it was called a fooler.
DICAEOPOLIS: So that's why you were making fools of *us*, and
   drawing two drachmas a day for it.   90
AMBASSADOR: And now we have come back, bringing with us
   Pseudartabas,
the King's Eye.
DICAEOPOLIS: May a raven knock it out with his beak,
and your ambassadorial eye along with it!
HERALD: The King's Eye!

[*Enter Pseudartabas; his mask has no nose or mouth, only an enormous eye set roughly where the mouth should be and partly swathed. He is attended by two eunuchs*]

DICAEOPOLIS: Lord Heracles!   95
Heavens, man, what are you doing looking like a warship?
Are you rounding a point and on the look-out for a
   ship-shed?

78 A mythical king of Athens.
79 The ambassador's word for 'oven' was *krībanos*, which usually means an oven for
   making bread rather than the kind of furnace-like oven in which the Persians,
   according to Herodotus (1.133.1), roasted oxen whole.
80 A politician noted for his weight.

I suppose that's an oarport sleeve you've got down there round
your eye![81]

AMBASSADOR: Come now, Pseudartabas, say what the King
has sent you to tell the Athenians.

PSEUDARTABAS: Iartaman exarxas apisona satra.   100

AMBASSADOR: Did you understand what he says?

DICAEOPOLIS: By Apollo, *I* didn't.

AMBASSADOR: He says the King is going to send you gold.

[*To Pseudartabas*] Speak louder, and plainly, about the gold.

PSEUDARTABAS: You not vill get goldo, you open-arsed Iaonian.[82]

DICAEOPOLIS: Good grief! That's plain all right!

AMBASSADOR: Why, what does he say?

DICAEOPOLIS: What does he say? He says that the Ionians are   105
open-arsed dodderers
if they expect gold from the barbarians.

AMBASSADOR: No, he says open carts full[83] of gold.

DICAEOPOLIS: Open carts, my foot! You're a great big liar.
Be off with you; I'll examine this man myself.

[*Exeunt Ambassadors*]

Here, you, tell me distinctly in the presence of this witness
[*his fist*],
or else I'll dye you Sardian purple:
is the King going to send us gold?   111

[*Pseudartabas throws back his head, indicating 'no'*][84]

So we're just being deceived by our ambassadors?

---

81 The features of contemporary Greek warships, on which this joke is based, are (1)
that they regularly had large eyes on their port and starboard bows (sometimes
painted on the timbers, sometimes on marble blocks fitted to the hull) and (2)
that the oarports nearest the waterline had leather covers (*askōmata*) to keep out
the sea. The actor playing Pseudartabas is walking blind (since his mask has no
eyes in the normal positions) and reminds Dicaeopolis of a ship feeling her way
into harbour; but unlike a normal ship, he has what looks like an *askōma* over his
eye.

82 *Ia(w)ones* ('Ionians') was the Greek phonetic equivalent of the Persian name for
the Greeks.

83 The ambassador claims that when Pseudartabas said *khaunoprōkte* 'open-arsed' he
was trying to say *akhănai*; the *akhănē* was a unit of capacity equivalent to about
2.35 cubic metres (such a volume of gold would weigh about 45 tonnes).

84 This and the next stage direction are, exceptionally, marked in the Greek text
(by single words meaning 'nods back' and 'nods forward').

[Pseudartabas and the eunuchs nod]

Very Greek, the way these fellows nod. 115
I'm quite sure they come from this very city –
and one of the eunuchs, this one,
I know who he is –
[unswathing the face of the 'eunuch'] Sibyrtius' boy Cleisthenes![85]
O thou that shav'st thy hot-desiring arse,[86]
dost thou, O monkey, with a beard like thine[87] 120
come among us dressed up as a eunuch?
And who may this one be? Surely not Strato?
HERALD: Silence! Sit down!
The Council invite the King's Eye
to the Prytaneum.[88]

[Pseudartabas and the eunuchs go out]

DICAEOPOLIS: Doesn't that just choke you? 125
Do you think I'm dallying here,
when no host's door is ever closed to *them*?
I'm going to do a great and fearful deed.
Where do I find Godschild?
GODSCHILD *[who has slipped back into the Assembly]*: Here I am.
DICAEOPOLIS: Take these eight drachmae and make peace 130
with the Spartans for me, myself alone,
and my children and my consort.
You lot can have your embassies and your gaping mouths!

The Wasps, ll. 1015–1059

In the *parabasis* of Aristophanes' earlier comedies the chorus leader regularly speaks
in praise of the author, sometimes wholly or partly identifying himself with the author
by speaking of him in the first person. Here we reproduce the main speech from the
parabasis of *The Wasps*, where Aristophanes reviews his career from its beginnings,

85 Cleisthenes (and Strato, below) were beardless men with a reputation for
effeminacy. Sibyrtius was a noted wrestling trainer: Cleisthenes may either have
been, or be being satirically or sarcastically described as, his son or his boyfriend
or his pupil.
86 Parodied from a tragic line.
87 Adapted from a line of Archilochus (fr. 187), with 'beard' substituted for the
original 'rump'; monkeys were proverbially 'rumpless', and similarly in the case
of Cleisthenes 'a beard like thine' means in effect 'no beard'.
88 The building in which the Athenian state dispensed public hospitality.

through the savage attack on 'the Jag-toothed One' (Cleon) in *The Knights*, to the
failure of the more intellectual *Clouds* which had been his most recent production.

Now then, all ye folk, pay attention, if you like some plain
    talking.   1015
Today our poet desires to reproach his audience.
He says that he has suffered an unprovoked injury after conferring
    many favours on them.
At first it was not openly but secretly, giving assistance to other
    poets,
slipping into other people's stomachs in imitation of the method
of the seer Eurycles,[89] that he poured forth many comic
    words;   1020
after that he did try his luck openly on his own,
holding the reins of a team of Muses that were his, not someone
    else's.
And when he was raised to greatness, and honoured as nobody has
    ever been among you,[90]
he says he didn't end up getting above himself, nor did he puff up
    with pride,
nor did he gallivant around the wrestling-schools, making
    passes;[91] and if a man   1025
who had had a lovers' quarrel pressed him to satirize the youth
    concerned,
he says he never complied with any such request, having in this
    the reasonable purpose
of not making the Muses he employs[92] into procurers.
And when he first began to produce, he did not, he says, attack
    mere men,
but with a spirit like that of Heracles he tackled the greatest
    monsters,   1030
boldly facing up right from the start to the Jag-toothed One
    himself,

89 Apparently the name of a spirit, who was supposed to speak ventriloquially
  through mediums.
90 Possibly by being the first person to hold the Dionysian and Lenaean comic crowns
  at the same time.
91 That is, at attractive boys.
92 Or 'the Muses with whom he consorts', since *khrēsthai* ('use, employ') can also
  mean 'enjoy sexually'.

from whose eyes shot terrible rays like those of the Bitch-star,[93]
while all around his head licked serpent-like a hundred head
of accursed flatterers; he had the voice of a torrent in destructive
    spate,
the smell of a seal, the unwashed balls of a Lamia,[94] and the arse
    of a camel.   1035
On seeing such a monstrosity he did not, he says, take fright and
    betray you for a bribe;
no, he's fought for you right through till now. And he says that
    after the monster,
last year,[95] he tackled the agues and the fevers,
the demons that by night throttled fathers and strangled
    grandfathers,
that lay down on the beds of the peaceable folk among you   1040
and stuck together affidavits, summonses and depositions,
so that many jumped up in terror to go to the polemarch.[96]
Such was the deliverer from evil, the cleanser of this land,[97]
    whom you had found;
but last year you let him down, when he sowed a crop of
    brand-new ideas,
which you blighted through not understanding them
    clearly –   1045
though he still swears by Dionysus, over any number of libations,
that no one ever heard better comic poetry than that.
So that puts *you* to shame, for not having recognized it
    immediately;
but our poet is none the worse thought of by the wise,
if while overtaking his rivals he wrecked his new concept.   1050
        But for the future, my dear sirs,
        cherish and foster more
        those poets who seek

93 Literally 'of Kynna' (a courtesan), a surprise substitute for 'of the Dog-star' (Greek
    Kynos) whose rays, when it began rising before the sun in July, were supposed to
    cause summer fevers.
94 An ogress [*sic*] who ate children; 'the . . . balls of a Lamia' may thus mean 'no
    balls at all'.
95 At the Lenaea of 423; the play cannot be identified with certainty. The 'demons'
    are *sūkophantai*, professional accusers who prosecute the innocent for personal gain.
96 The polemarch was the magistrate in charge of many types of lawsuit involving
    non-citizens, so there is an insinuation that many *sūkophantai* were exercising the
    rights of citizens without being entitled to them.
97 Designations often applied to Heracles.

to find something new to say;
save up their ideas   1055
and put them into your clothes-boxes
along with the quinces;[98]
and if you do that, then after a year
your cloaks
will be scented with cleverness.

The Birds, ll. 209–262

From *The Birds* we select the song in which the Hoopoe (alias Tereus), with the
assistance of his wife the Nightingale (alias Procne), summons the birds to a meeting
in a song of varied rhythm full of bird-calls. Between the introduction and the song
itself, his two human visitors, Peisetaerus and Euelpides, make brief comments.

HOOPOE: Come, my consort, leave your sleep
    and let forth the melodies of sacred song   210
    with which from your divine lips you lament
    your child and mine, the much-bewailed Itys,[99]
    quavering with the liquid notes
    of your vibrant throat.

[*The song of the nightingale is now heard, played by the piper*]

    Through the leaf-clad green-brier comes   215
    the pure sound, reaching the abode of Zeus,
    where golden-haired Phoebus hears
    and in response to your elegies plucks
    his ivoried lyre and stirs the gods
    to make music together; and from immortal lips   220
    issues as one voice the harmonious
    swelling divine refrain of the Blest Ones.

98 Packed with clothes when they were put away in storage, to protect them against
    moths and mustiness.
99 Procne, together with her sister Philomela, had killed Itys in revenge for Tereus'
    rape of Philomela, and had served his flesh to his father to eat. Tereus angrily
    pursued the two women intending to kill them, but they were saved by the gods,
    who turned Tereus into a hoopoe, Philomela into a swallow, and Procne into a
    nightingale, who laments eternally for Itys. In this play, however, typically of
    comedy, 'those whom the myth makes the greatest of enemies . . . have become
    friends' (Aristotle, *Poetics* 1453a36–39), and Tereus and Procne appear as a happily
    married couple.

[*The piper plays on, solo*]¹⁰⁰

EUELPIDES: Lord Zeus, what a voice that bird has!
How she filled the whole thicket with her sweetness!
PEISETAERUS: I say –
EUELPIDES: What is it?
PEISETAERUS: Keep quiet, won't you?
EUELPIDES: Why?   225
PEISETAERUS: The hoopoe's getting ready to sing an aria this time.
HOOPOE: Epopoi, popopopopoi, popoi!
    Io, io, ito, ito, hither, hither,
    hither let all my feathered fellows come!
    All who dwell in the country plough-lands   230
    rich in seed, the myriad tribes of barleycorn-eaters
    and the races of seed-gatherers
    that fly swiftly and utter soft notes,
    and all who in the furrows often
    gently twitter over the turned soil   235
    with joyful voices, like this,
    tio tio tio tio tio tio tio tio!
    And all of you who find their food
    in gardens on the ivy branches,
    and you of the hills, the eaters of oleaster and arbute,   240
    hurry, come flying to my call:
    trioto trioto totobrix!
    And you who in the marshy valleys swallow
    the sharp-biting gnats, and all you who inhabit   245
    the well-watered regions of the land and the lovely meads
        of Marathon,
    and the bird of patterned plumage, francolin, francolin!
    And you whose tribes fly with the halcyons¹⁰¹   250
    over the swell of the open sea,
    come hither to learn the news;
    for we are assembling here all the tribes
    of long-necked fowls.

---

100 This represents another of the rare ancient stage-directions, again a single Greek
     word ('one pipes').
101 The halcyon was a mythical bird, believed to build its nest on the surface of the
     sea; those in antiquity who tried to identify it with an actual bird usually selected
     the kingfisher.

For a sharp-witted old man has come here,   255
novel in his ideas
and an attempter of novel deeds.
Come to the meeting, all of you,
hither, hither, hither, hither!
Torotorotorotorotix!
Kikkabau, kikkabau!
Torotorotorolililix!

The Women at the Thesmophoria, ll. 1098–1135

In *Women at the Thesmophoria* Euripides is shown attempting to rescue his brother-in-law (here labelled 'Inlaw'), who has been condemned to death for infiltrating the all-female festival of the Thesmophoria, disguised as a woman, to defend Euripides against the women's accusations that he slanders them. Euripides' method is to enact rescue scenes from some of his own recent plays in the hope that his friend's captors may succumb to the theatrical illusion and allow the rescue to take place. In this scene Euripides plays Perseus while his (elderly) in-law plays Andromeda, whom Perseus rescued when she had been left chained to a rock to be devoured by a sea-monster; unfortunately the Scythian archer who is guarding the prisoner is not susceptible to the magic of drama . . .

[*The theatrical flying-machine swings Euripides into view. He is costumed as Perseus, wearing winged cap and winged sandals, carrying in his hand a scimitar and over his shoulder the leather bag in which Perseus kept the Gorgon's head*]

EURIPIDES: What barbarous land is this, O gods, where I
    swift-sandalled have arrived? Cleaving a path
    across the heavens I ply my wingèd foot,   1100
    Perseus, to Argos voyaging, my freight
    the Gorgon's head.
ARCHER:[102]   What you say? You garryin' de 'ead
    of Gorgo de segretar'?[103]
EURIPIDES: The Gorgon's,
    I say.
ARCHER: Yes, I dell you, Gorgo, dass what *I* say.

---

102 The archer speaks broken Greek, marked especially by an inability to aspirate
    the consonants *ph*, *th*, *kh*, by the omission or mangling of inflectional endings,
    and by total confusion regarding grammatical gender.
103 Secretary, that is, to some administrative body in the state apparatus (possibly
    to the Council of Five Hundred, whose orderly the speaker is). The man's name
    was probably Gorgus.

EURIPIDES [*descending to the ground in front of the stage-house, on the far side of the stage from Inlaw, and beholding him with affected astonishment*]:
But ah, what rock do I see? who is this maiden,   1105
fair as a goddess, ship-like moored to it?
INLAW: Good sir, take pity on my wretched plight,
release me from my bonds!
ARCHER [*threateningly*]:
                              Stop dalkin', will you?
You dare dalk, damn you, when you soon be dead?
EURIPIDES: Maid, I thee pity, seeing thee hanging here.   1110
ARCHER: She no maid, she a wicked ol' man,
a t'ief, a villain.
EURIPIDES: Nonsense, O Scythian:
this is Andromeda, the child of Cepheus.
ARCHER [*lifting up Inlaw's lower garments*]: Look at her fig![104] Don'
look all dat small, do it?
EURIPIDES: Give me her hand here; let me touch the maid.   1115
Come now, O Scythian. Every man on earth
hath some affliction, and so too have I:
love of this maid has ta'en me prisoner.
ARCHER: I don' envy you.
Now if 'is arse'ole was durned roun' dis way,
I no grudge you dake 'im an' bugger 'im.   1120
EURIPIDES: Why, Scythian, wilt thou not let me release her
to fall upon the bed and nuptial couch?
ARCHER: If you wan' all dat much bugger de ol' man,
den bore a 'ole in de board[105] an' fuck her from be'ind.
EURIPIDES: Nay, but I'll loose her bonds.

[*He approaches Inlaw, but the Archer, whip at the ready, blocks him*]

ARCHER: Den I whip you.   1125
EURIPIDES: Yet will I do it.

---

104 The archer's problems with Greek grammar result in his confusing the neuter noun *sūkon* 'fig, [*slang*] vulva' with the feminine noun *sūkē* 'fig, [*slang*] penis'.
105 Inlaw is clamped (by the neck, wrists and ankles) to a large board which has been stood up vertically, leaving him to a slow death by (most likely) dehydration, unless at some stage he is given a comparatively merciful release and strangled by the tightening of the neck-clamp.

ARCHER [*brandishing his sword*]: Den your 'ead,
    I jop 'im off wid dis sabre.
EURIPIDES: Alack! what shall I do, to what words turn? –
    But no, his barbarous mind won't take them in:
    'To feed slow wits with novel subtleties   1130
    is effort vainly spent.'[106] No, I must bring to bear
    some other scheme, more suited to this man. [*He departs*]
ARCHER: De foxy villain! de mongey drick 'e dried on me!
INLAW [*calling after Euripides*]: Perseus! remember the wretched
    plight you leave me in!
ARCHER [*cracking his whip*]: You still fancy geddin' de whip, do
    you?   1135

MENANDER

The Curmudgeon (Dyskolos), ll. 189–232

From *The Curmudgeon (Dyskolos)*, the only play by Menander to have survived virtually complete, we select the scene (at the end of Act I) in which young Sostratus gets his first (and, in the play, his only) chance to speak to the girl with whom he has fallen in love, the daughter of the misanthropic Cnemon. Cnemon's house adjoins a cave-shrine of Pan and the Nymphs, in which there is apparently a spring. The other house on stage belongs to the girl's half-brother Gorgias (Cnemon's stepson) and his mother; their slave Daos sees Sostratus talking to the girl and misunderstands his intentions. Daos' final words are a cue for the entrance of the chorus, whom Menander regularly introduces in similar terms but who have no role in the play except to perform intermezzi between the acts.

GIRL [*coming out of Cnemon's house with a water-jar*]: Help, poor me,
    what a pickle I'm in!
    What shall I do now? Nurse was hauling up   190
    the bucket, and she dropped it in the well!
SOSTRATUS [*aside*]:   O Father Zeus
    and Phoebus the Healer, O dear Sons of Zeus,[107]
    what irresistible beauty!
GIRL: And when daddy went out, he or[dered me]
    to heat up water.
SOSTRATUS [*confidentially to the audience*]: [I'm trembling,] people!

---

106 Adapted from Euripides' *Medea* (lines 298–299).
107 The Dioscori (Castor and Pollux).

GIRL: And if he realizes what's happened, he'll [absolutely]
    beat the life
    out of her! I haven't got time for id[le chatter.]   195
    Dearest Nymphs, I must g[et it] from you.
    I'm ashamed, though, to bother anyone who m[ay be]
    sacrificing in there –
SOSTRATUS [*coming forward*]: Well, if you g[ive it] to me, I'll dip
    t[he jar right away and c]ome back with it.
GIRL [*giving him the jar*]: Yes, by the gods, [but] h[urry].   200
SOSTRATUS [*aside, as he goes into the shrine*]: Rather well-bred, she is,
    for a country girl. You [glor]ious gods,
    what [pow]er can save me?

[*A noise is heard as if a door were being opened*]

GIRL: Oh dear,
    who made that noise? Is daddy coming?
    If so, I'll get hit, if he finds me
    outside!   205

[*She moves over to stand in her own doorway. Daos comes out of Gorgias' house*]

DAOS [*addressing Gorgias' mother, who is inside*]:
          I've been wasting a lot of time doing odd jobs here
    for you, while he's digging on his own. I've got to go
    to him. Oh, damnable Poverty,
    why did we run into such a lot of you?
    Why have you been sat in our house with us   210
    for such a long time, without a break?
SOSTRATUS [*returning, having filled the jar; to the girl*]: Take it,
    here.
GIRL: Give it over.

[*Sostratus takes the jar over to her*]

DAOS [*aside*]:   What on earth is this fellow
    up to?
SOSTRATUS: Keep well, and look after your father.

[*The girl disappears inside*]

    Wretched me! – Stop lamenting, Sostratus!
    It'll be all right.
DAOS [*aside*]:   *What* will be all right?
SOSTRATUS [*to himself*]:   Don't worry.   215

Do what you were just meaning to do; go home and get
Getas,[108] telling him the whole story plainly.

[*Exit, towards the city*]

DAOS: What fishy business is this? I don't like it
at all. Young lad doing job
for girl? That's bad. Cnemon, may all the gods   220
make you perish wretchedly for your wretched behaviour,
letting an innocent girl loose alone in the middle
of nowhere, keeping no watch on her
as would be proper. I suppose he got wind of it
and rushed here, thinking he'd had   225
a marvellous stroke of luck! Anyway, I *must*
tell her brother as soon as possible, so that
we can take care of the girl.
I think I'll go and do that right away,
because I can see some worshippers of Pan   230
coming this way, rather the worse for drink,
and I think it would be prudent not to bother them.

[*Exit, towards the fields*]

The Arbitration (Epitrepontes), ll. 218–360

Our next scene is that from which *The Arbitration* (*Epitrepontes*) takes its name. Two
slaves – Syrus, a charcoal-burner, and Daos, a shepherd – are in dispute over possession
of a baby whom Daos had found in the woods (and of some trinkets found with it),
and submit the matter to the arbitration of an elderly gentleman, Smicrines, whom
they happen to meet. In due course, from the initial clue provided by the trinkets, it
will be established that the child is Smicrines' own grandson, and that its father,
who had raped the mother at an all-night festival, is the same man who, all unknowing,
had subsequently married her. The plot is modelled on Euripides' (lost) *Alope*, in which
Alope's father Cercyon arbitrated a dispute between two shepherds over a foundling
child's valuable clothing, and the clothing enabled the child to be identified as Alope's
son.

SYRUS: You're trying to evade justice.
DAOS: You're making bogus charges,
                                       you wretch.
You've no right to have what's not yours.

---

108 A slave belonging to Sostratus' father, whom Sostratus regards as an expert
    intriguer (but who, as it proves, will be no help to him at all!).

SYRUS: We should submit this
to someone to arbitrate.

DAOS: I agree to that; let's get it judged.   220

SYRUS: Who, then?

DAOS: Anyone will do me. I've got
what I deserved: why did I give you a share?

SYRUS [*pointing to Smicrines, who has not so far noticed the pair*]: Do you
    want to have
this man as judge?

DAOS: With fortune's blessing!

SYRUS [*going up to Smicrines*]:   If you please,[109]
my good sir, could you spare us a little time?

SMICRINES: You? What about?

SYRUS: We have a bit of a dispute.   225

SMICRINES: So what has that to do with me?

SYRUS: We're looking for an
                                   impartial person
to judge it; *if* you're not otherwise engaged,
please do resolve our differences.

SMICRINES: You damnable fellows,
do you go around pleading lawsuits when you wear
leather jerkins?[110]

SYRUS: All the same, do. It's a small matter   230
and easy to understand. Give us this favour, father;[111]
don't despise us, we beg you. Everywhere,
on every occasion, justice ought to prevail,
and it's a universal rule of life
that anyone, however uninvolved,[112] should have a concern   235
for this principle.

DAOS: A fairly expert orator I've got myself tangled
                         up with!
Why did I give you a share?

SMICRINES: Tell me, will you abide
by my decision?

---

109 Literally 'in the gods' name', but here conveying an earnest rather than an
importunate request.

110 Smicrines is evidently of a somewhat 'oligarchic' disposition (cf. Theophrastus,
Characters 26) and thinks that poor men (he does not yet know they are slaves)
have no business concerning themselves with such things when they ought to
be working.

111 A respectful form of address to an older man.

112 Literally 'that the person who happens by . . .'

SYRUS: Certainly.
SMICRINES: I'll hear it. What is there
    to stop me? [*To Daos*] You, the silent one, speak first.
DAOS: I'll go back a bit, telling you more than just my dealings   240
    with this man, so that the whole business will be clear to you.
    I'd been shepherding my flock, all by myself,
    in the woods near this place
    for perhaps a month, sir,
    and I found this baby boy lying in the open   245
    together with a necklace and some ornaments
    of that sort.
SYRUS: They're what's in dispute.
DAOS: He won't let me speak!
SMICRINES: If you interrupt, I'll go for you
    with my stick!
SYRUS [*cowed*]:   You're quite right.
SMICRINES [*to Daos*]:   Speak on.
DAOS: I will.
    I picked it up, I went home with it,   250
    I was going to rear it. That was my intention at the time.
    But during the night, as happens to everyone,
    I reflected and thought to myself: 'Why should I
    have all the troubles of child-rearing? Where shall I get
    all the money I'd need to spend? Why should I have the
        bother?'   255
    That was how I felt. In the morning
    I was back with my flock. Then this man came (he's a charcoal-
        burner)
    to the same place, to saw some logs there;
    we already knew each other.
    We talked together. He saw I was looking glum   260
    and said 'What's worrying you, Daos?' 'Why,' I said,
    'I've bitten off more than I can chew' – and I explained the
        situation to him,
    how I found the baby, how I picked it up. And then,
    right away, before I'd finished speaking, he was begging me,
    saying 'so may you be blessed, Daos' every few words: 265
    'Give me the baby. So may you be happy,
    so may you be free. You see,' he said, 'I've got
    a wife, and she had a baby, but it died' –
    meaning her, the one that's holding the baby now.

Did you beg me, my dear Syrus?[113]

SYRUS: I did.

DAOS: He spent the whole day   270

at it. He argued with me, he wheedled me,
I promised him, I gave it him, and he went away
wishing ten thousand blessings on me; he took my hands
and kept kissing them. Did you do that?

SYRUS: I did.

DAOS: And he went off.

Now suddenly he meets me, along with his wife,   275
and demands to be given the things that were put out
together with the baby – they were little things, fripperies,
nothing really – and says he's being treated unfairly
because I won't hand them over. But I say I'm entitled to
    them.
I say he ought to be grateful   280
for the share he begged for and received; if I didn't give
    him
the whole lot, that's no cause for interrogating me!
If we'd been walking together and found these things,
'finding's sharing' as it were,[114] he [would have] taken one
    share
and I the other; but I found them on my own, you weren't there
    a[t the time],
and yet you think you should have the lot, with nothing at all
    for me!   286
The long and short of it is: I gave you something of mine.
If you're satisfied with that, keep it.
If you're not, if you've changed your mind, give it back;
you'll have done no wrong and suffered no loss. But have the
    lot –   290
part of it with my consent, the rest taken by force –
that you shouldn't. I have said what I have to say.

SYRUS: Has he finished?

SMICRINES: Didn't you hear? He's finished!

113 In the Greek, Daos addresses Syrus by the diminutive form 'Syriscus'.
114 Literally 'shared Hermes': Hermes was the god of lucky finds, and it was an
    accepted principle that if property was found and its owner could not be
    discovered, it belonged to the finders in equal shares.

SYRUS: Good.
   Then it's now my turn. This man found the baby
   all by himself, and everything he says now   295
   is true; that's how it happened, father,
   I don't dispute it. I begged, I pleaded,
   and I received it from him; he's telling the truth.
   I was told by a shepherd, who he'd been talking to,
   one of those who worked with him, that he'd found   300
   some ornaments with the baby. Father, he's here
   in person to claim them. (Wife, give me
   the baby.) Daos, he demands back from you
   the necklace and the recognition-tokens. He says
   that they were put there to adorn him, not to feed you.   305
   I join in his demand, as his guardian:
   you made me that by giving him to me. Now, sir,
   this is what you have to decide, as it seems to me.
   This gold stuff, or whatever it is – should it,
   in accordance with the wish of the mother, whoever she
      was,   310
   when she gave it, be kept for the child until he grows up,
   or should the man who robbed him have it
   just because he was the first to find someone else's property?
     Why then, you ask,
   didn't I demand these things from you when I received the
     baby?
   I wasn't then in a position to speak for him.   315
   But I come now, and I'm not asking you for a single thing
   that belongs to *me*. 'Finding's sharing'? You can't talk of
   finding anything, when there's also a person who has been
     wronged.
   That's not finding, it's stealing!
   And also, father, look at it this way. Perhaps this boy   320
   is above us; after being reared among working men,
   he will despise that station, rush to fulfil his inherited nature,
   and have the daring to do something worthy of a gentleman,
   hunting lions, bearing arms, running
   in competition. You've seen tragedies, I'm sure,   325
   and you know all that stuff. There was that Neleus or
     someone,
   and Pelias, who were found by an old man,
   a goatherd, wearing a leather jerkin as I am now,

but when he became aware that they were his superiors,
he told them the story, how he'd found them, how he'd
   picked them up;   330
and he gave them a little wallet of recognition-tokens,
thanks to which they learned the whole truth about
   themselves
and, having once been shepherds, they became kings.[115]
If Daos had taken those things from them and sold them
so he could make a profit of twelve drachmas,   335
those boys of such great standing and birth
would have remained in obscurity all their lives.
It's not proper that I should be rearing
this baby physically, while his hope of a good life
is taken by Daos and thrown away, father.   340
A man has been stopped from marrying his sister
through recognition-tokens, another came across his mother
   and saved her,
another his brother.[116] Everyone's life, father,
is precarious by nature, and one has to watch it carefully,
foreseeing its possibilities well before they come.   345
And he says 'If you're not satisfied, give it back', thinking
   this
is a strong and relevant argument.
It's not fair. If you're expected to return some of his property,
will you also want to take *him*,
so that next time you can play the villain with greater
   safety,   350
if this time Fortune has preserved some of his possessions?[117]
I have spoken. Judge where you think justice lies.

115 Neleus and Pelias were the twin sons of Tyro and Poseidon; they became kings of Pylos and Iolcus respectively. The story of their birth and identification was told in one or both of two plays by Sophocles called *Tyro*.
116 Situations of this kind provided plots for several tragedies (notably Euripides' surviving *Iphigeneia in Tauris*); compare also Menander's own *Perikeiromene*, in which the young man Moschion is in love with Glycera until it is discovered that she is his sister.
117 In other words: if the judge decides (as in fact he will) that the tokens must not be separated from the baby, Syrus expects (rightly) that Daos will want to have both, in the hope (according to Syrus) of then being able to rob the baby with impunity.

SMICRINES: It is easy to decide. Everything which was put out
    with the baby
    belongs to the baby. That is my decision.
DAOS: Good;
    and the baby?
SMICRINES: I'm not going to adjudge him, by Zeus, to you   355
    who tried to wrong him, but to him who came to his aid
    and opposed your intended crime.
SYRUS: May you have many blessings!
DAOS: A dreadful [judgement],
    by Zeus the Saviour! [I] found the lot,
    I've had the lot wrenched away, and the one who didn't find
    them, gets them!   360

Shorn (Perikeiromene), ll. 486–525

This scene from *Shorn (Perikeiromene)* shows the despair of the soldier Polemon after being deserted by his mistress Glycera, angry because he had abused her and cut off her hair after seeing her kissing a young man named Moschion who, unknown to him (and unknown to the young man himself), was her brother. She has now taken refuge in the house of Myrrhine, Moschion's foster-mother. Here Polemon is being counselled by an older friend, Pataecus; later in the play Pataecus will discover that he is the father of Moschion and Glycera, and will give Glycera to Polemon in lawful marriage. Unusually, the play is set at Corinth rather than Athens, probably because it would have been improper to present the daughter of an Athenian citizen living with a man as his mistress.

PATAECUS: If the situation really was as you say it was,
    Polemon, and it was actually your wedded wife who –
POLEMON: What a thing to say, Pataecus!
PATAECUS: It makes a bit of a difference!
POLEMON: I've treated her *as* my wife!
PATAECUS: Don't shout.
    Who gave her to you?
POLEMON: To me? She gave herself.
PATAECUS: Very well.   490
    She liked you before, perhaps, and now she doesn't any more.
    You didn't treat her satisfactorily, and
    she's left.
POLEMON: What do you mean, not satisfactorily? That's hurt
    me
    more than anything you've said.

PATAECUS: You're in love.
I know that very well. The result is, the way you're behaving
   now   495
is crazy.

[*Polemon begins to move towards Myrrhine's house*]

     Where are you off to? Who do you mean
to take away? She's her own mistress!
For someone who's in love and in a bad way
the only solution is persuasion.
POLEMON: And the man who corrupted her
in my absence – has he not done me wrong?
PATAECUS: Yes, he's wronged you,
so complain about it, if you ever come face to face.   500
But if you use force, he'll sue you and win. This injury
is a case for complaint, not for vengeance.
POLEMON: Not even now?
PATAECUS: Not even now.
POLEMON: I don't know what
to say, by Demeter, except 'I'm going to choke!'
Pataecus, Glycera has *left* me,   505
she's *left* me, Glycera has! But if that's really what you think
I should do – you know her well, you've often
talked to her before – go and speak to her,
be my ambassador, I beg you!
PATAECUS: That's what I think
we should do, don't you see?   510
POLEMON: And you certainly have a way with words,
Pataecus.
PATAECUS: So-so.
POLEMON: But really, Pataecus, you *must*.
This is the only way to save the situation.
If I've ever done her any wrong at all . . .
if I don't always have the highest aims . . .
if you could see what she wears . . . [118]
PATAECUS [*soothingly*]:   Everything's all right!   515

---

118 Polemon is rambling incoherently, unable to finish a sentence without changing
    the subject.

POLEMON: Take a look at it, Pataecus, in the gods' name;
you'll pity me even more!

[*He tries to drag Pataecus towards his own house*]

PATAECUS: Poseidon!
POLEMON: Come this way!
What dresses! And the way she looks, when she
puts one of them on! You probably haven't seen it.
PATAECUS: I have.   520
POLEMON: And her height, that was certainly
remarkable.[119] But why am I now making an issue
of her height, idiot that I am, talking about things that
don't matter?
PATAECUS: They don't, by Zeus.
POLEMON: They don't? But, Pataecus, you *must*
see them! Come this way.
PATAECUS: Lead the way; I'm coming.

525

The Necklace (Plokion), fr. 296.1–16

In *The Necklace* (*Plokion*) the central character is an elderly widower, Laches, who has married an ugly *epikleros* (a brotherless heiress, who was automatically given, together with her father's estate, to the nearest relative who chose to claim her) for the sake of her money, and has found her, as he says in another surviving fragment, to be an 'ogress' both to him and to her stepchildren. Here he complains of how she has forced him to sell a good-looking maidservant with whom she suspected him (we do not know how justly) of having an affair.

This lovely heiress now intends to sleep
on both sides of the bed! She's done a great
and glorious deed – she was vexed by someone,
she wanted rid of her, and she threw her out of the house,
so that everyone would have their eyes on Crobyle's
face, and everyone would know that my wife   5
owns me. And the looks she's got!
As the proverb says, she's an ass among monkeys![120]
I want to say nothing about the night

---

119 Tallness was considered beautiful and shortness ugly, both in men and in women.
120 That is, the ugliest of the ugly ('lovely' in line 1 was sarcastic).

that was the beginning of so many evils. Dammit, why
did I marry Crobyle, with that thick nose of hers,   10
even if she did <bring me> ten talents! And then
her hoity-toity ways,[121] how can they be endured? By Zeus
on Olympus, by Athena, they can't!
Little girl, good servant, answers
before you call – get rid of her!   15

Unknown play, fr. 602.1–18

In this fragment of an unknown play, preserved both in a quotation by Plutarch and
on a papyrus, a slave advises his young master to bear up under a misfortune, arguing
that misfortune is the lot of all mortals and this one (a disappointment in love perhaps?)
is far from being the worst imaginable.

Young master, if you, alone among mankind,
when your mother gave birth to you, were born on the terms
that you would always do what you liked and enjoy good fortune –
if some god had struck this bargain with you –
then you're entitled to grumble, because he's cheated you
and acted improperly. But if you breathe the air we all share   5
(if I can speak to you in rather elevated[122] tones)
under the same conditions as the rest of us,
you should bear these things better and be rational.
To sum the whole thing up, you're a human being,
than whom no animal experiences more rapid changes   10
in the direction of pride and then of humiliation.
Quite rightly too; for he is the weakest of creatures
by nature, and yet builds the biggest structures;[123]
so when he falls, he smashes a great many goods.
The good things *you've* lost, young master,   15
aren't exceptional, and your present troubles are moderate;
so you really should keep your grief moderate too.

121 Literally 'neighing'.
122 Literally 'tragic'.
123 Literally (perhaps) 'organizes himself in the biggest affairs'.

Unknown play, fr. 804

It was in accordance with traditional wisdom, from Hesiod onwards, to discover what one could about a woman's character before offering to marry her, but this father of a marriageable girl has taken the logic of this principle to conclusions which most of his contemporaries would find extremely eccentric.

We really ought all to make marriages,
O Zeus the Saviour, in the same way as we make purchases.
Don't ask questions about things of no importance –
who's the bride's grandfather, who's her grandmother –
while not examining or asking about the character   5
of the actual girl you're going to be living with!
Don't, either, take the dowry to the bank
for the tester to see if the silver is good,[124]
silver that won't stay in the house for five months,
while not testing anything at all about the woman   10
who's going to stay in the house all her life, but just taking
  her anyway,
selfish, bad-tempered, difficult, loose-tongued,
whatever. I'm going to take my daughter
all round the city. Anyone who wants to marry her,
talk to her, see in advance what grade of pest   15
you'll be getting – because a wife is bound to be a pest,
but you're lucky if yours is as mild a pest as possible!

MINOR COMEDIANS

Telecleides, *The Amphictyons*, fr. 1

The second/third century AD writer Athenaeus quotes a long series of passages from fifth-century comedy on the theme of a Utopia in which all good things, and especially food, come to man of their own accord (*automata*) without labour. One of them is this extract from *The Amphictyons*, a comedy by Telecleides, probably produced in the 430s; the idea of food cooking itself and/or coming of its own will to the consumer and asking to be eaten is a typical feature of writing on this theme. The identity of the speaker is uncertain, but it may well be the god Cronus; 'the life in the days of Cronus' was the ancient Greek phrase for a utopian or paradisal lifestyle.

I will speak, then, beginning at the beginning, about the life that
  I used to provide for mortals.

124 That is, of proper weight and fineness.

First of all, like water over the hands,[125] there was peace.
The earth bore no plagues and no terrors; everything that was
    needed came of its own accord.
Every brook flowed with wine; barley-cakes fought with loaves
for access to men's mouths, begging them to swallow   5
the whitest, if they liked. Fish roasted themselves to a turn
on the way home, and lay ready on the tables.
A river of broth flowed past the dining-couches, rolling down hot
    meat,
and there were channels of sauces for these for anyone who wanted
    them,
so it was easy to moisten the stuff till it was tender and swallow it
    down.   10
There were <   > in little bowls, sprinkled with seasonings.
Roast thrushes with little milk-cakes flew down your throat,
and the flat-cakes jostling round your jaws made a right
    hullabaloo!
The boys would play dice with slices and titbits of sow's womb.[126]
Men were fat then, real giants of people.   15

Cratinus, *Cheirones*, frs 258 and 259

Aristophanes' older contemporary **Cratinus** was noted for his relentless satire on
Pericles. These two quotations from his play *Cheirones* (probably meaning *Cheiron and
his Companions*, indicating a chorus of centaurs) combine several common themes: the
comparison of Pericles to Zeus; references to his odd-shaped head; and attacks on his
mistress, Aspasia of Miletus.

And Faction and ancient
Cronus joined in union
and begot that greatest of tyrants
who is called the Head-gatherer[127]
by the gods . . .   5

and Nymphomania bore Aspasia to be his Hera,
a bitch-eyed[128] concubine.

125 Immediately before a meal, water was brought in for the diners to pour over their
     hands; hence 'water over the hands' could refer to the beginning of any activity.
126 In classical Athens a great delicacy; in this account, apparently so common as
     not to be worth eating!
127 Playing on Zeus' Homeric epithet 'cloud-gatherer'.
128 Playing on Hera's Homeric epithet 'ox-eyed'.

Eupolis, *The Flatterers (Kolakes)*, fr. 172

Eupolis was Aristophanes' greatest rival until he died on naval service in or about 411. This fragment comes from *The Flatterers (Kolakes)*, with which he defeated Aristophanes' *Peace* at the City Dionysia of 421. The play was built around the figure of the wealthy and extravagant Callias, whose patronage of sophists is well known from Plato's dialogue *Protagoras* which is set at his house, and who seems to have been a target, over many years, for male and female spongers of many kinds. In this passage, probably a speech from the *parabasis* of the play, the chorus explain some features of the life of a sponger (or, as later comedy would call the type, a 'parasite'), ending with a joke at the expense of the tragic dramatist Acestor.

We will tell you the way of life that spongers have in relation to
    you.
Just listen and hear what clever men we are
in every way. First of all, my footboy[129]
belongs mostly to someone else, though I have a small share of
    him.[130]
I have two smart cloaks; of these   5
I take one every day and march out
to the Agora. There, when I see a man
who's rich and stupid, I'm on to him right away.
Whatever the rich bloke says, I praise it tremendously,
and I make out that his words amaze me with delight.   10
Then we go to dinner, one here, one there,
to alien grub, where the sponger immediately has to say
a lot of witty things, or else he's turfed out.
I know that once happened to Acestor, him with the tattoo:[131]
he cracked a bawdy joke, and then the boy[132] put a collar on him,   15
took him outside, and handed him over to Oeneus.[133]

129 A slave who accompanied his master about, carrying his impedimenta.
130 The sponger induces a rich man to contribute the lion's share to the purchase price of a slave of whom the sponger himself will have sole use.
131 Insinuating that Acestor (whose right to Athenian citizenship appears to have been disputed by some) was by origin a slave, who had been forcibly tattooed after running away and being recaptured or for other serious misbehaviour.
132 The host's slave (*pais*, like 'boy' in more recent slave societies, could denote a male slave of any age).
133 That is, apparently, to the executioner/torturer – with allusion, probably, to Periboea, daughter of Hipponous of Olenus, who 'having lost her virginity to Hippostratus son of Amarynceus was sent by her father Hipponous to Oeneus [at Calydon] with instructions that she should be put to death' (Apollodorus, *Library* 1.8.4, citing Hesiod; Oeneus disobeyed the instructions and kept Periboea as his own wife, eventually to bear him Tydeus).

Plato, *Phaon*, fr. 188.5–21

The central character of *Phaon*, produced in 391 BC by the comic dramatist **Plato**, was a man to whom Aphrodite had granted the gift of being irresistible to women. In this extract, a goddess (probably Aphrodite herself), acting in effect as Phaon's pimp, tells (the chorus of?) women what they will have to pay/sacrifice in order to get an assignation with Phaon.

If you want to see Phaon, you must first 5
make substantial preliminary sacrifices of the following kind.
In the first place, offered to myself as Nurturer of the Young,
an uncastrated flat-cake, a pregnant sponge-cake,[134] sixteen
whole thrushes mixed with honey,
twelve helpings of hare with crescent-shaped cakes. After that 10
the rest is very cheap; listen to it.[135]
To Orthannes[136] three gallons of edible bulbs;
to Conisalus[137] and his two supporters
a tray of myrtle-berries plucked by hand[138]
(because gods don't like the smell of the lamp);[139] 15
to the Dogs and the Huntsmen[140] <   >;
to Bendback a drachma, to Bendover three obols,
to the hero Jockey a skin and meal-offerings.
Those are the costs. If you're willing to pay them,
you can come in; otherwise, you are free
to feel vacantly randy to no good end!

Antiphanes, *Poetry (Poiesis)*, fr. 189

Comedy delighted in deflating the pretensions of its sister genre Tragedy. In *Poetry (Poiesis)*, by the fourth-century Middle Comedy poet **Antiphanes**, a comic dramatist (less probably Comedy herself) is made to complain that comedy is much harder to

---

134 The cakes are spoken of as if they were animal victims.
135 From this point on both the offerings and the names of their recipients are mostly obscene, either directly or by *double entendre*.
136 Orthannes ('the upright one') was an ithyphallic divinity worshipped in Attica and elsewhere.
137 Another phallic god known from other sources (e.g. Aristophanes, *Lysistrata*, line 992). His two 'supporters' are of course testicular gods (possibly invented *ad hoc*).
138 *Murton* ('myrtle-berry') also meant 'clitoris'.
139 Women often used lamp flames for rapid depilation.
140 These were minor divinities associated with Asclepius; but *kuōn* ('dog') could also mean 'penis'. The words describing the offering to be made to them are corrupt and cannot be restored with confidence.

write than tragedy because tragedies are based on myths already familiar to their
audiences.

> Tragedy is a very lucky kind
> of poetry in every way. For a start,
> the audience already know the plots,
> before anyone has said a word, and all the poet needs to do
> is put them in mind of the story. Let him just mention Oedipus, 5
> they know all the rest: his father was Laius,
> his mother Iocaste, who were his sons and daughters,
> what's going to happen to him, what he's done in the past. Again,
> if someone mentions Alcmeon,[141] he's as good as said already
> who all his children were, how he went mad and killed 10
> his mother, how an angry Adrastus will shortly
> come and go away again <   >.
> Then when they've run out of things to say
> and when their play has completely exhausted itself,
> they throw up the sponge, or rather the flying-machine,[142] 15
> and the audience are satisfied.
> *We* don't have all that; we have to
> invent the lot, new names and all <
>   >, including the story-so-far,
> the initial situation, the opening of the action 20
> and its conclusion. If some Chremes or Pheidon
> leaves any of that out, he's hissed off the stage;
> whereas Peleus and Teucer can do what they like!

Epicrates (unknown play), fr. 10

As Socrates had been a butt in Old Comedy, so Plato was in Middle Comedy. In this
extract from an unknown play (written in chanted anapaests, a type of verse which
Middle Comedy seems to have favoured more than either Old or New) a character
describes a Platonic seminar in taxonomy (a subject of considerable interest to Plato

---

141 Son of the prophet Amphiaraus, who was tricked by his wife Eriphyle into joining
  the expedition of the Seven against Thebes (led by Adrastus), from which he did
  not return; Alcmeon, like Orestes, took revenge for his father by killing his
  mother. The audience's 'knowledge' of the story appears distinctly shaky: in all
  versions we know of, Alcmeon went mad, if at all, *after* killing his mother, and
  his children are differently named in different sources.
142 Literally 'they raise up the flying-machine like a finger' (i.e. they bring on a *deus
  ex machina*); in combat sports, raising one finger indicated that a contestant was
  ready to accept defeat.

in his later years, notably in the *Sophist*). The play, whose title was not known, will thus have been written during the last two decades of Plato's life (367–347); the author, **Epicrates**, appears to have been a fairly undistinguished dramatist (the Lenaean victor-list, on which all his leading contemporaries figure, does not include his name).

(A): What about Plato
    and Speusippus and Menedemus?[143]
    What are they spending their time on just now?
    What thoughts, what arguments
    are being investigated among them?   5
    Tell me this precisely, if you have come
    with any knowledge of it, in the name of Mother Earth!
(B): I know, and can tell you truly about these things.
    At the Panathenaea, I saw a herd
    of adolescent lads   10
    among the gymnasia of the Academy[144]
    and heard talk that was extraordinary, incredible.
    They were establishing definitions in the natural world
    and classifying the lives of animals,
    the natural qualities of trees, and the different kinds of
        vegetables;   15
    and then, in the course of this, they were examining the
        question
    what category the pumpkin belonged to.
(A): And how did they define the plant? To what category
    did they assign it? Tell me, if you have any information.
(B): At first they all stood still   20
    and speechless, with their heads bowed,
    thinking it out for quite a long time.
    Then suddenly, while the lads
    were still head down and thinking,
    someone said it was a round vegetable;   25
    a grass, said another; a tree, said a third.
    Hearing this, a doctor
    from the land o' the Sicels[145]

143 Close associates of Plato in his later years. Speusippus, Plato's nephew, succeeded him as head of the Academy.
144 The *Akadēmeiā*, the precinct of the god Academus, had been laid out as a park by Cimon, probably in the 460s, with a stream, shaded walks, and running-tracks (Plutarch, *Cimon* 13.8); when Plato established his school in the area, the school came to be known by the same name.
145 The phrase is said in the Doric dialect which most Sicilian Greeks spoke.

broke wind at them as if to say 'what twaddle!'
(A): I suppose they were terribly angry, and complained loudly that
    they were being made fun of?   30
    It's hardly proper to do that sort of thing in the middle of a
    discussion like that!
(B): The lads couldn't have cared less.
    Plato was there, and very mildly –
    he wasn't stirred up at all – he instructed them
    to do another definition exercise: 35
    what category does a <fart> belong to?
    And they started taxonomizing it.

Alexis, *Linus*, fr. 140

Alexis of Thurii is reported to have written 245 plays in a career spanning eight decades, beginning in the 350s. *Linus*, from which the following quotation derives, was unusual among them in being a mythological burlesque, centred on the traditional comic figure of the gluttonous Heracles. In this scene Linus, tutor to the young Heracles, invites his pupil to choose a book for study; Heracles knows what he likes . . .

LINUS: Go and take
    any book you want from here
    and then read it, examining them carefully,
    slowly, unhurriedly, by the labels.
    There's Orpheus[146] here, Hesiod, tragedies,   5
    Choerilus,[147] Homer, Epicharmus, prose works
    of all kinds. In this way you will show the main bent
    of your nature.
HERACLES [*taking a book*]: I choose this one.
LINUS: First show me what it is.
HERACLES: *Cookery*,
    as the label says.
LINUS: You're a lover of wisdom,[148]   10
    it's clear, if you pass over so many writings
    and choose a technical work by Simus.

---

146 That is, the religious/mystical poetry of the Orphic sect, supposed to be the work
    of its mythical founder.
147 Choerilus of Samos, a fifth-century epic poet; his most famous work was on the
    great Persian war.
148 Greek *philosophos*.

HERACLES: And who *is* Simus?
LINUS: A very talented man. He's now launched himself
   into tragedy; among actors he's by far
   the best cook, in the opinion   15
   of those who use him, and among cooks the best actor.[149]

[*After some further dialogue*]

LINUS: The man's insatiable![150]
HERACLES: Say what you like;
   what I know is, I'm hungry!

Philippides, *The Lover of Euripides* (*Phileuripides*), fr. 25

Philippides was both a dramatist and a politician; there survives an inscribed decree (*IG* ii² 657) awarding him lavish honours (a golden crown, a bronze statue in the theatre, privileged seating at all public spectacles, and meals at public expense in the Prytaneum for him and his eldest descendant in perpetuity) in recognition of his services to Athens over a period of twenty years. In a play produced close to the year 300 a character bitterly attacked the politician Stratocles for his servility towards the Macedonian ruler Demetrius Poliorcetes: when Demetrius visited Athens to be initiated in the Eleusinian Mysteries, Stratocles had moved and carried a decree manipulating the Athenian calendar so that the two festivals which an initiand had to attend would both fall at convenient times, and another permitting Demetrius to lodge on the Acropolis. The last line of the passage indicates that attempts were yet again being made to restrict freedom of speech in comedy; but Philippides' attack may not have been as bold as it seems – Demetrius had by now been defeated at Ipsus, both he and Stratocles were in eclipse, and the dominant figure in the Aegean and Asia Minor was Lysimachus who was Philippides' personal friend.

The man who cut down the year to a single month,
the man who turned the Acropolis into a hotel
and brought courtesans into the house of the Virgin,
because of whom the hoar-frost ruined the vines,
because of whose impiety Athena's robe[151] was torn through –   5
the man who gave the honours of the gods to mortals!
That, not comedy, is what subverts democracy!

---

149 Somewhat equivocal praise, since Simus must in fact have been virtually the only
   man of his time to have practised both professions!
150 Probably Heracles is now insisting on his lesson being ended and a large meal
   served.
151 The *peplos* presented to Athena at the Panathenaea.

Philemon, *The Soldier (Stratiotes)*, fr. 82

The boastful cook, inordinately proud both of his profession and of his personal skill, was an extremely frequent figure both in Middle and in New Comedy. Here we present a typical monologue by a cook from the play *The Soldier (Stratiotes)* by **Philemon**, describing the (allegedly) brilliant success of a fish dish he has just served.

What a longing has come over me to come here
and tell heaven and earth of the dish I have created!
By Athena, it's nice to be successful
in all respects! How tender my fish was,
how it looked when I served it! Not cosmeticized   5
with cheeses or dolled up with seasonings:
like it was in life, so it was when roasted!
So soft and gentle the fire I supplied
when roasting the fish, you just won't believe me!
It was like when a hen has picked up   10
something too big to swallow: she runs round in circles
keeping an eye on it, anxious to swallow it,
and the others chase her. It was the same.
The first of them to discover how delightful
the dish was, jumped up and ran around   15
holding the dish, with the others chasing at his heels.
You could have cheered: some of them were snatching a bit,
some got nothing, some got the lot. And yet what they were
    taking
was freshwater fish that eat mud:
if they'd been taking wrasse, or Attic   20
greyfish[152] (O Zeus the Saviour!) or catfish from Argos,[153]
or conger-eel from beloved Sicyon, which Poseidon
takes to heaven for the gods,
then everyone who ate it would have *become* gods!
I've discovered immortality: those who are already dead,   25
when they so much as sniff it, I make them live again.

152 Greek *glaukiskos*; this fish cannot be identified.
153 Not Argos in the Peloponnese (which is well inland), but Amphilochian Argos
    at the head of the Ambracian Gulf in north-western Greece.

Anonymous, fr. 1000 from *Comica Adespota*

Our final extract is a fragment of a New Comedy by an unknown author, preserved
in a papyrus (P. Louvre 7172, also known as the Didot papyrus) written in the second
century BC, perhaps not very long after the play was composed. A young wife is
resisting her father's attempt to terminate her marriage to a husband who has lost his
wealth. There is a rather similar, but poorly preserved, scene in Menander's *The
Arbitration* (Act IV), where the father's reason for intervening is that the husband is
supposedly keeping a mistress and an illegitimate child.

Father, the things that I am going to say,
it should be *you* saying them; for properly you should have
more intelligence than me, and be the one to speak, when
    necessary.
Since you have failed to do so, I imagine there remains no
    alternative
but for me, myself, to say what is right.   5
If my husband has done something seriously wrong,
it is not my responsibility to punish it;
but if he has done some wrong to *me*, I should have noticed it!
Perhaps I'm just ignorant and stupid;
well, I won't deny it, but still, Father,   10
even if a woman has no sense to judge other things,
perhaps she has some about her *own* affairs at least.
But let that be as you will. What wrong has he done me? Tell me.
There is a law laid down for man and wife:
he must always and ever cherish the wife he has,   15
she must do what pleases her husband.
Well, he has been to me just what I thought he ought to be,
and what pleases me, Father, is what pleases him.
But though he's good to me, he's lost his wealth;
and you, so you say, are now giving me to a rich man,   20
so that I won't live out my life in grief.
Yet where can there be a quantity of possessions, Father,
the having of which will give me more pleasure than a husband?
Or how can it be right or proper
that I should have my share of the good things he had   25
but not have a share in his impoverishment?
Tell me, if the man who's going to take me now –
but may that never happen, dear Zeus – and it never *will* happen,
certainly not with my consent while I have power to avoid it –
if he, in his turn, loses his property,   30
are you going to give me to a third man? And if he does too,

to a fourth? How long, Father, are you going to use my life
for the purpose of testing fortune?
When I was a girl, then it was proper for you to seek
a man to give me to; the choice was yours then.   35
But once you did give me, then, Father,
it's for *me* to take care of the matter, and rightly; for if
I judge things badly, it's my own life I'll be ruining.
That's what I have to say. So I beg you, in the name of Hestia,[154]
don't deprive me of the man to whom you united me;   40
this just and humane favour, Father,
I ask of you. If you refuse, you will be imposing
your will by force,[155] but I shall try to bear
my fortune as I should, without incurring shame.

---

154 Goddess of the hearth and the household (from which her father is trying to
remove her).
155 The language may be designed to suggest that a father who acted thus would
be spiritually no better than a rapist.

5

TESTIMONIA

Below are presented some extracts from the ancient sources, literary and
inscriptional, concerning the life and work of the five principal dramatists.
Much of the material in the literary sources, especially in the 'Lives' (*Vitae*)
found in medieval manuscripts of the poets' works (dating from the tenth
century onwards), is highly unreliable and full of legendary accretions –
though the *Vitae* also preserve a fair amount of authentic material deriving
from public records, lost contemporary or near-contemporary writings,
and the researches of Hellenistic scholars. The following selection, so far
as possible, concentrates on texts which are either early or based on early
sources; from the *Vitae*, only extracts are printed. Full collections of
evidence relating to the life and work of the various dramatists (except,
for the present, Euripides) will be found in *Tragicorum Graecorum Fragmenta*
or *Poetae Comici Graeci* as the case may be (see Chapter 6, pp. 172–3);
testimonia for Euripides are collected in D. Kovacs, *Euripidea* (Leiden,
1994), and *Euripidea Altera* (Leiden, 1996). Reference numbers at the
beginning of each extract are keyed to these collections.

AESCHYLUS

1. **Vita Aeschyli.** (1) Aeschylus the tragic poet was by birth an Athenian,
from the deme of Eleusis, the son of Euphorion and brother of Cynegeirus,
of Eupatrid descent.[1] . . . (9) He went . . . to Sicily at the time when
Hieron[2] was founding Aetna and presented *The Women of Aetna* as an
augury of a happy life to those joining in the foundation of the city. (10)
He was highly honoured both by the tyrant Hiero and by the people of

---

1 Descended, that is, from the traditional nobility of Athens.
2 Hieron I of Syracuse (reigned 478–467).

Gela, and in the third year of his residence[3] he died at an advanced age
. . . (11) When he died, the Geloans gave him a lavish burial in the public
cemetery, and honoured him magnificently, inscribing the following
epitaph:

> In Gela, rich in wheat, he died, and lies beneath this stone:
> Aeschylus the Athenian, son of Euphorion.
> His valour, tried and proved, the mead of Marathon can tell,
> The long-haired Persian also, who knows it all too well. . . .

(12) The Athenians so loved Aeschylus that after his death they passed a
decree whereby anyone wishing to produce works of Aeschylus could
receive a chorus. (13) . . . In all he won thirteen victories; he also gained
not a few victories after his death.

54a. Marmor Parium = *FGrH* 239 A 50 (third century BC). Since
Aeschylus the poet won his first victory in tragedy . . . 222 years, the
archon at Athens being Philocrates [485/4].

93a. Aristotle, *Nicomachean Ethics* 1111a8–10 (fourth century BC).
Or a person may not know what he is doing, as when people say that a
remark 'accidentally escaped them' or that 'they did not know it was a
secret', as Aeschylus said about the Mysteries.[4]

100. Aristotle, *Poetics* 1449a15–18 (fourth century BC). Aeschylus
was the first to increase the number of actors from one to two; he reduced
the choral parts, and gave speech the predominant role.

112. Athenaeus, *Deipnosophistae* 8.347d (*c.* AD 200). . . . the words
of the admirable and glorious Aeschylus, who said that his tragedies were
slices from the great banquets of Homer.

114. Porphyry, *On Abstinence* 2.18 (third century AD). They say
that when the Delphians asked Aeschylus to write a paean for their god,
he said that there was already an excellent one composed by Tynnichus,
and that when he compared it to his own he felt much as he did when
comparing old cult-statues with new ones: the old, though crudely made,
were thought to be divine, whereas the new ones, made with great artistry,
were much admired but were not thought so numinous.

---

3 This seems to confuse two separate visits by Aeschylus to Sicily, one about 470 BC
at the invitation of Hieron, the other beginning in 458 (when Hieron had been
dead nine years) and ending with Aeschylus' death at Gela in 456/5.

4 Various later sources speak of Aeschylus being put on trial for having allegedly
divulged the secrets of the Eleusinian Mysteries. This passage proves that the story
was already current in the time of Aristotle.

149a. **Plutarch, *Moralia* 79d** (*c.* AD 100).[5] When Aeschylus was watching a boxing contest at the Isthmian Games, and the spectators shouted out when one of the boxers was hit, he nudged Ion of Chios and said 'Do you see what training does? The man who was struck is silent, and the spectators cry out!'

SOPHOCLES

1. **Vita Sophoclis.** (1) Sophocles was an Athenian by birth, the son of Sophillus . . . of the deme Colonus . . . (2) He is reported to have been born in the second year of the seventy-first Olympiad [495/4], when Philippus was archon at Athens . . . (3) As a boy he was trained both in wrestling and in music, and won crowns for both, according to Istros. He was taught music by Lamprus, and after the battle of Salamis, when the Athenians dedicated a trophy, he led a chorus singing a paean in honour of the victory, naked, anointed, and carrying a lyre. (4) . . . And he made many innovations in theatrical practice; for example, he put an end to the custom of the poet acting in his own plays, because of his weak voice . . . ; he increased the chorus from twelve to fifteen, and he introduced a third actor. (5) He is said to be painted in the Stoa Poikile[6] with a *kithara* . . . (7) And to put it simply, there was so much charm in his character that he was loved everywhere and by everyone. (8) He won twenty victories, according to Carystius,[7] and frequently also came second, but never third . . . (10) His Athenian patriotism was so intense that though he received invitations from many kings, he was never willing to leave his own country. (11) He held the priesthood of Halon,[8] a hero who < > with Cheiron together with Asclepius . . . (18) According to Aristophanes[9] there are 130 plays of his, of which seven[10] have been regarded as spurious.

2. **Suda σ815** (tenth century AD). . . . And he wrote an elegiac poem, and paeans, and a prose treatise about the chorus, in which he took issue with Thespis and Choerilus.

---

5   The source of this anecdote may well be Ion himself (cf. Sophocles 75 on p. 162 below).
6   A building in the Agora, commissioned by Cimon and built in the second quarter of the fifth century, containing murals of the war between Theseus and the Amazons, the Trojan War and the battle of Marathon.
7   Eighteen according to the Dionysian victor-list (*IG* ii² 2325); higher figures cited here and elsewhere probably include victories at the Lenaea.
8   This hero is otherwise unknown.
9   That is, the Hellenistic scholar Aristophanes of Byzantium.
10 Most manuscripts give this figure as seventeen, but a figure of seven spurious plays out of 130 would tally with the Suda's statement that Sophocles wrote 123 plays.

18. **The Athenian Tribute Lists no. 12, line 36** (443/2 BC). [S]ophocles [of] Colonus was [*hellenotami*]*as*.[11]

19. **Androtion, *FGrH* 324 F 38** (fourth century BC). The names of the ten generals at Samos [441/0] . . . : Socrates of Anagyrus,[12] Sophocles of Colonus (the poet), Andocides of Cydathenaeum,[13] Creon of Scambonidae, Pericles of Cholargus . . .[14]

27. **Aristotle, *Rhetoric* 1419a25ff.** (fourth century BC). As when Sophocles, asked by Peisander whether he had agreed with the decision of the other *probouloi*[15] to establish the Four Hundred, said that he had. 'Well, don't you think that was a bad decision?' 'Yes.' 'So you did this thing, which was bad?' 'Yes,' said Sophocles, 'because there was no alternative that was better.'

53a. **Aristotle, *Poetics* 1460b32–34** (fourth century BC). Sophocles said that while he portrayed people as one ought to, Euripides portrayed them as they were.

75. **Ion of Chios, *FGrH* 392 F 6** (fifth century BC). I met Sophocles the poet on Chios, when he was en route for Lesbos as general [441/0]; he was a clever and playful man when in his cups. At a party given for him by Hermesileos, who was both a personal friend and a local representative of Athenian interests,[16] the boy who was pouring the wine, who was standing near the fire, was going visibly red in the face. Sophocles said to him 'Do you want me to enjoy my drinking?' The boy said yes, and Sophocles continued, 'Then be slower about giving me the cup and taking it away.' The boy's face became much redder still, and Sophocles said to his neighbour: 'How well Phrynichus put it when he said "The light of love shines on crimson cheeks"'! [This leads to a discussion on

---

11 One (and since he alone is mentioned on the inscription, apparently the most prominent) of the treasurers of the funds of the alliance of states headed by Athens; by the 440s these funds, derived mainly from the tribute payments of allied states, were held at Athens and used at the Athenians' discretion.

12 No connection with the philosopher; he was again a colleague of Pericles in the generalship ten years later (Thucydides 2.23.2).

13 Grandfather of the orator Andocides.

14 Six [*sic*] further names follow.

15 The emergency board of ten magistrates instituted after the Sicilian disaster of 413. In 411 they, along with others, became part of a constitutional commission whose report opened the way to the creation of the short-lived oligarchy of the Four Hundred, of which Peisander was a leading member. Sophocles was then in his mid-eighties.

16 This phrase translates *proxenos*, a citizen of one state (here Chios) who assumes responsibility for promoting there the interests of another state (here Athens) and protecting its citizens when they visit his own state's territory.

poetry, after which] Sophocles turned the conversation back to the boy, who was about to take a twig out of the cup with his little finger. Sophocles asked him 'Can you see the twig?' and, on his saying that he could, told him to *blow* it away, so as not to get his finger wet. Then, when the boy brought his face close to the cup, Sophocles brought the cup closer to his own lips, so as to bring their two heads closer together; and when the boy's head was very close to his, Sophocles took hold of it and kissed him. Everyone applauded, with laughter and shouting, and said how cleverly he had led the boy into his net. 'I'm practising generalship, gentlemen,' he said, 'since Pericles says I know how to write poetry but not how to be a general. Hasn't this stratagem of mine been successful?' He said and did many clever things of this kind when he was drinking or <   >; but in political matters he was not specially gifted or active, but just like the average upper-class Athenian.

80a. Plato, *Republic* 329b–c (fourth century BC). I[17] was once present when someone asked Sophocles the poet: 'How are things with you, Sophocles, so far as sex is concerned? Are you still capable of performing?' And he replied: 'Mind what you say, my man.[18] I am delighted to have escaped from all that, like a slave running away from a savage, raving master.'

105. Phrynichus (comic dramatist), *Muses*, fr. 32 (405 BC).

Blest is Sophocles, who lived a long life
and died a happy and accomplished man:
he wrote many excellent tragedies
and died a good death, having suffered no troubles.

EURIPIDES

1. Vita Euripidis. (1) Euripides the poet was the son of Mnesarchides . . . and was an Athenian. (2) He was born on Salamis in the archonship of Calliades [480/79][19] in the seventy-fifth Olympiad, at the time when the Persians and Greeks fought their naval battle . . . (6) It is said that

---

17 The speaker is Cephalus, father of the orator Lysias. But Plato himself probably knew Sophocles: he was twenty-one or twenty-two years old when Sophocles died, he belonged to the highest stratum of Athenian society, and he is said to have aspired to a career as a dramatist.

18 Sophocles is professing to be afraid that the act of uttering the name of the 'savage master' may magically restore its power and subject him anew to its tyranny.

19 Another tradition puts his birth about five years earlier; cf. 25 on p. 165 below.

... (9) he began ... to compete at the age of 25. (10) He migrated to Magnesia, and was honoured with the title of *proxenos*[20] and exemption from taxes. (11) From there he went to Macedonia, to the court of Archelaus, lived there, gratified him by writing a play of the same name, and was very well treated by him ... (12) He was said ... (13) to have married Melito as his first wife, Choerile as his second. (14) And he left three sons: the eldest, Mnesarchides, was a merchant; the second, Mnesilochus, was an actor; the youngest, Euripides, produced some of his father's plays. (15) He[21] began to produce in the archonship of Callias [456/5], the first year of the Eighty-first Olympiad; the first play he produced was *The Daughters of Pelias*, and he came third. (16) His plays numbered ninety-two in all, of which seventy-eight survive; of these, three are considered spurious, *Tennes*, *Rhadamanthys* and *Peirithous*.[22] (17) He died aged over 70 (according to Philochorus) or 75 (according to Eratosthenes), and was buried in Macedonia ... (20) It is said that Sophocles, on hearing that he had died, made his appearance at the *proagōn* in dark clothing, and brought his chorus and actors on without garlands, and that the people burst into tears.[23]

2. **Suda ε3695** (tenth century AD). ... It is not true ... that his mother was a vegetable-seller;[24] she was actually of very noble birth, as Philochorus shows ... He gained five victories, four during his lifetime and one after his death when the play[25] was presented by his nephew[26] Euripides. He presented plays for a total of twenty-two years.[27]

4. **Satyrus, *Life of Euripides* (*POxy* 1176)** (third century BC). (11) ... [a husband] against his w[i]fe and a father against his s[o]n and a ser[van]t against his m[as]ter, or c[ases] of dramatic r[ev]ersals, r[a]pes

---

20 See note 16.
21 This refers to Euripides senior, not his son.
22 *Peirithous* was also attributed (probably correctly) to Critias, as was another play not mentioned here, *Sisyphus*; *Tennes* and *Rhadamanthys* may have been his also.
23 If this story is true, it must refer to the City Dionysia of 406, since by the time of the next dramatic festival (the Lenaea of 405, when Aristophanes' *Frogs* and Phrynichus' *Muses* were staged) Sophocles was dead.
24 As repeatedly alleged in comedy (Aristophanes, *Acharnians*, line 478, *Frogs*, line 840, etc.).
25 The lexicographer, or his source, has forgotten that an entry for the tragic contest at the City Dionysia consisted of *four* plays.
26 Contrast 1.(14) above.
27 Another misunderstanding, since Euripides' career was actually over twice as long as this; the source must have said that he produced plays (at Athens) on twenty-two *occasions*.

of vir[g]ins, child substitutions, recognitions by means of rings and necklaces; for these are of course the features that provide the framework of[28] recent comedy, and Euripides brou[g]ht them to their peak . . . (21) At any rate it is said that when Nicias led the expedition against Sicily and ma[n]y of the Athenians became prisoners, a large number of them were saved thanks to Euripides' poetry, those who knew some of his verses by heart and taug[h]t them to the sons of those who had taken them captive.

12. **Theophrastus, *On Drunkenness*, fr.** 119 **Wimmer** (*c*.300 BC). I find that Euripides the poet himself poured wine at Athens for the so-called Dancers (*orchēstai*). These men, who were some of the leading men of Athens, used to dance around the temple of Delian Apollo, wearing cloaks of the Theran kind . . . And a painting on this subject is preserved at Phlya[29] in the Daphnephorium.

25. **Marmor Parium, *FGrH* 239 A 60** (third century BC). Since Euripides, being 44 years old, won his first victory in tragedy . . . 178 years, the archon at Athens being Diphilus [442/1].

49. **Plutarch, *Life of Alcibiades* 11** (*c*. AD 100) cites a lyric poem attributed to Euripides on the spectacular Olympic chariot-racing victory won by Alcibiades in 416 BC:

> I admire you, son of Cleinias!
> Noble was your victory, but the noblest thing, which no other
> of the Greeks <had achieved>,
> was to run first and second and third[30] in the chariot race,
> and to go without toil, crowned with the olive of Zeus,
> to give the herald cause to proclaim you.

58. **Aristophanes, *Frogs* 944, 1407–9, 1451–3** (405 BC).

(a) *Euripides*: Then I fed it [namely Tragedy] up again on a diet of arias, mixing in some Cephisophon.
(b) *Aeschylus*: Yes, and I'll have no more line-by-line stuff now! Let *him* climb on to the scales

---

28 Literally 'that hold together'
29 The deme (district) of Attica to which, according to the lexicographer Harpocration, Euripides belonged.
30 So the manuscripts of Plutarch (*trita*, usually emended on metrical grounds to the synonym *tritata*); but Euripides may actually have written *tetrata* ('fourth') (cf. Thucydides 6.16.2).

and sit there – himself, his children, his wife, Cephisophon, and he can take his books with him too . . .

(c) *Dionysus*: Splendid, you Palamedes, you intellectual genius! Did you think of that yourself, or was it Cephisophon?

Euripides: Myself entirely; but the vinegar-cruets were Cephisophon's idea.

Scholia to 944: Cephisophon, who was a slave, was thought to have helped him in composition, particularly with the lyrics; he is also accused in comedy of having had an affair with Euripides' wife.[31]

59. Aristotle, *Rhetoric* 1416a28–35 (fourth century BC). As Euripides did to Hygiaenon in the *antidosis* case[32] when he was accused of impiety on the score of his having encouraged perjury by writing 'My tongue has sworn, but my heart is not on oath'.[33] He said that his opponent was doing wrong to bring the judgements of the Dionysiac competitions into the courts: 'I have rendered my accounts for these words there [namely, in the theatre], or will do so if you want to accuse me.'

77. Aristophanes, *Frogs* 1069–82 and 1491–9 (405 BC).

(a) *Aeschylus*: Then again, you've taught people the habit of chatter and babble,

which has emptied the wrestling-schools and worn down young men's buttocks

as they sit blabbering – and has encouraged the crew of the *Paralus*

to talk back to their officers.[34] Why, in the old days, when I was alive,

---

31 There is sufficient comic evidence (cf. also *Frogs*, lines 1046–1048 and Ar., fr. 596) that Cephisophon was believed by contemporaries to have collaborated in the composition of Euripides' plays and to have seduced his wife; but no source before Satyrus gives any indication that he was a slave.

32 A person who had been designated to be a *chorēgos*, or to perform some other compulsory public service, was entitled to challenge any other person to choose between performing the service himself and accepting an exchange (*antidosis*) of all his property for the challenger's property. If such a challenge was refused, the challenger could ask a court to enforce it.

33 *Hippolytus*, line 612, a line that Euripides was never allowed to forget (cf. Aristophanes, *Thesm.*, lines 275–276, *Frogs*, lines 101–102, 1471). Euripides' retort refers to the fact that *Hippolytus* won first prize in the tragic competition.

34 The *Paralus* was one of two extra-fast 'sacred' triremes, often used for special duties such as the despatch of news or the transport of ambassadors. Aeschylus seems to be referring to an occasion in 411 when the Four Hundred sent three ambassadors to Sparta on board the *Paralus*, and the crew instead imprisoned the ambassadors, handed them over to the Argives, and sailed off to join the democratic forces (opposed to the Four Hundred) at Samos.

all they knew how to do was call for their grub and shout
'yo-ho!' . . .
   And what evils is he *not* responsible for?
   Has he not displayed women playing the bawd,[35]
   giving birth in sanctuaries of the gods[36]
   having sex with their brothers,[37]
   saying that life is not life?[38]
(b) *Chorus*: So it isn't stylish to sit
      beside Socrates[39] and blabber away,
      discarding artistry
      and ignoring the most important things
      about the tragedian's craft.
      To spend one's time fecklessly
      on pretentious talk
      and nit-picking humbug
      is to act like a lunatic.

90. **Hieronymus of Rhodes**, *Historical Notes*, fr. 36 Wehrli (third
century BC). When someone said to Sophocles that Euripides was a hater
of women, Sophocles replied: 'Only in his tragedies; in his *bed* he's a *lover*
of them!'

ARISTOPHANES

1. **Vita Aristophanis**. (1–2) Aristophanes the comic poet was son of
Philippus, an Athenian by birth, from the deme of Cydathenaeum . . .
(7–10) At first he put plays on stage through Callistratus and Philonides;
for which reason Aristonymus and Ameipsias made fun of him, saying
that he had been born on the fourth of the month[40] (as the proverb has
it), because he toiled for others. Later he also competed himself . . . (35–39)

---

35 Such as Phaedra's nurse in *Hippolytus*.
36 Like Auge in the (lost) play of that name.
37 Like Canace in *Aeolus*.
38 Cf. Eur., fr. 638: 'Who knows whether life may be death, and whether in the world
    below death may be regarded as life?'; also fr. 833.
39 Contemporary comedy several times associates Euripides with Socrates, apparently
    for no other reason than that both were intellectuals who often called into question
    deep-rooted certainties of conventional wisdom.
40 Like Heracles, who spent much of his life 'toiling for others' (Eurystheus,
    Omphale).

He was officially commended and crowned with a wreath of sacred olive, which is considered equal in honour to a gold crown, when he said the celebrated words in *The Frogs* about the disfranchised:

> It is right and proper for the sacred chorus to take part in giving much good advice to the community.[41] . . .

(49–51) He wrote a comedy called *Cocalus*, in which he introduces rape, recognition, and all the other things that Menander imitated . . . (54–56) And in this play he brought his son Araros before the public. And so he departed this life, leaving three sons behind him, Philippus (who bore the same name as his grandfather), Nicostratus, and Araros (through whom he had produced *Wealth*) . . . (59–61) He wrote forty-four plays, of which four are disputed and said not to be his; these are *Poetry*, <*Dionysus*> *Shipwrecked*, *The Islands* and *Niobus*, which some say are the work of Archippus.

9. *IG* ii² 1740.21–24 (list of councillors from the tribe Pandionis, *c*.390 BC). Of Cydathenaeum . . . Aristophanes.

52. Plato, *Symposium* (*c*.382 BC).[42]

(a) 176b [Aristophanes speaking] That was well said, Pausanias, that we should at all costs provide ourselves with a little easing-off on the drink; I'm another of those who got well dipped yesterday.

(b) 177a [Socrates replies to a suggestion by Eryximachus that everyone should give a speech in praise of Eros] Nobody, Eryximachus, will vote against you. I certainly couldn't say no, when I claim to know nothing about anything except erotics; nor, I am sure, would Agathon and Pausanias,[43] nor yet Aristophanes, whose whole time is spent in the service of Dionysus and Aphrodite,[44] nor anyone else among those I see before me.

---

41 *Frogs*, lines 686–687; the reference is not merely to these words but to the whole speech which begins with them, and which goes on to advocate the restoration of citizen rights to those who had lost them as a result of their involvement with the regime of the Four Hundred. The didascalic hypothesis of *The Frogs* (see p. 91) refers to another provision of the same honorific decree.

42 The dialogue purports to describe a party held at the house of the tragic dramatist Agathon in 416 BC, attended by (among others) Socrates, Aristophanes and Alcibiades.

43 It was well known that these two were lovers (*Symposium* 193b; cf. Plato, *Protagoras* 315d–e).

44 This may refer to Aristophanes' professional concerns as a dramatist, or to his private life, or to both at once.

(c) 189a-b [Ar. has humorously thanked Eryximachus for having cured his attack of hiccups] 'My good Aristophanes,' said Eryximachus, 'watch what you're doing. You're joking before you've started to speak, and you're forcing me to stand guard over your speech, in case you make more jokes, when you might have been left to speak in peace.' Aristophanes laughed and said, 'You're quite right, Eryximachus; cancel what I just said. But don't stand guard over me, because I'm apprehensive about what I'm going to be saying, not for fear that what I say may be funny – that would be something on the profit side, right in my own Muse's territory – but for fear it may seem ridiculous.' [Aristophanes proceeds to narrate a myth, full of fantastic and grotesque features, 'explaining' the origin of sexual attraction and of the various sexual orientations.]

79. Platonius, *On the Different Styles of Comic Dramatists* (third century AD?). Cratinus . . . is harsh in his abuse; for unlike Aristophanes he does not remove the vulgarity of his condemnations by making charm (*kharis*) run at the heels of his jokes . . . Eupolis' plots show an extremely high level of imagination . . . and as he has elevation, so too he has charm, and his jests are very well aimed. Aristophanes steers a middle course between their respective styles: he is neither excessively harsh like Cratinus nor pleasant like Eupolis, but towards wrongdoers he had both the intensity of Cratinus and something of the attendant charm of Eupolis.

MENANDER

1. Suda μ589 (tenth century AD). Menander . . . an Athenian, son of Diopeithes and Hegestrate, about whom all authors have a great deal to say, a comic poet of New Comedy, who suffered from a squint in the eyes but was mentally acute and mad about women.[45] He wrote 108 comedies.

2. IG xiv 1184 (Rome, date uncertain). Menander, son of Diopeithes, of Cephisia, was born in the archonship of Sosigenes [342/1] and died at the age of 52 in the archonship of Philippus [292/1] in the thirty-second year of King Ptolemy Soter.[46]

3. Prolegomena de Comoedia III Koster (date uncertain). Menander . . . famous both for his descent and for his life, spent much of his time with Alexis and was apparently trained by him. He was the first to produce a play when an ephebe,[47] in the archonship of Philocles [322/1].

---

45 No other source mentions any liaison except that with Glycera; see **16** on p.170 below.

46 Of Egypt; he reckoned the years of his reign from the death of Alexander, though he did not assume the title of King until long after.

47 This shows that he was eighteen or nineteen years old at the start of that year, confirming that he was born no earlier than 342/1.

8. Pamphila, *Historical Notes,* **fr. 10 Müller** (first century AD). Theophrastus was . . . the teacher of the comic poet Menander.

9. Diogenes Laertius, *Lives of the Philosophers* **5.79** (third century AD; on Demetrius of Phalerum). When malicious accusations were made against him in Athens[48] . . . Menander the comic poet was very nearly brought to trial, simply because he was his friend, but Telesphorus, the cousin of Demetrius,[49] successfully pleaded for him to be spared.

16. Aristodemus, *Comic Anecdotes* (first century AD; cited by Athenaeus 13.585c). When Menander the poet came home after having had a bad day, Glycera brought him milk and invited him to drink it. He declined, because the milk had skim on it; and she said 'Blow it off and use what's underneath.'

23. Ovid, *Ibis* **591–592** (early first century AD).

As the comic poet perished while swimming in the wet waves,
so may the waters of Styx suffocate your mouth!

Scholium: Menander, the Athenian comic poet, was drowned while swimming in the harbour of Piraeus; about this there have been handed down some very famous elegiac verses of Greek authorship, and an epigram by Callimachus.[50]

46. Aulus Gellius, *Attic Nights* **17.4.4** (second century AD). We read these verses about Menander in the book entitled *Chronica* by the very celebrated writer Apollodorus [second century BC]:

Being of Cephisia, the son of Diopeithes,
he wrote five plays over the hundred
and expired aged fifty-two years.[51]

But the same Apollodorus, in the same book, writes that of this total of 105 plays, Menander was victorious with only eight.

70. Plutarch, *Moralia* **347e** (*c.* AD 100). It is said that one of Menander's acquaintances said to him: 'Well, Menander, it's close to the Dionysia, and you haven't composed your comedy?' and he replied: 'Oh,

---

48 After his fall from power in 307.
49 The cousin, that is, of Demetrius Poliorcetes, not of Demetrius of Phalerum.
50 The epigram by Callimachus has not survived, but there is no reason to doubt that he wrote one; thus our source for this account of Menander's death goes back to a virtual contemporary (Callimachus was probably born in the last years of the fourth century).
51 Gellius, though himself writing in Latin, has left Apollodorus' lines in Greek.

yes, by the gods, I've composed the comedy. The plot's worked out; I've just got to provide the little matter of a verse accompaniment.'

71. Aulus Gellius, *Attic Nights* 17.4.1 (second century AD). Menander was frequently defeated in the comic contests by Philemon, a much inferior writer, because of lobbying, favouritism and cliques.[52] When they happened to meet, Menander said: 'Please, Philemon, pardon my asking this, but when you beat me, don't you blush?'

83.8–9. Aristophanes of Byzantium (*c.*200 BC; cited by Syrianus, *Commentary on Hermogenes*, II p. 23 Rabe):

O Menander, O life,
which of you, pray, imitated the other?

103. Plutarch, *Moralia (Comparison of Aristophanes and Menander)* 853d–f (*c.* AD 100). But Menander's language is so polished, so harmoniously blended, that as it moves through many emotions and character-types, fitting under all kinds of masks, it still gives the impression of being one, and keeps its uniformity in the employment of common, familiar words in ordinary use. If the topic requires some portentousness and bombast, he opens, as it were, all the stops of his pipe, and then quickly and credibly closes them again, returning his voice to its normal tones. There have been many craftsmen of note, but none who has been able to make a single shoe, or mask, or cloak that will fit, without alteration, a man, a woman, a youth, an old man or a slave; and yet Menander has so blended his language that it matches every nature, every disposition, every time of life, and that although he began his career at an early age and died at the height of his powers as a poet and producer, at the very time when (according to Aristotle) the linguistic abilities of writers advance most rapidly. If you compare Menander's middle and late plays with his early ones, you will perceive from them how much more he was destined to add to his achievements had he lived.

---

52 It is not clear that Philemon was much, or at all, more successful than Menander; we know, for example, that in a career of about seventy years he won only three victories at the Lenaea.

6

SELECT FURTHER READING[1]

TEXTS AND TRANSLATIONS

There are now up-to-date critical editions of the surviving plays of all three major tragic dramatists: M.L. West, *Aeschyli Tragoediae* (1990); H. Lloyd-Jones and N.G. Wilson, *Sophoclis Fabulae* (1990); J. Diggle, *Euripidis Fabulae* (3 vols., 1981–94). The collection *Tragicorum Graecorum Fragmenta* (*TrGF*) so far includes the fragments of Aeschylus (S.L. Radt, 1985), of Sophocles (S.L. Radt, 1977), of the minor tragic poets (B. Snell and R. Kannicht, 2nd edn, 1986), and of tragic and satyric texts whose author is not identifiable (B. Snell and R. Kannicht, 2nd edn, 1986). For fragments of Euripides, pending the appearance of Kannicht's *TrGF* volume, it is still necessary to consult A. Nauck, *Tragicorum Graecorum Fragmenta* (*TGF*) (1889; 2nd edn, with appendix by B. Snell, 1964) and editions of individual plays of which papyri have greatly augmented our knowledge since 1889, e.g. *Telephus* by E.W. Handley and J. Rea (1957), *Hypsipyle* by G.W. Bond (1963), *Phaethon* by J. Diggle (1970), *Cresphontes* and *Archelaus* by A. Harder (1985); see also D.L. Page, *Greek Literary Papyri I* (1941), C. Austin, *Nova Fragmenta Euripidea in Papyris Reperta* (1968), C. Collard *et al.*, *Euripides: Selected Fragmentary Plays* (2 vols., 1995– ; with facing translation), and J. Diggle, *Tragicorum Graecorum Fragmenta Selecta* (1998).

R. Kassel and C. Austin, *Poetae Comici Graeci* (*PCG*) (9 vols. in 10, 1983–) will eventually include everything that survives of Greek comedy (and the related genres, mime and phlyax-drama). The volumes so far

---

1 This chapter does not attempt to list editions of, commentaries on, or books about, individual plays, except where they are essential tools for the broader study of the author or genre, or where (in the first section) there is no adequate edition of an author's complete works.

published cover the whole of Attic comedy except for the eleven surviving plays of Aristophanes and the twenty best preserved plays of Menander; the latter can be found in W.G. Arnott, *Menander* (3 vols., 1979–2000; with facing translation), and eighteen of them in F.H. Sandbach, *Menandri Reliquiae Selectae* (2nd edn, 1990). There is at present no complete modern critical edition of Aristophanes' surviving plays, those of V. Coulon (5 vols., 1923–30) and R. Cantarella (5 vols., 1949–64) being seriously inadequate; pending the appearance of *PCG* iii.1, the gap is gradually being filled by the Oxford series of editions of individual plays, which so far includes *Clouds* (K.J. Dover, 1968), *Wasps* (D.M. MacDowell, 1971), *Peace* (S.D. Olson, 1998), *Birds* (N.V. Dunbar, 1995), *Lysistrata* (J.J. Henderson, 1990), *Frogs* (K.J. Dover, 1993), and *Ecclesiazusae* (R.G. Ussher, 1973). For Epicharmus and other western Greek comic dramatists it is still necessary to rely on G. Kaibel, *Comicorum Graecorum Fragmenta I* (1899) and A. Olivieri, *Frammenti della commedia greca e del mimo nella Sicilia e nella Magna Grecia* (2nd edn, 2 vols., 1946–7), supplemented by C. Austin, *Comicorum Graecorum Fragmenta in Papyris Reperta* (1973).

Translations of extant Greek dramas are now innumerable,[2] and vary much in their objectives, the extent to which they attempt to be faithful to the original, and the extent to which they achieve such fidelity. For study purposes the most useful are generally the more recent volumes of the Loeb Classical Library and the volumes of the Aris & Phillips (A&P) Classical Texts series (both with facing Greek text), but neither series has yet achieved full coverage. Recommended are the following (*denotes facing Greek text):

Aeschylus: M. Ewans (2 vols., 1995–6); *E.M. Hall, *Persians* (A&P, 1996); C.M. Dawson, *Seven against Thebes* (1970); P. Burian, *Suppliants* (1991); H. Lloyd-Jones, *Oresteia* (1979); *G. Thomson, *Prometheus Bound* (1932). *H. Weir Smyth, *Aeschylus II* (Loeb, 1926; 2nd edn, 1957, with appendix by H. Lloyd-Jones) includes most of the substantial fragments of lost plays.

Sophocles: *H. Lloyd-Jones (3 vols., Loeb 1994–6; vol. 3 includes all substantial fragments of lost plays); M. Ewans (2 vols., 1999–2000); *A.F. Garvie, *Ajax* (A&P, 1998); *A.L. Brown, *Antigone* (A&P, 1987).

Euripides: *D. Kovacs (6 vols. when complete, Loeb, 1994–); J. Morwood (4 vols., 1997–2001); the Aris & Phillips series *The Plays of Euripides*

---

2 For fragments of lost plays, on the other hand, reliable translations are often not available; where they are, they have been included in the lists below.

(1985– ; general editor, C. Collard) now contains twelve volumes by various hands, including one of *Selected Fragmentary Plays* by C. Collard, M.J. Cropp and K.H. Lee (1995; a second is to follow).

Aristophanes: *J.J. Henderson (4 vols. when complete, Loeb, 1998–); *A.H. Sommerstein (11 vols. with index volume to follow, A&P, 1980–).

Menander: *W.G. Arnott, *Menander* (3 vols., 1979–2000); M.G. Balme, *Menander: The Plays and Fragments* (2001); *S. Ireland, *The Bad-Tempered Man* [*Dyskolos*] (A&P, 1995).

DRAMA AND THEATRE

A wide range of translated ancient texts bearing on all aspects of drama is collected by E.G. Csapo and W.J. Slater in *The Context of Ancient Drama* (1994). Good comprehensive introductions to Greek drama, each by several hands, will be found in G.A. Seeck ed., *Das griechische Drama* (1979) and P.E. Easterling and B.M.W. Knox eds, *The Cambridge History of Classical Literature: Greek Drama* (1989). Almost all other general works deal with tragedy or comedy separately (see the following sections).

On the physical conditions of production see A.W. Pickard-Cambridge, *The Theatre of Dionysus in Athens* (1946), a good guide to what was known and conjectured up to that time; N.G.L. Hammond, 'The conditions of dramatic production to the death of Aeschylus', *Greek, Roman and Byzantine Studies* 13 (1972), 387–450; S. Melchinger, *Das Theater der Tragödie* (1974); H.J. Newiger, 'Drama und Theater', in G.A. Seeck ed., *Das griechische Drama* (1979), 434–503; E. Simon, *The Ancient Theatre* (Eng. tr. 1982); S. Scullion, *Three Studies in Athenian Dramaturgy* (1994). The evidence of the dramatic texts is put to good use by O.P. Taplin, *The Stagecraft of Aeschylus* (1977), R. Rehm, *Greek Tragic Theater* (1992), and D. Wiles, *Tragedy in Athens* (1997); C.F. Russo, *Aristophanes: An Author for the Stage* (3rd edn, 1994), while often unconvincing, is always thoughtful and thought-provoking. On the festival competitions, see A.W. Pickard-Cambridge, *The Dramatic Festivals of Athens* (3rd edn, 1988, rev. J. Gould and D.M. Lewis), and P.J. Wilson, *The Athenian Institution of the Khoregia* (2000). For the evidence of art, see A.D. Trendall and T.B.L. Webster, *Illustrations of Greek Drama* (1971); O.P. Taplin, *Comic Angels and Other Approaches to Greek Drama through Vase-paintings* (1993), and especially J.R. Green and E.W. Handley, *Images of the Greek Theatre* (1994); also the catalogues in T.B.L. Webster, *Monuments Illustrating Tragedy and Satyr-Play* (2nd edn, 1967); T.B.L. Webster, *Monuments Illustrating Old and Middle Comedy* (3rd edn, 1978, rev. J.R. Green); T.B.L. Webster,

Monuments Illustrating New Comedy (2nd edn, 1969; 3rd edn, 1995, rev. J.R. Green and A. Seeberg). On the Hellenistic theatre see B. Le Guen ed., *De la scène aux gradins: théâtre et représentations dramatiques après Alexandre le Grand* (1997).

There is no good modern study of tragic costuming. For comedy, see L.M. Stone, *Costume in Aristophanic Comedy* (1981), and D. Wiles, *The Masks of Menander* (1991); the use made by Wiles (and by Webster and many others) of the mask-catalogue preserved by the lexicographer Pollux is criticized by J.P. Poe, 'The supposed conventional meanings of dramatic masks: a re-examination of Pollux 4.133–54', *Philologus* 140 (1996), 306–328.

On dramatists' theatrical techniques, see O.P. Taplin, *The Stagecraft of Aeschylus* (1977), and *Greek Tragedy in Action* (1978); D. Seale, *Vision and Stagecraft in Sophocles* (1982); N.C. Hourmouziades, *Production and Imagination in Euripides* (1965); and K. McLeish, *The Theatre of Aristophanes* (1980). Of unique value are the new Everyman translations by Michael Ewans of Aeschylus (2 vols., 1995–6) and Sophocles (2 vols., 1999–2000) which are accompanied by a detailed study of the staging of the plays, with particular reference to movements ('blocking'), based on production experience and taking full account of the findings of more traditional scholarship. On an important and little-studied aspect of performance, see A.L. Boegehold, *When a Gesture was Expected* (1999).

On the verse of Greek drama see M.L. West, *Greek Metre* (1982), esp. 77–137, and A.M. Dale, *The Lyric Metres of Greek Drama* (2nd edn, 1968). Dale analysed all the choral songs in surviving tragedies in *Metrical Analyses of Tragic Choruses* (3 vols., 1971–83); for analyses of Aristophanes' lyrics see L.P.E. Parker, *The Songs of Aristophanes* (1997).

DRAMA AND SOCIETY

Four collections of papers which show between them a number of important trends in current thinking on this subject are J.J. Winkler and F.I. Zeitlin eds, *Nothing to do with Dionysos?* (1990); A.H. Sommerstein *et al.* ed., *Tragedy, Comedy and the Polis* (1993); R.S. Scodel ed., *Theater and Society in the Classical World* (1993); and C.B.R. Pelling ed., *Greek Tragedy and the Historian* (1997). C. Meier, *The Political Art of Greek Tragedy* (1993), is particularly valuable on Aeschylus, on whom see also A.J. Podlecki, *The Political Background of Aeschylean Tragedy* (1967), and C.W. Macleod, 'Politics in the *Oresteia*', *Journal of Hellenic Studies* 102 (1982), 122–144; on Euripides, J. Gregory, *Euripides and the Instruction of the Athenians* (1991); on drama and the Dionysiac, T.H. Carpenter and

C.A. Faraone eds, *Masks of Dionysus* (1993), especially the contributions by Seaford and Zeitlin, also A.F.H. Bierl, *Dionysos und die griechische Tragödie* (1991), and I. Lada-Richards, *Initiating Dionysus* (1999); on a wide variety of aspects of the relationship between tragedy, ritual and society, R. Seaford, *Reciprocity and Ritual* (1994). For a sceptical view of the trend of much recent scholarship see J. Griffin, 'The social function of Attic tragedy', *Classical Quarterly* 48 (1998), 39–61; there have been combative responses by R. Seaford, 'The social function of Attic tragedy: a response to Jasper Griffin', *Classical Quarterly* 50 (2000), 30–44, and by S.D. Goldhill, 'Civic ideology and the problem of difference: the politics of Aeschylean tragedy, once again', *Journal of Hellenic Studies* 120 (2000), 34–56.

Discussions of the relationship between Old Comedy and Athenian culture, society and politics are innumerable. In addition to those offered by various contributors to the Winkler–Zeitlin and Sommerstein *et al.* volumes (see above), see S. Halliwell, 'Comic satire and freedom of speech in classical Athens', *Journal of Hellenic Studies* 111 (1991), 48–70, and M. Heath, 'Aristophanes and the discourse of politics', in G.W. Dobrov ed., *The City as Comedy* (1997), 230–249, who both take the view that comedy neither affected nor was expected to affect the public life of the state (a more nuanced view is C. Carey, 'Comic ridicule and democracy', in R.G. Osborne and S. Hornblower eds, *Ritual, Finance, Politics* (1994), 69–83); against this, see especially A.T. Edwards in R.S. Scodel ed., *Theater and Society in the Classical World* (1993), also P.A. Cartledge, *Aristophanes and his Theatre of the Absurd* (1990), and A.H. Sommerstein, 'How to avoid being a *komodoumenos*', *Classical Quarterly* 46 (1996), 327–356. There has been less on New Comedy, whose social connections are more ethically than politically oriented; but see W.G. Arnott, 'Moral values in Menander', *Philologus* 125 (1981), 215–227, and P.G.McC. Brown, 'Love and marriage in Greek new comedy', *Classical Quarterly* 43 (1993), 189–205. Both periods are examined from a Marxist (or at least *marxisant*) standpoint in D. Konstan, *Greek Comedy and Ideology* (1995).

Two aspects of 'drama and society' that have attracted great attention in recent years concern drama's 'discourse' of ethnicity (especially Greek versus barbarian) and of gender. On the former, see E.M. Hall, *Inventing the Barbarian* (1989); on the latter, N. Loraux, *Tragic Ways of Killing a Woman* (1987), S. des Bouvrie, *Women in Greek Tragedy* (1991), V. Wohl, *Intimate Commerce: Exchange, Gender, and Subjectivity in Greek Tragedy* (1998), L. McClure, *Spoken like a Woman: Speech and Gender in Athenian Drama* (1999), C.A. Powell ed., *Euripides, Women and Sexuality* (1990), N.S. Rabinowitz, *Anxiety Veiled: Euripides and the Traffic in Women* (1994), and J. Bonnamour and H. Delavault eds, *Aristophane, les femmes et la cité*

(1979); on both, P.A. Cartledge, *The Greeks: A Portrait of Self and Others* (1993).

On the problems and principles of using drama (and other literary texts) as sources of evidence about contemporary society, see C.B.R. Pelling, *Literary Texts and the Greek Historian* (2000).

For an entirely different approach see J.R. Green, *Theatre in Ancient Greek Society* (1995), which examines evidence from the visual arts for the social setting and function of theatre throughout Antiquity.

TRAGEDY AND SATYR-DRAMA

On tragedy the best introduction remains A. Lesky, *Greek Tragic Poetry* (Eng. tr. 1983); the smaller introductory text by B. Zimmermann, *Greek Tragedy* (Eng. tr. 1991), has useful bibliographies. M.S. Silk ed., *Tragedy and the Tragic* (1996), offers a wide variety of approaches to the problem of defining the concept of the tragic, and in the process sheds light on many aspects of the genre; P.E. Easterling ed., *The Cambridge Companion to Greek Tragedy* (1997), focuses more on the relations between tragedy and the society in which it was composed and received. A valuable collection of essays, most of them on the interpretation of individual plays, is E. Segal ed., *Oxford Readings in Greek Tragedy* (1983).

Origins: a good starting-point is A.F. Garvie, *Aeschylus' Supplices: Play and Trilogy* (1969), ch. 3; two recent works which approach the subject from different angles are R. Seaford, *Reciprocity and Ritual* (1994), and C.J. Herington, *Poetry into Drama* (1985). C. Sourvinou-Inwood, 'Something to do with Athens: tragedy and ritual', in R.G. Osborne and S. Hornblower eds, *Ritual, Finance, Politics* (1994), 269–290, offers an innovative discussion of the ritual context of early tragedy.

Structure: the most comprehensive treatment is W. Jens ed., *Die Bauformen der griechischen Tragödie* (1971). There are a number of recent studies of particular structural elements. For example, on choral songs, H. Parry, *Lyric Poems of Greek Tragedy* (1978), and W.C. Scott, *Musical Design in Aeschylean Theater* (1984), and *Musical Design in Sophoclean Theater* (1996); on formal debates, M. Lloyd, *The Agon in Euripides* (1992); on messenger-speeches, I.J.F. de Jong, *Narrative in Drama* (1991). There have also been a series of attempts at a completely new style of structural analysis of tragic drama, of which only O.P. Taplin, *The Stagecraft of Aeschylus* (1977), takes adequate account of performance factors; J.P. Poe, 'The determination of episodes in Greek tragedy', *American Journal of Philology* 114 (1993), 343–396, shows that no universal system of analysis can satisfactorily account for the evidence. On plot and story patterns, see R. Lattimore, *Story Patterns in*

Greek Tragedy (1964); M. Heath, *The Poetics of Greek Tragedy* (1987); A. Machin, *Cohérence et continuité dans le théâtre de Sophocle* (1981); and A.P. Burnett, *Catastrophe Survived: Euripides' Plays of Mixed Reversal* (1971). On *satyr-drama* see D.F. Sutton, *The Greek Satyr Play* (1980); B. Seidensticker ed., *Satyrspiel* (1989); R. Krumeich *et al.*, *Das griechische Satyrspiel* (1999); and R. Seaford, *Euripides: Cyclops* (1984), 1–48.

INDIVIDUAL TRAGIC DRAMATISTS

Aeschylus: A.H. Sommerstein, *Aeschylean Tragedy* (1996), aims to be comprehensive (except as regards language and style); C.J. Herington, *Aeschylus* (1986), is a helpful, though highly personal, broad-brush introduction; T.G. Rosenmeyer, *The Art of Aeschylus* (1982), concentrates on poetic and dramatic technique; R.P. Winnington-Ingram, *Studies in Aeschylus* (1983), is a collection of extremely sensitive separate essays; O.P. Taplin, *The Stagecraft of Aeschylus* (1977), is an unmatched study of many aspects of Aeschylus' dramatic and theatrical technique.

Sophocles: Among numerous general studies may be noted K. Reinhardt, *Sophokles* (1933); R.P. Winnington-Ingram, *Sophocles: An Interpretation* (1980); C.P. Segal, *Tragedy and Civilization: An Interpretation of Sophocles* (1981), and *Sophocles' Tragic World* (1995); B.M.W. Knox, *The Heroic Temper* (1964), on the 'Sophoclean hero'; and M. Whitlock Blundell, *Helping Friends and Harming Enemies: A Study in Sophocles and Greek Ethics* (1989).

Euripides: No modern introductory work on Euripides can be recommended, though D.J. Conacher, *Euripidean Drama* (1967), was good in its day. Useful collections of essays are P. Burian ed., *Directions in Euripidean Criticism* (1985), C.A. Powell ed., *Euripides, Women and Sexuality* (1990), and especially M.J. Cropp *et al.* eds, *Euripides and Tragic Drama in the Late Fifth Century* (= *Illinois Classical Studies* 24/25 [1999/2000]). On more or less broad aspects of Euripides' technique and thought, see A. Rivier, *Essai sur le tragique d'Euripide* (2nd edn, 1975); S.A. Barlow, *The Imagery of Euripides* (2nd edn, 1986); A.N. Michelini, *Euripides and the Tragic Tradition* (1987); and J. Gregory, *Euripides and the Instruction of the Athenians* (1991).

Minor tragic poets: Specialized studies are few. Among the most important are H. Lloyd-Jones, 'Problems of early Greek tragedy: Pratinas and Phrynichus', most easily found in *The Academic Papers of Sir Hugh Lloyd-Jones* i (1990), 225–237; A. von Blumenthal, *Ion von Chios* (1935); P. Lévêque, *Agathon* (1955); G. Xanthakis-Karamanos, *Studies in Fourth-Century Tragedy* (1980); C. Collard, 'On the tragedian Chaeremon', *Journal of Hellenic Studies* 90 (1970), 22–34; H. Jacobson, *The Exagoge of Ezekiel* (1983).

ARISTOPHANES AND OLD COMEDY

Three good general introductions, in many ways complementary, are K.J. Dover, *Aristophanic Comedy* (1972), G. Mastromarco, *Introduzione a Aristofane* (1994), and D.M. MacDowell, *Aristophanes and Athens* (1995); a recent major critical study is M.S. Silk, *Aristophanes and the Definition of Comedy* (2000). Three useful collections of essays are J.M. Bremer and E.W. Handley eds, *Aristophane = Entretiens de la Fondation Hardt* 38 (1993), E. Segal ed., *Oxford Readings in Aristophanes* (1996), and P. Thiercy and M. Menu eds, *Aristophane: la langue, la scène, la cité* (1997). Also deserving of special notice are K.J. Reckford, *Aristophanes' Old-and-New Comedy I* (1987), which concentrates on elements of fantasy, and A.M. Bowie, *Aristophanes: Myth, Ritual and Comedy* (1993), which concentrates on elements related to myth and religion. A short treatment of remarkable breadth and judgement is N.J. Lowe, 'Greek stagecraft and Aristophanes', in J. Redmond ed., *Themes in Drama 10: Farce* (1988), 33–52.

Two key elements in the structure of Old Comedy are discussed by T. Gelzer, *Der epirrhematische Agon bei Aristophanes* (1960), and G.M. Sifakis, *Parabasis and Animal Choruses* (1971); see also T.K. Hubbard, *The Mask of Comedy: Aristophanes and the Intertextual Parabasis* (1991). On Aristophanic plot and story patterns, see C.H. Whitman, *Aristophanes and the Comic Hero* (1964); P. Thiercy, *Aristophane: fiction et dramaturgie* (1986); G.M. Sifakis, 'The structure of Aristophanic comedy', *Journal of Hellenic Studies* 112 (1992), 123–142; and P. von Möllendorff, *Grundlagen einer Ästhetik der Alten Komödie* (1995).

Recently there has been an upsurge of interest in the Old Comic dramatists other than Aristophanes, and in J. Wilkins and F.D. Harvey eds, *The Rivals of Aristophanes* (2000), twenty-eight scholars examine numerous aspects of their work. G.W. Dobrov ed., *Beyond Aristophanes: Transition and Diversity in Greek Comedy* (1995), explores continuities and developments linking Old to Middle Comedy.

MIDDLE COMEDY

H.G. Nesselrath, *Die attische Mittlere Komödie* (1990), is now the standard work on this period in the history of Greek comedy; there are also two major commentaries on the fragments of individual poets, *Eubulus* (by R.L. Hunter, 1983) and *Alexis* (by W.G. Arnott, 1996).

MENANDER AND NEW COMEDY

R.L. Hunter, *The New Comedy of Greece and Rome* (1985), is an excellent introduction, treating Menander, Plautus and Terence together. A.W. Gomme and F.H. Sandbach, *Menander: A Commentary* (1973), is the standard commentary on the plays and fragments contained in the first edition (1972) of F.H. Sandbach's *Menandri Reliquiae Selectae* (2nd edn, 1990), but is now in need of revision. Literary and dramatic studies include S.M. Goldberg, *The Making of Menander's Comedy* (1980); A. Blanchard, *Essai sur la composition des comédies de Ménandre* (1983); E.W. Handley and A. Hurst eds, *Relire Ménandre* (1990); G. Vogt-Spira, *Dramaturgie des Zufalls: Tyche und Handeln in der Komödie Menanders* (1992); and N. Zagagi, *The Comedy of Menander* (1995).

INDEX

In all the indexes, major discussions are indicated by **bold**. The indexes do not cover the dramatic texts anthologized in Chapter 4, though they do cover the introductions and annotations to these texts.

I Ancient dramatists and dramas

Tragic and comic poets are marked (t) and (c) respectively. It may be assumed that tragic poets of the fifth century also composed satyr-dramas; if a later poet had significant satyric output, this is indicated by (s).

---

1 The position of "Apollodorus" in the inscription here cited, only two places below Menander, shows that Apollodorus of Gela is meant, not his much younger (and more famous) namesake of Carystus.

II Other persons

For historical persons the entry indicates, by a bracketed Roman numeral or numerals, the century/centuries when they were active (BC unless otherwise indicated by a superscript [P] for post 'after').

Alope, mother by Poseidon of Hippothoon 138
Amarynceus, father of Hippostratus 150 n.133
Amphiaraus, prophet who joined the Seven against Thebes 152 n.141
Amphitheus ('Godschild'), peacemaker sent by the gods 125
Amphitryon, foster-father of Heracles 22, 52, 58
Anaxagoras, philosopher (v) 62
Andocides, general (v) 162
Andocides, his grandson, politician (vi–v) 162 n.13
Andromache, wife of Hector 19, 51, 52, 55
Andromeda, daughter of Cepheus, afterwards married to Perseus 134
Androtion, Athenian historian and politician (iv) 162
Antigenes, archon in 407/6 (v) 91
Antigone, daughter of Oedipus 17, 35 n.2, 42, 43, 44, 45, 53, 57, 58, 102
Antiphon, political thinker, speechwriter and activist (v) 126 n.74
Aphrodite 18, 28, 35, 50, 92, 151, 168
Apollo 24, 35, 46, 47, 51, 52, 53, 58, 165
Apollodorus, Athenian/ Alexandrian scholar (ii) 170
Apollodorus, pseudo-, mythographer (i–ii^P?) 49, 150 n.133
Archedemides, archon in 464/3 (v) 89 n.2
Archelaus, king of Macedon (v–iv) 49, 60, 113, 164
Archilochus, iambic poet (vii) 25, 129 n.87
Aristarchus, Alexandrian scholar (ii) 16
Aristodemus, collector of anecdotes (i^P) 170
Ariston, son of Sophocles (v) 42
Aristophanes of Byzantium, Alexandrian scholar (iii–ii) 161, 171
Aristotle, philosopher (iv) 1, 11, 15,

16 n.4, 17, 18, 20, 31, 37, 48, 55, 56, 60, 61, 132 n.99, 160, 162, 166, 171
Artemis 50, 52, 54 n.9, 96
Asclepius, healing hero/god 42, 66, 151 n.140, 161
Aspasia, mistress of Pericles (v) 148
Astyanax, son of Hector 52
Athena 21, 28, 35–6, 40, 42, 47, 51, 52, 54, 92, 101 n.27, 155
Athenaeus, antiquarian writer (ii–iii^P) 31, 76, 148, 160, 170
Atreidae see Agamemnon, Menelaus
Atreus, father of Agamemnon 39
Auge, mother by Heracles of Telephus 167 n.36
Augustus, Roman emperor (i–i^P) 3

Bacchus see Dionysus
Basileia ('Princess'), embodiment of universal power 66
Bdelycleon, son of Philocleon 65
Bellerophon, hero 10, 58, 91–2

Cadmus, founder of Thebes 58
Calliades, archon in 480/79 (v) 163
Callias, archon in 456/5 (v) 164
Callias, archon in 406/5 (v) 91
Callias, son of Hipponicus, a rich and extravagant Athenian (v–iv) 150
Callimachus, poet and scholar (iii) 170
Callistratus, producer for Aristophanes (v) 63, 167
Canace, daughter of Aeolus 167 n.37
Candaules, king of Lydia (vii) 122–3
Capaneus, one of the Seven against Thebes 58
Carion, cook in Menander's *Epitrepontes* 74
Carystius, collector of historical information (ii) 161
Cassandra, daughter of Priam 10, 35, 37, 39, 52, 100 n.24, 109
Castor see Dioscuri
Celeus, father of Triptolemus 125 n.71
Cephalus, father of Lysias (v) 163 n.17

Cephisophon, collaborator with
Euripides (v) 165–6
Cercyon, father of Alope 138
Chaereas, young man in Menander's
Aspis 71
Chaerestratus, old man in
Menander's *Aspis* 71
Charisius, young husband in
Menander's *Epitrepontes* 71, 73
Cheiron, virtuous centaur and tutor
of heroes 161
Choerile, wife of Euripides (v) 164
Choerilus of Samos, epic poet (v)
154 n.147
Chremylus, hero of Aristophanes'
Wealth 66–7
Chryseis, briefly Agamemnon's
captive at Troy 100 n.24
Chrysis, mistress of Demeas in
Menander's *Samia* 72
Cimon, Athenian statesman (v) 40,
41, 153 n.144, 161 n.6
Cleinias, father of Alcibiades (v) 165
Cleisthenes, tyrant of Sicyon (vi) 2,
15
Cleisthenes, a beardless Athenian (v)
129 nn.85, 87
Cleon, Athenian politician (v) 27,
63, 64–5
Cleonymus, Athenian politician (v)
127
Cleostratus, young man in
Menander's *Aspis* 71
Clouds, goddesses/personifications 65
Clytaemestra, wife of Agamemnon
10, 16 n.4, 17, 18, 35–6, 37, 39,
40, 43, 46, 51, 54, 58, 98–100
Cnemon, title character of
Menander's *Dyskolos* 10, 71, 136
Comedy, personification 75, 151
Conisalus, a phallic god 151
Corianno, courtesan in Pherecrates'
Corianno 29
Corneille, Pierre, dramatist (xvii[P])
4
Cranaus, king of Athens 127
Crateia, Thrasonides' mistress in
Menander's *Misoumenos* 71–2
Creon, brother of Iocaste 42, 43, 44,
45, 46, 47, 48, 53, 102

Creon, Athenian general (v) 162
Creusa, mother (by Apollo) of Ion 52
Cronus, father of Zeus 76, 96, 148
Cyclops (Polyphemus), one-eyed
giant blinded by Odysseus 27, 53,
114–17
Cyllene, a mountain nymph 24
Cynegeirus, brother of Aeschylus (v)
33, 159
Cynna *see* Kynna

Danaids (daughters of Danaus) 18,
35, 38, 39
Danaus, king of Egypt 35, 39, 40,
61
Dardanus, king of Troy 117 n.56
Daos, slave in various Menandrian
plays 73, 136, 138–44
Darius I, king of Persia (vi–v) 9, 34,
93
Death, god/personification 50
Deianeira, wife of Heracles 16, 42,
44, 45, 46
Demeas, old man in various
Menandrian plays 71–2, 73
Demeter 125 n.71
Demetrius of Phalerum, autocrat of
Athens (iv) 8, 70, 170
Demetrius Poliorcetes, king of
Macedon (iv–iii) 70, 76, 155, 170
Demodocus, *chorēgos* in 459/8 (v) 87
Demos, personification of the
Athenian people 64–5
Demosthenes, Athenian politician
and orator (iv) 76
Dexion, hero (later identified with
Sophocles) 42
Dicaearchus, polymath (iv–iii) 91
Dicaeopolis, hero of *Acharnians* 64,
125–9
Dido, foundress of Carthage 107
Diogenes Laertius, biographer (iii[P])
170
Diomedes, Trojan War hero 54
Dionysus (Bacchus, Bromius) 2, 6–7,
22, 23, 24, 28–9, 34, 53, 64, 66,
92, 112–14, 116 n.52, 166, 168,
175–6
Diopeithes, father of Menander (iv)
70, 169

INDEX

Syrus, slave in Menander's
Epitrepontes 73, 138–44

Tecmessa, concubine of Ajax 45, 46,
100
Telesphorus, cousin of Demetrius
Poliorcetes 170
Tereus, king of Thrace, afterwards a
hoopoe 132
Teucer, half-brother of Ajax 102
n.30
Themistocles, Athenian statesman
(v) 20, 26, 40, 60
Theoclymenus, king of Egypt 19,
52, 58
Theonoe, sister of Theoclymenus 52,
58
Theophrastus, philosopher (iv–iii)
139 n.110, 165, 170
Theron, parasite in Menander's
Sikyonios 72
Theseus, king of Athens 17, 18, 22,
43, 44, 47, 48, 50, 51, 52, 55,
58, 161 n.6
Thetis, sea-goddess 36, 118 n.58
Thettalus, tragic actor (iv) 88
Thoas, king of the Tauri 52
Thrasonides, soldier in Menander's
Misoumenos 71
Thucydides, historian (v) 165 n.30
Thyestes, brother of Atreus 18, 39,
122

Treaty, personification 13
Triptolemus, Eleusinian hero 125
n.71
Trygaeus, hero of Aristophanes' *Peace*
65
Tydeus, one of the Seven against
Thebes 150 n.133
Tyndareos, husband of Leda 112
n.44
Tynnichus, lyric poet (vi?) 160
Tyro, mother of Neleus and Pelias
143 n.115

Uranus, grandfather of Zeus 96

Victory (Nike),
goddess/personification 75
Virgil (P. Vergilius Maro), Roman
epic poet (i) 107

War, god/personification 10, 65
Wealth, god/personification 66–7

Xenocles of Aphidna, Aeschylus'
chorēgos in 459/8 (v) 88
Xerxes, king of Persia (v) 34, 39, 93,
94
Xuthus, son of Hellen and husband
of Creusa 52

Zeus 36, 47, 56, 65, 67, 111, 112
n.44, 117 n.56, 118, 148, 165

III Dramatic and theatrical terms
Terms are normally indexed only where they are explained, or where the
features they refer to are the subject of significant discussion.

actors 12–13, 36, 37, 41, 88, 160,
161
acts 11, 74
agōn 21, 55, 68–9, 176, 179
amoibaion 20
anapaestic verse 15, 68, 74, 152
antidosis 166 n.32
antilabē 21
antistrophe 14
archon, eponymous 7
Artists of Dionysus 6–7
aulos (pipe) 11, 14

chorēgos 8, 30, 87–8
chorodidaskalos 8
chorou 11, 69
chorus 11–12, 20, 37–8, 41, 45–6,
57, 74, 136, 160, 161
City Dionysia 2, 6–9, 22, 87–8, 130
n.90

dactylic verse 38, 74
deus/dea ex machina 10–11, 43, 51,
54, 55, 152 n.142
didascalic hypotheses 89
Didaskaliai 88